THE DEATH
OF THE ARMY

Edward L. King

THE DEATH
OF THE ARMY

A Pre-Mortem

☆ ☆ ☆ ☆ ☆ ☆ ☆ ☆ ☆ ☆ ☆ ☆

Saturday Review Press

New York

To the Soldiers of the U.S. Army

Library of Congress Catalog Card Number: 70–154256
ISBN 0–8415–0168–8

Saturday Review Press
230 Park Avenue
New York, New York 10017

PRINTED IN THE UNITED STATES OF AMERICA

Design by Margaret F. Plympton

Preface

☆ ☆ ☆ ☆ ☆ ☆ ☆ ☆ ☆

Quiet resolution.
The hardihood to take risks.
The will to take full responsibility for decisions.
The readiness to share its rewards with subordinates.

An equal readiness to take the blame when things go adversely.

The nerve to survive storm and disappointment and to face toward each new day with the scoresheet wiped clean, neither dwelling on one's successes nor accepting discouragement from one's failure.

To give it everything, though not quite making the grade personally, is merely an exercise in character building. But to have the mission fail because of false pride is inexcusable.

—THE ARMED FORCES OFFICER

These old tenets of military leadership apply more than ever before to a U.S. Army beset on all sides by past mistakes

and faced with a loss of public confidence brought about by
false pride. The Army is at a crossroads. It has been the victim of selfish leadership. Slowly, painfully, it is realizing it
must turn from the wrong road it has been following for
over fifteen years if it is to regain its self-respect and the
public's confidence. How it makes this turn will determine
whether it continues as an accepted national institution or
ceases to exist.

The following pages are an attempt to trace how the
Army arrived at its present point of virtual disintegration,
to examine the causes of some of its past mistakes, the price
of those failures, and what the future may hold in store.
This book is the culmination of years of increasing personal
concern over what has been happening in the U.S. Army.
Many are now trying to oversimplify the problem by saying
that the Army's troubles began in Vietnam. My own lifetime
of service has convinced me that this is not the case. The
low morale which afflicts the Army today is not solely the
result of the war in Vietnam, or merely a reflection of
the increase in drug abuse and crime that are part of contemporary American society. The sickness that is consuming
the Army is the result of years of false leadership and parochial self-interest.

There are thousands of honest, brave, dedicated men and
women serving in the U.S. Army. They can and will save it
if given the chance. The danger is that they may not have
such a chance. It is all too likely that any mandate to reform
the Army will become a ploy in the hands of the same false
leaders, who will make only superficial changes while using
the "reform bandwagon" as yet another means toward promotion and the furthering of their careers.

This book is written in the hope that it may help to prevent a charade of reform by raising issues and helping to
dispel some of the misconceptions caused by years of hypocritical Army rhetoric. To reform an institution effectively
it must first be understood. If this book assists in achieving
a better public understanding of the Army and a conse-

quent thorough reform, then the labor and personal sacrifice that have gone into it will have been more than worthwhile.

The conversations recorded in the book are as I noted or recollect them. In some instances due to the passage of time they may not be verbatim.

I wish to acknowledge my deep gratitude to my wife and the small group of loyal friends who have contributed so unselfishly of their time and understanding during the difficult and trying period of the writing of this book. Without their help and friendship it could not have been completed.

September 1971   EDWARD L. KING
                                   Lieutenant Colonel
                                   U. S. Army, Retd.

Contents

☆ ☆ ☆ ☆ ☆

PART I

Chapter 1

The Past Weighs
on the Present

☆ ☆ ☆ ☆ ☆ ☆ ☆ ☆ ☆

"Colonel, your orders to Vietnam arrived this morning." That was the first message I received from my office after being in the hospital a week.

It was January 14, 1969. I was being ordered to a staff job in the headquarters of the Military Assistance Command in Saigon with a reporting date of August 6, 1969. After hanging up the phone I sat on my hospital bed for a minute staring out the window through the bright winter sun, watching the people bundled up in overcoats walk into the wind. It suddenly seemed like I was being faced with the most critical decisions of my life. And I wondered if my wife would be coming to visit me that evening. There was a lot we needed to talk over.

I was in Walter Reed Army Hospital to find out what was wrong with my liver. It had been damaged by amoebic dysen-

tery in Korea. Now there was the possibility of cancer. I still
had several more days of tests to endure before the doctors
could make a diagnosis. During those days I would have an opportunity to think over what I would do about the orders.

Since 1963 I had been doubtful about the wisdom of the
course the nation and the Army had been following in Vietnam. For a much longer time I had been growing increasingly
more disillusioned with conditions of service in the U.S. Army.
In July 1965 I had remained on a military-assistance assignment
rather than accept an offer of a voluntary assignment to the 4th
Infantry Division, a division that a friend in Washington had
privately told me would be ordered to Vietnam in a few
months. As a professional soldier I knew that the essential pre-
requisite for promotion in the Army was service in the most recent war. But was it right for an officer to take part in a war
under the guise of duty and to be responsible for the deaths of
other Americans in an effort to advance his own career? I had
returned from the war in Korea disillusioned by the callous disregard for the lives of our soldiers that I had seen there, and
had decided then that I would not again be responsible for
leading young Americans to their deaths for reasons having little to do with the defense of our true national security. Vietnam, to me, had all the earmarks of another Korea.

My thoughts wandered back to Korea and the frozen hills of
the "Iron Triangle" in 1951. I remembered a cold, cloudy September morning on Hill 432, northwest of the rubble of the
town of Kumwha. I could almost hear the clink of canteens
being filled and the groaning of straps as weapons and ammunition belts were slung over the shoulders of the men of the third
platoon of Easy Company. It was a couple of hours till daylight
but the third platoon had been awake since midnight. We had
been assigned the mission of seizing Hill 582—the "Ice Cream
Cone" as it was called by the GI's. Captain Tony Cavallo, the
company commander, had given me the brief typewritten
order from battalion headquarters that ordered one platoon to
"attack and seize" Hill 582. By the glow of a flashlight Tony
had gone over the attack details with me. I would get five minutes of artillery preparatory fires on the hill when I was in the

attack position and I could have a few rounds of 4.2-mortar-harassing fire while I moved down off Hill 432 and crossed the open valley that lay between us and the Chinese soldiers on Hill 582. Tony had finished briefing me by saying "It's going to be a tough uphill fight, Ed. You've got to keep climbing and moving all the way."

This was to be a "limited-objective" attack to throw the Chinese off-balance and convince them of the United States resolve to continue fighting in Korea, even though all eyes were then on the peace talks going on at the village of Panmunjon. But why did we have to attack now, I asked myself? Why not just hold the ground we had—which was north of the original 38th Parallel dividing line between North and South Korea—and wait for the war to end? Why go out and get some more of us killed? What would it accomplish to seize Hill 582? We didn't need the real estate. And while nothing had been said in my orders about holding the hill, it seemed likely that I would, in the tradition of U.S. Infantry, be expected to dig in and hold the hill until I could be reinforced. Well, I had told myself there must be a damn good reason to take the hill or I wouldn't be ordered to risk the lives of forty men. At least I had hoped there was a good reason and that it was not another mission dreamed up by the regiment and battalion commanders to make themselves look tough and aggressive.

I thought about my birthday just a little over a month away; I kind of wanted to live to be twenty-three and there were several men in my platoon still looking forward to becoming twenty-one. I couldn't help but wonder how attacking Hill 582 would make my countrymen across the Pacific any safer back there in their nice warm homes. I knew from hard-earned experience that it was normal to dread a coming attack and to think of reasons for not making it and risking your life and the lives of your men. I also knew that once the fighting started the doubts would disappear and the orders would come instinctively. But that cold gray morning I could not shake the thought that this attack really wasn't necessary.

By the flickering light of a candle I finished shaving, read the 23rd Psalm, and put my Bible in my field pack that would be left behind with my sleeping bag and the metal machine-gun ammunition box containing my few personal possessions. If I didn't make it back, the personal things would go to graves registration for return to my next of kin. I repeated to myself, "Yea, though I walk through the valley of the shadow of death, I will fear no evil: for thou art with me." But there was no more time to dwell on my doubts, it was time to move down into the valley and up onto the steep slopes of Hill 582. I climbed out of my sandbag and log bunker to find my platoon messenger, Corporal Vacanti, and platoon medic, Private First Class Hildenbrand, waiting. Hildenbrand was a conscientious objector who served reluctantly but efficiently as the platoon aidman. He absolutely refused to carry any type of weapon and went into battle armed only with his first-aid kit. He was one of the bravest men I have known.

From Sergeant Green, the platoon sergeant, I learned that everyone had finished their breakfast of cold C-rations and that two additional cans of C-rations had been issued to each man in case there was a chance to eat again before nightfall. All of us knew that for some men in the platoon this cold can of beans or hash would be their last meal on earth. The only question was whose number would come up—who would die that day? Each man believed it would be someone else.

As I walked around the back of Hill 432 checking my squads I had a chance to talk with most of the men in my platoon. I joked with some, kidded others, and tried to buck up the ones that were new and frightened; for these three or four this would be their first combat action, and with them I tried to be especially reassuring. These men were my responsibility and over the next hours they would risk their lives to carry out orders that I would have to give them supposedly to carry out our role in defending the national security.

Captain Cavallo suddenly appeared out of the morning fog with a frown on his forty-two-year-old face, yet filled with words of fatherly encouragement. Tony Cavallo was a "retread inactive reservist" who had spent four years in the infantry in World War II only to be involuntarily called back to active duty when the Korean War broke out. He despised the Army but he tried hard to run a good company. Now he wanted to tell me that the battalion and regimental commanders were coming up to the company CP (command post) to watch me attack 582. Tony was nervous and urged me to move as fast as I safely could so everything would look all right and the "wheels" wouldn't get restless waiting for the fighting to start. I had mumbled something about doing my best, but wondered what was bringing old "get-me-promoted" Sinclair up to watch a platoon attack. All the old-timers in the battalion remembered Lieutenant Colonel Sinclair telling us before we left Japan that "all of you are going to help me make colonel." He had been a staff officer in World War II and had failed to get an infantry combat command on his record before the war ended. So he was still a lieutenant colonel while most of his West Point classmates were already colonels or generals. He had arrived from XIV Corps Headquarters a few days before the battalion sailed for Korea. We all knew that his command tour would last only about six months. He had to look good to the regimental and division commanders in that period and make no glaring mistakes, if he hoped to wear the coveted colonel's eagles. He had previously volunteered the battalion twice for attacks of doubtful value south of Kumwha. And I had been told the day before by a friend in the operations section that the limited-objective attack I was going to make had been Lieutenant Colonel Sinclair's idea. He was bringing the regimental commander up to watch his operation.

I looked at my watch: 0500 hours. Time to begin moving down into the valley. The third platoon was strung out along the backside of the hill. I waved my lead scouts out toward the perimeter of the company position, and the heavily armed platoon began moving down the trail. As we cleared the barbed-wire barrier that marked the limit of Easy Company's domain on Hill 432, I slipped the bolt of my M-2 carbine back and loaded a bullet into the chamber. We then began the descent into the fog-filled valley below. Not a word had been spoken. Everyone was taut with anxiety—the Chinese had a bad habit of ambushing patrols moving out to attack them. The scouts signaled back that the trail down to the valley appeared clear.

As I motioned the platoon down into the valley we heard the whoosh of the first mortar shells plummeting into the crest of Hill 582. This was the harassing fire that we hoped would keep the Chinese soldiers down in their bunkers while we moved across the exposed valley floor.

Our pants' legs were quickly soaked with the morning dew that clung to every bush and blade of grass. The crisp clean smells of the Korean dawn blended with the smell of stale perspiration rising from unwashed bodies. It had been over two weeks since anyone in the third platoon had had an opportunity to bathe.

The thin stream of perspiration running down my armpit was not purely the result of the exercise—I felt nervous and tense. We were at the valley floor and the sun began to filter through the morning haze. We had to get across the valley before the fog lifted. I motioned one light-machine-gun team to set up a position covering the valley and prepared to order the first squad to begin crossing. At that moment Vacanti told me that the company commander wanted to talk to me on the SCR-300 radio. I had asked that there be no radio transmissions until I reached the attack position because frequent conversations before attacks usually warned the Chinese when and where we were attacking. But now I had to break silence and say "Red Dog Easy Three" into the handset. Tony Cavallo sounded anxious, "Where are you, Ed? I can't see you in all that fog." I dug into the front of my field jacket and brought out the dog-eared map and figured out where I was at that moment. I gave Tony the map coordinates of my position. There was a note of annoyance in his voice, "You mean you're not across the valley?" I replied I was in the process of trying to cross, but couldn't do so while I was talking to him on the radio. "Red Dog Six [battalion commander] is here and wants you to get across at once." I replied that I would make a check for mines and then start crossing. "Never mind the mines, move across at once so you won't look too slow in crossing. Remember who is up here watching you," he replied. "Roger, over," I said. "Out," he answered, ending the conversation.

The platoon sergeant came up at this point to tell me the

scouts had found antipersonnel mines along the bank of the stream that ran in the center of the valley. He asked, "Do you want to clear some of them out before we start trying to get across?" "No, they want us to get across the valley on the double, mines or no mines," I answered. I told the first-squad leader to start moving his squad across and to avoid the mines the scouts had found. He nodded and moved forward into the fast-dissolving haze. I took my binoculars from the case on my belt and began scanning the valley and lower slopes of Hill 582. I was hoping that the Chinese had neglected to put out forward listening posts. The next few minutes would tell as the nine members of the first squad began moving. They reached the stream that came rushing down from the nearby mountains, and began wading across. Now would be the moment any Chinese listening posts would open fire. I waited tensely for the familiar sound of a Chinese submachine-gun burst. None came and the first squad was across the hip-deep stream. The men lying flat on their bellies around me sucked in their breath as their friends in the first squad waded out of the water and started picking their way toward the foot of Hill 582. Now came the mines.

Again Vacanti was passing up the radio handset, "It's Red Dog Easy Six," he said, frowning. Tony Cavallo wanted to know if I was across the valley yet. I replied that I was in the act of crossing. "Red Dog Six and Dragon Six [regimental commander] are here and want you to hurry up," he answered. I swallowed the temptation to tell him that if they were in such a hurry why didn't they come down and join me in crossing the minefield. But instead I said, "I'll cross as fast as I can but I'm not going to risk my men's lives just to please Red Dog Six." I got an "Out" in reply. I handed the handset back to Vacanti and motioned the second squad to follow me across the valley. The weapons squad would follow us and then the third squad would cross. Ahead I could see the first squad taking up covering positions at the foot of Hill 582. Then we were in the swiftly flowing, icy water of the stream, stumbling over the smooth round stones that shifted about on the bottom. We stumbled out soaked to the waist and started looking for the telltale marks of raised box-mine lids, tripwires, or the small thin metal prongs showing where a captured U.S. "Bouncing Betty" mine had been buried to maim or kill those who had manufactured it. Mostly we tried to follow the trail of the first squad through the wet knee-high grass.

The sun began to burn off the last of the morning fog. We would soon be plainly visible to anyone on the summit of Hill 582 who cared to look. I waved the first squad up the steep finger of the hill and looked back to see how fast the weapons squad was crossing the stream. The heavily loaded weapons and ammunition bearers stumbled and slipped in the water. The mortar gunner fell and struggled up drenched, trying to retrieve his carbine. They were out of the water and starting toward us when a black cloud of dirt and smoke flew up between two of the advancing ammunition bearers. A second later the sharp "thump-whump" of an exploding Bouncing Betty reached our ears. Four men had gone down as if brushed over by the wind. For a minute there was silence. Then the anguished scream of "Medic!" broke the silence.

I frantically motioned the first and second squads to keep climbing up through the trees and underbrush to the attack position, and then pumped my right arm up and down in the direction of the third squad, which was just starting to cross, to tell them to hurry. It would be only minutes before Chinese mortar and artillery fire hit the valley. Any hope of surprise was gone.

I scrambled down the finger and ran back out to the valley to find out how badly the men in the weapons squad were hurt and to speed up the movement of the rest of the platoon. Vacanti waved the handset and said, "Red Dog Six." "Tell him I'm too busy to talk," I said, running to one of the men lying face down in the weeds. I turned him over as gently as I could to find that his face and chest were only a mangled mass of bloody flesh riddled with dozens of small ball-bearing-size holes. I checked his pulse—there was none I could feel. I tried to find a heartbeat, but could hear nothing; he was dead. I picked him up and dog-trotted toward the base of the hill where I laid him down.

Men of the third squad were helping two of the other wounded toward the same protected spot. Hildenbrand was carrying the lifeless form of another soldier. I was putting a belt tourniquet around the upper part of Private Franklin's shattered right arm when the first mortar shells came "whooshing" into the valley behind us. At about the same instant the crackle of machine-gun fire began from the top of Hill 582. Vacanti tugged at my sleeve and stuck the radio handset into my hand. "The captain again," he said.

"What's your situation, Easy Three?" Before I could answer, Cavallo continued, "What's holding you up? Red Dog Six wants you to get up that hill on the double."

When I could break in I said, "This is Red Dog Easy Three. Listen, Captain, I've got two dead and three wounded from those goddamn mines and in a couple of minutes those mortars you see hitting in the valley are gonna be on us. Request permission to move right through the attack position, and how about giving me my preparatory artillery fire right now to get those bastards' heads down so we can get up this ridge."

"Roger on attack position and prep fires," he answered. "Quit worrying about the mines and get your asses up that hill."

I made no reply.

The angry whine and buzz of machine-gun bullets ricocheting from trees and rocks increased as we struggled higher up the long ridge. A few moments later we heard the whistling rush of the incoming preparatory artillery fire. This was followed by the resounding thump of exploding shells on the top of the hill as the ground under our feet trembled from the shock. As the last salvo of shells came in some of the rounds fell short of the top of the hill and exploded slightly in front of the second squad. The blast threw nearly everyone to the ground and was followed by the scream of "Medic! Medic!" I shouted to Vacanti, and told him to tell them to shift the fire to the back of the hill.

As we broke out of the last of the timberline and started moving steadily uphill, running from tree stump to rocks, firing as we advanced, the Chinese directed a heavy volume of fire at

us from the trenches. Through my binoculars I could see a
group of Chinese soldiers setting a Maxim machine gun in
place to fire toward us.

I looked around for Corporal Johnson and his 57mm. Recoilless Rifle. We had to get that Maxim before he got us. I saw
Johnson crouched behind an ancient Korean grave mound and
started running toward him, hugging low to the ground. About
halfway there, a string of machine-gun bullets tore up the
ground between us and several more buzzed angrily by my
head. I dove to the ground behind a fallen tree and stuck my
nose into the gravelly ridge. The bullets kept singing about two
feet over me. I fearfully raised my head and shouted "Johnson!" at the top of my lungs. He looked at me and I motioned
toward the machine gun—he nodded and reached back for his
heavy 57 rifle. I didn't see how he was going to get off a shot
with the Maxim raking the ridge with burst after burst of fire.

But Corporal Johnson was a very unusual soldier. He was
black and, until a few weeks before, he had been serving in one
of the last all-black units in the American Army, the 24th Infantry Regiment. The platoon I was leading had been inte-
grated only a short time before and now 35 percent of the platoon was composed of black soldiers from the 24th Regiment.
This was our first combat action together. I had spent some
time with the "Deuce Four" (as the 24th Regiment was
known); I had heard their song of "When the old gook mortars
begin to thud, the old deuce four begins to bug," sung to the
tune of "I'm Moving On," a popular country-western song of
that era. I remembered the low morale that had permeated this
regiment of black soldiers commanded by white officers. I had
heard about how a company of black soldiers had quit up on
Hill 1062 after being sent forward on a third assault in one day,
and I had heard stories that black soldiers wouldn't fight.

I went flat against the ground again as the Maxim sent another burst my way. As I lay there I saw a large ant crawl un-
concernedly along the ground in front of my face. I thought
how nice it would be to be an ant, and in a way I felt like an
ant in a world gone mad. But we had to get moving; we dared
not remain pinned down by the machine-gun fire. It was only a

matter of time before the mortars would start firing at us. I motioned to Johnson again to try to get off a shot at the machine-gun bunker. He raised up to a half crouch behind the grave mound and "Spoons" Davis (so called because he played music on a pair of GI mess spoons) loaded a round into the breech of the heavy, long-barreled recoilless rifle. The Maxim swept the ridge again and as it did Johnson was on his feet and a round went winging into the corner of the bunker. The Maxim stopped firing.

Again Johnson was on his feet and another round went slamming into the bunker. A burst of fire came back and Johnson fell to the ground, rolling over on his side with one arm extended trying to stop the stream of bullets that churned up the ground around him. Then little Davis grabbed up the rifle and crouched on one knee as he got off a shot at the Maxim.

Hildenbrand ran out across the ground toward Johnson and knelt down beside him even as the bullets kept coming. He rolled him over and calmly began to bandage his chest. Davis and another loader had the 57 firing again and yet the machine gun kept firing at Hildenbrand. I watched in amazement as he picked up Johnson's carbine, knelt, and began firing back. Everyone was firing at the top of the ridge. Suddenly to my right I heard the steady pitch of a BAR (Browning Automatic Rifle) slightly to the front of where we were strung out along the ground. Private First Class Dunaway was walking crouched over his BAR and firing burst after burst into the bunker where the Maxim was firing from. Then we were on our feet screaming and running up toward the top of the hill. "Let's go! Let's go! Get 'em! Kill 'em!" I screamed, as I emptied my carbine at the enemy positions. The third platoon, with Dunaway leading the others forward, went up the hill. Some crouched as though walking into a wind; others fired as they ran, stooping to fumble with ammo clips as they reloaded their M-1 rifles. Nearly everyone was screaming as we reached the brush and barbed-wire barricade in front of the Chinese trenches.

Dunaway was firing as fast as he could reload, then he suddenly went down, hit by a burst from a submachine gun. Momentarily halted, we crouched behind the brush fence that sur-

rounded the Chinese positions as they tried to drive us back
with concussion grenades. It was then that Vacanti reached me
and handed me the radio handset again. It was Red Dog Six
himself and he sounded angry as he said, "What the hell is
holding you up on that ridge, King? You should be on top by
now. Now I'm ordering you to stop screwing around and get
up there—all in the hell you have to do is to charge the bastards!"

I struggled to hold my temper as I replied, "I'm up to the
brush now and I'm trying to work a squad around to their flank
before I go in, otherwise I'm going to get all the fire on the
front and take a lot more casualties." The reply came back
sharply, "Quit worrying so much about casualties. You're up
there to take that hill, now get your ass in there and take it.
We've waited around here long enough." Old "get-me-promoted" was pretty jumpy with the regimental commander at
his elbow. Vacanti made a sour face and said, "His radio operator says he's mad because he told the regimental commander
we'd have this pimple before lunch and it's making him look
bad—guess we got to get with it, sir, or the colonel ain't gonna
get promoted."

Before I could answer him there was a fresh burst of firing
from the flank of the Chinese trenches. The third squad had
managed to get behind them. I rose to my feet and shouted
"Let's go!" and the rest of the third platoon went piling over
the brush and into the Chinese trenches. Scattered shots
greeted us as the Chinese ran along the trenches toward the
rear of the hill. I can still feel the cold fear that gripped me
when I encountered a Chinese soldier coming out of a firing
bunker. He had a grenade in one hand, and at the sight of me
he began frantically unscrewing the cap which would enable
him to pull the firing ring and throw the grenade. Somewhere
in the assault I had left my carbine behind. I fumbled desperately for the 45-caliber automatic pistol I carried in a belt holster. I got it out of the holster and aimed it at arm's length at
the crouched Chinese—it wouldn't fire.

Frantically, I pulled back the slide and let it snap forward.
The grenade arched forward as I felt the recoil of the pistol and

saw jets of dust squirt from the quilted jacket of the Chinese soldier. He was spun around and slammed against the wall of the trench. Even as he fell he was trying to shove himself toward me but his legs buckled under him. His grenade was a dud that hit me in the leg and rolled harmlessly to the ground. For some reason which I still do not understand my life had been spared. My hand which held the suddenly heavy pistol began to shake uncontrollably. This was not the first time I had looked over a gun barrel and seen a man die after I pulled the trigger—and it was not to be the last time—but each time I felt a sickening remorse.

I looked down at the sprawled bodies of the dead Chinese and I wondered why Americans had to kill so many other people and so many die themselves to keep America safe and free.

The "Ice Cream Cone" was ours. Ten men lay in the shelter of a Chinese-built bunker. Hildenbrand had bandaged their wounds as best he could. Dunaway was the worst hit. Bloody bandages covered his chest and the wheeze of his breathing told me he was dying. I knelt down and cradled his head in my arms and told him he was going to be okay. He was nineteen and had married just before coming overseas. He asked that I take a letter from his pack that had been left back at the company, and send it to his wife. I promised him I would.

Vacanti motioned me to the radio and I listened to Red Dog Six congratulate me for getting on top of the hill. He said, "All right now, count the bodies of the Chinks, collect all the weapons you can and get busy blowing up the bunkers, then pull off as soon as you can." I didn't understand. I said, "But, sir, I can hold up here. All I need is to get my dead and wounded out and get some ammo and food sent up while the artillery covers that ridgeline to the north." "No," he said. "Your mission is to destroy the positions; it's a limited-objective attack." I tried to argue that I could hold the hill and didn't see any reason to pull off and give it back to the Chinese after the dead and wounded I had taken. "Goddammit, you are to pull off that hill before dark. It doesn't have any tactical value and besides the damn thing will be on the enemy side of the truce line, anyway, once the peace talks end."

I had been standing outside the bunker while I argued with the battalion commander. When I finished giving orders to blow the bunkers I went back inside to see how the wounded were doing. Hildenbrand was getting them ready to be carried down on the litters that were on the way up the hill. We had asked for an air-evac chopper to pick up Dunaway and Franklin just as soon as they got back off the hill. Dunaway was bleeding from the mouth but he managed to gasp out, "Are we really pulling off and giving it back?" I nodded dumbly. As the realization sunk in that his efforts had been for little more than a training exercise, he asked, "Doesn't anyone care what happens to us anymore, sir?" I didn't have an answer. All I could do was let helpless tears of rage course down my cheeks. Outside the bunker I was stopped by another soldier who said, "Why the hell are we pulling off and giving this fucking hill back to the bastards?" I said it was orders and he wept too as he said, "But they killed Johnny, they killed Johnny, the fucking sonsabitches, and now we're gonna give it all back to them so we can come take it again. What kind of a fucking war is this, sir?" Then he turned away saying, "Aw shit, what's the use, what's the fucking use?" And walked toward the side of the hill. I felt the same way.

Dunaway died before he reached the bottom of Hill 582. Four other young Americans died with him that day as did over a score of young Chinese. The survivors came down off the Ice Cream Cone, crossed the minefield once more, and climbed wearily back up to the holes on Hill 432 that we called home. As I walked I made a vow that never again would I order more young Americans to their deaths in futile missions like this one. Back on Hill 432 I sat down to eat a cold can of C-ration ham and lima beans. As I was putting a spoonful of this greasy mess into my mouth I glanced at my hands. They were brown and sticky with dried blood. I stuck the plastic spoon in the can, set it down, and tried to wipe off the blood, but it wouldn't come off—and I went back to eating. A few days later I would write to Dunaway's young wife, "Your husband died bravely with no pain. He died fighting for his country and I promise you we will

not forget him and we will square his death with the enemy."
Brave young words, hollow words, hypocritical words. Dunaway hadn't died in defense of his country. The Chinese had already reoccupied Hill 582 and soon another limited-objective
attack would be sent against it. He and the others had died because of a commander's desire to make the battalion look "aggressive."

I couldn't believe that the Army to which I had decided to
dedicate my life could really be this callous and uncaring of its
soldiers. It had to be only a few climbers like Lieutenant Colonel "Get-me-promoted" who thought solely of their careers. It
would take me until 1966 to find out that I was wrong.

I came back to the United States to be asked in New York,
"Where you stationed, soldier boy?" And when I said I was just
in from Korea to be asked, "Yeah, where's that?" My thoughts
often went back to Dunaway. He had been right; no one did
care. Only the wives and parents of the dead really grieved and
no one seemed to notice. Even the Army didn't seem to care.
The truce talks ground on as we argued over the prisoners, and
the limited-objective attacks continued on "Heartbreak
Ridge," "Papasan," "Old Baldy," and "Pork Chop Hill." The
casualty rate went down to "only" forty deaths a week and any
of the American public that had thought about the fighting at
all began forgetting it.

As the war ground to a close, Army promotions and decorations became fewer. Many officers who had not yet gotten
"combat command" on their records tried to volunteer for
service in Korea before the war ended. Those who didn't go to
Korea knew they would have to resign themselves to being
"book soldiers" and to feeling self-conscious in the presence of
their beribboned contemporaries who had gotten the magical
"combat experience" on their records. Based on past United
States history, there didn't appear much possibility that officers
would have another chance to gain combat command and a
share of Combat Infantry Badges and ribbons that the World
War II and Korean veterans now imperiously sported. It looked

like the U.S. Army was faced with thirty years of peace, or at best only a cold war in Europe which would bring neither promotions nor decorations.

After returning from Korea I was sent to Fort Benning, Georgia, to attend the company-officer course and learn what I should have known before going to Korea two years before. After combat experience I found the course repetitive and so far removed from the reality of war as to be almost ridiculous. From Fort Benning I went to Fort Riley, Kansas, to serve as an infantry-training officer and an instructor in a leadership battalion. Here I saw the conversion of the Army from a combat orientation to a peacetime status quo. Noncommissioned officers who had been quickly promoted for combat leadership in Korea were just as rapidly demoted because of their inability to adjust to the spit-and-polish barracks life that the book soldiers now instigated. Decorated soldiers were placed on endless details picking up trash or cutting grass—there was apparently nothing else to do with them. Those who showed their displeasure by getting drunk or going home without permission were court-martialed.

One afternoon while serving as officer of the guard I chanced upon one of the soldiers who had served in my platoon in Korea. His name was Wells and he had been a sergeant when I had last seen him. But now he wore the stripe of a private first class. I asked him what had happened. He replied, "Well, I'm not much good at all this saluting, shining, and polishing, Lieutenant, so I got busted 'cause they said I wasn't qualified to be a noncom." I recalled that he had been deemed well qualified when leading men up steep rocky ridges under enemy fire.

At Fort Riley I made plans to leave active duty when my period of voluntary service ended. While I waited I frequently voiced my complaints over the many wrongs I believed existed in the Army system. One afternoon I explained to Brigadier General John L. Whitelaw that I planned to leave the Army because, after what I had seen in Korea and Fort Riley, I didn't feel I could remain even though I had once planned to make the Army my career. The general was a quiet, erudite man and he looked at me with his kindly grin and said, "But it is because of people like you, Lieutenant, that nothing ever changes in the Army. You come in from civilian life and don't like what you see and so you leave. If you really cared what happened in the Army you would stay and work to set things right. You don't convince me of the sincerity of your convictions when you tell me everything is wrong with the Army, but you haven't the courage to stay and work to make things better. You're a capable young officer, exactly the kind of man the Army needs, and if you really believed what you say you would stay rather than leave the Army."

The more I thought over his words the more convinced I became that he was right. It seemed true that all those who were perceptive enough to question what went on in the Army quickly left. They in effect left the Army to the unchallenged control of the very people they disliked and mistrusted. Maybe this was one of the reasons there seemed so little evidence of a chance for improvement in the conditions of service in the Army. I decided I would apply for a Regular Army commission and try to do whatever I could to change and improve the things that I had come to believe were wrong in the Army. Eighteen years later I would wonder how I could have been so naïve, but from the lowly, uninformed position of a twenty-four-year-old first lieutenant all things seemed possible if one was just willing to work hard enough.

The constant emphasis on mopping and waxing rotting wood floors in barracks built in 1940 to last a maximum of ten years, and of lining up footlockers, buttoning all the buttons on shirts hanging up in wall-lockers, and so forth, grew very tiresome. This minutia plus the repetitive boring classes I was required to teach did not seem essential to the development of effective leadership. Another annoyance was the conformity-conscious rank-climbers and their wives who were constantly trying to impress the battalion commander and his wife. The wives of West Point officers always made it a point to remind the less fortunate officers and their wives that "they" had graduated from "the Academy" in 1949 or 1950.

After a year I volunteered for duty in Europe. I received orders to Austria and was elated. Then the orders were canceled

and I was ordered to Germany instead. But I was still pleased
to be leaving Fort Riley. In Germany I was assigned to the 28th
National Guard Division (soon to be redesignated the 9th Infantry Division). I waited for three days at division headquarters to see the division commander. He had wanted to talk to
all regular officers being assigned to the regiment I was going
to. When he did see me, his talk had hardly been reassuring.
He said, "You probably have never seen a regiment quite as
bad as the 112th Infantry. Don't let it get you down. I've sent a
new regimental commander there and he will need your help
to improve things—do your best to make things better." After
that peptalk I rode the train to Heilbronn expecting the worst
and that was exactly what I found.

I quickly learned what it meant to be a regular Army officer
assigned to a National Guard division. There were no available
family quarters and it would be at least a year before any
would be available. In the meantime I would not be authorized
to bring my family at my own expense because the German
housing shortage was critical. And though I was the senior first
lieutenant assigned to the regiment, I was not given a company
command even though companies were commanded by Guard
officers junior to me in rank and experience.

I reasoned that all of this would be balanced by the possibility of getting back to field duty. For years I had been reading
about the vaunted combat efficiency of the U.S. Seventh Army.
I had been anxious to get into the field and see the units in action. My anticipation was short-lived. Not only were the troops
poorly trained and discipline lax, but command leadership was
practically nonexistent. Many of the field-grade officers were
more concerned with drinking bouts and chasing Fräuleins
than they were about field operations or the welfare of their
troops. Despite stringent rules to the contrary, headquarters'
staffs frequently put up for the night in German inns while
their troops slept outside on the ground. And there were constant racial problems.

One night while serving as officer of the guard I was ordered
to Heilbronn with all off-duty guards to quell a disturbance in a
"black" *gasthaus,* one of the three bars in the town that ca-

tered to Negro soldiers. The rest were for whites only. Trouble
had erupted when several white soldiers entered the bar and
tried to become friendly with one of the German prostitutes
who frequented the place. The ensuing fight had gone beyond
the normal punching and bottle-breaking and had developed
into a chair-throwing, knife-wielding free-for-all. Additional
white and black soldiers quickly joined the fight and it grew
beyond the control of the U.S. Military Police and the local
German police. When I arrived with about thirty armed guards
the regimental commander was already there issuing orders
through a bullhorn. His voice was resonant as he shouted,
"Ah'm ordering you to stop that gawddamned fighting and
come out of there with your hands over your heads." The reply
was a barrage of beer bottles. With this he ordered me to form
my guards into a single rank facing the *gasthaus*. Then he said,
"Have the guards lock and load" (place a clip of eight bullets
into the chamber of each M-1 rifle). His next command was
"Prepare to fire on my command." Since there were women inside, I walked over to him and asked if he was sure he wanted
to fire into the building. "We'll fire into the roof. I don't give a
goddamn about a bunch of niggers and their German whores.
You give the command to fire when I tell you," he said in
parting, as he walked to his parked jeep. I had decided I would
not give such an order, when the first of several black soldiers
began filing out of the *gasthaus* with their hands over their
heads. They were met at the door by waiting white military police who clubbed and kicked them into nearby Army trucks for
the ride back to the guardhouse. I thought of Corporal Johnson
and Spoons Davis and wondered why they had risked their
lives for this same Army.

Chapter 2

Why I Decided to Stop Making It in the Army

☆ ☆ ☆ ☆ ☆ ☆ ☆ ☆ ☆

My recollections were abruptly interrupted by the arrival of a nurse with pills I was supposed to take daily while in Walter Reed. After she left, an Argentinian lieutenant who was awaiting surgery stopped by to chat in Spanish. While he was there the Argentine military attaché, General Roberto Levingston (later to become president of Argentina), came by to visit the lieutenant. His visit reminded me that none of the three U.S. generals I worked for had taken time to call or visit, although two Brazilian generals that I worked with had come to see me.

I also noticed the apparent friendly air of courtesy and camaraderie that existed between the Argentine general and his officer. He listened attentively to the lieutenant's opinions and to my own. He may have given our opinions little consideration but he at least listened and gave an appearance of interest. I mentally contrasted this interest and the relaxed tone of the conversation with the subdued, nervous restraint that normally marked any conversation between a United States general or flag officer and a subordinate. A U.S. Army officer is not expected to take exception to any opinion expressed by an Army general. I recalled the time, during my first weeks of duty with the Joint Chiefs of Staff, when I inadvertently slipped and disagreed with my superior at a meeting by saying, "I think a better way to accomplish our goal might be to . . ." I got no further. He cut me off in front of the other members of the delegation by saying, "I don't give a goddamn what you think. I'm not interested in your opinions or ideas. I just want to hear whatever facts you can give me."

After the Argentines left I thought again of my orders to Vietnam. I did not believe in the badly led, mercenary war we were waging in South Vietnam. If I served there it would be as a fraud. I would not be serving in support of what I believed was best for the nation or the Army. I would be doing the same as many of my lieutenant colonel contemporaries who were anxiously volunteering for service in Vietnam in order to get some "command time" on their record. But if I did not serve, it meant I had to leave my profession at forty years of age and begin anew in an already tight job market. I weighed the financial aspects of leaving the service. Within a year I would be eligible for promotion to full colonel. If I served a Vietnam tour I was almost sure to be promoted. By law I would then have to remain on active duty two years from the date of my promotion. Since I already had nearly twenty-three years of total service that meant staying in the Army another five years and retiring at age forty-five with twenty-eight years of service. That would have entitled me to 75 percent of my base pay, or about $12,000 a year, for the rest of my life. And during the five more years of active duty I would have been drawing about $22,000 a year in pay and allowances before taxes, plus whatever military pay raises came out of the current talks.

I took pencil and paper and did some figuring. Assuming I lived twenty more years it could cost me up to $111,000 in re-

tirement pay to retire in 1969. If I hid my convictions and went
to Vietnam, I would be assigned to a safe headquarters staff job
in Saigon. But I would have still been authorized to collect an
additional $65 per month as "hostile fire pay." Also I would be
entitled to a reduction in my declared taxable federal income. I
would be allowed to deposit up to $5,000, returning 10 percent
interest annually, in the government-operated Soldiers', Sailors'
and Airmen's Deposits savings program. There were financial
as well as career incentives for duty in Vietnam.

I drew a line down the center of a piece of paper and wrote
at the top on one side of the line, "Reasons for going," and on
the other side of the line, "Reasons for not going." On the
"going" side I listed: (1) retention of my friends, reputation,
and continued career in the Army; (2) a probable assignment to
attaché duty in Spain or Latin America after my year in Vietnam; (3) serving one year would qualify me for almost certain
promotion to colonel and the consequent financial and retirement advantages. Among the reasons for not going I listed: (1)
my desire to be honest with myself, the Army, and my fellow
citizens by making known my beliefs about the war and conditions in the Army; (2) not wanting to be responsible for the
death of others chiefly so I could continue to profit and advance in my career.

But was I afraid to go to Vietnam—was I afraid of dying? I
thought about this and decided that I was not. I had faced
death before and, though I had been afraid, it had not been
enough to cause me to fear facing death again. Since my experiences in Korea I had been fatalistic about death. Like most
combat soldiers I believed that when your number came up it
didn't make any difference where you were—home in bed or in
Vietnam—you died from one thing or another. I had always assumed that I might someday die wearing my country's uniform;
that was what my profession was all about. Besides, there was
no use being foolishly dramatic. I would be in less physical danger in Saigon than I would late at night on upper Fourteenth
Street in Washington, D.C. There just wasn't much danger for
a lieutenant colonel living the good staff life in Saigon, unless
he drank or screwed himself to death. Even in a battalion com-

mand the chief danger was a helicopter crash and your chances there were better than in the rush-hour Washington beltway traffic. No, fear of death wasn't a reason for not going.

The shadows were lengthening across my bed when Floyd, the cheerful black ward orderly, brought in my dinner tray. "Hi, Colonel, you really look like you're thinking hard." "Yeah, I'm trying to make up my mind about Vietnam," I said. "Man that ain't no problem, ain't nothin' good about that hole," he said. "What did you do there?" I asked. "I was an aidman down in the Delta with the 9th Division." "What did you think of the war?" I asked again. "Well, if you was anything but a grunt it wasn't too bad. I mean all the lifers they was gettin' promoted and they could get a little whiskey when they wanted and the generals and colonels they was livin' high on the hog—but if you were a grunt—nothin' man. And we had to turn up the bodies; old General Ewell he was somethin' else about killin' gooks. The platoons they'd better turn in a good body count or else they stayed out in the brush forever. Didn't make no difference what kind of bodies—even pigs and chickens counted—just so you reported them as bodies." Then Floyd's usually smiling features turned hard and his black eyes took on a cold glitter as he said, "I ain't going back over there again; nobody gives a damn about the cats over there. They're just there so the lifers can get promoted. Look at all them cats up in the wards without no legs, or arms, or balls. Look at the lootenant down the hall there, no eyes left—a damn mine done nearly tore his head off—and what for, sir?—you don't see ol' General Westmoreland limpin' aroun' here with no plastic legs. Fuck no, ain't nothin' good about that war, sir."

Then afraid he might have offended me he said, "I didn't mean that against you, Colonel, you seem like a pretty fair guy, but you officers just don't know what it's like being an EM." I told him I hadn't always been an officer and I knew damn well what it was like. I hadn't forgotten being an eighteen-year-old private held from behind by one noncommissioned officer while another punched me in the stomach until I couldn't breathe and thought I was going to strangle in my own vomit. The two sergeants were having some fun with the "new men" in that isolated rifle company standing occupation duty in Korea. Oh no, I'd never forgotten being an enlisted man in the last all-volunteer "New Regular Army" of 1946.

Floyd's comments brought back a conversation I had with two young soldiers a few days earlier. We had all been sitting in a hospital waiting room. They both looked about nineteen years old and resembled hundreds of other forlorn-looking tousled-haired kids that I had seen over the years. They were the low-IQ kids usually referred to in the Army as "dumbshits" or "shitheads." Most infantry units receive a fairly large number of these soldiers. They make good infantry soldiers because they do not often grasp the danger they are in, and they seldom question anything. It is the dumbshits who frequently bear the brunt of infantry combat. Vietnam has been no exception. It was their arms, legs, and eyes that President Johnson and his general, "Westy," risked in trying to find the light at the end of the tunnel. And it was chiefly through their lives that Westy and his classmates and friends were gaining their promotions, decorations, fame, and glory.

Now these two who had each given a leg, and one an arm as well, to our "crusade" in Vietnam were sitting in rumpled blue bathrobes waiting to be patched up before being sent out to struggle for their continued existence at "home." Each wore a plastic leg with a shiny new black GI shoe on the end of it. That plastic leg and a small bronze Purple Heart medal were a grateful nation's way of thanking them for their part in the crusade. Later there would be modest monthly disability payments from the Veterans Administration, and a special price on a new car they could drive with plastic legs and arms. And if things didn't work out there would be a VA hospital where they could go to die. And at the last the nation would help to bury them and finally remove them from the national conscience.

But at that point they sat there in the stifling hot waiting room inhaling the smell of rubbing alcohol and unwashed feet. No one seemed to be getting in to see the doctor and since it was mid-morning that meant he was having a cup of coffee. There was no hurry, for we were being paid to sit there and wait—and we were used to waiting. You were always waiting

for something in the U.S. Army. I looked at them and smiled.
They both smiled back uneasily. There was no way of telling by
my rumpled blue bathrobe what kind of a creature I was. The
gray in my temples told the cautious pair that I might be an active or retired officer or noncommissioned officer. Dumbshits
learn by bitter experience to avoid contact with officers and
noncommissioned officers whenever possible. To become involved with these creatures nearly always results in some un-
pleasantness or pain for the dumbshit. It may mean an extra
detail cleaning latrines or kitchen grease-traps, or it may mean
having to charge a blazing AK-47, depending on where they
run afoul of one of those people wearing stripes, bars, oak
leaves, or stars.

These two looked quickly away hoping, I suspect, that I
would leave things at a smile. For an opener, I asked, "Who
were you with in Vietnam?" One replied, "Americal Division,
sir." He was playing it safe and adding the "sir" just in case.
They both were trying to figure out what my angle was and
how to avoid being hurt. I realized that they expected me to
ask about their wounds, give them a little congratulatory peptalk, and then dismiss them from existence as nearly everyone
in the Army did.

I think they were taken aback when I said, "Do you think
you lost your arm and legs for a purpose—was it necessary?"
"Well, I don't know, sir," one began. I cut him off. "What do
you mean you don't know? Surely a man who has been to Vietnam and been through what you have must have some idea of
what goes on there. I'm interested in knowing what you feel—
and you don't have to 'sir' me, I'm not wearing any insignia of
rank." I had rankled the one in the wheelchair who had lost
both an arm and a leg. "Well, I think the fuckin' war stinks,"
he said. "They promised me I wouldn't be in the infantry if I
volunteered for three years. The recruiting sergeant, he said I'd
go to school. But that was a bunch of shit. Soon's I finished
basic they sent me to infantry advanced trainin'—and from
there to Nam. When I got to Nam I told them I wanted to be a
truck driver or somethin' good like that. But they stuck me in a
company packin' a damn rifle—and we had this sergeant who

was all the time tellin' me I was a shithead and couldn't do nothin' right. And everybody was always talkin' about killing gooks. The platoon had to kill a certain number every month or we got the shit details." He grinned. "The Cong had a lot of water buffaloes an' pigs an' chickens fightin' with 'em."

At that point the other soldier, who was sitting on the plastic couch with a pair of chrome arm-brace crutches stacked next to him, broke in and said, "Everybody was gung ho for gettin' a good body count. We had a battalion commander who used to go out cruising in his helicopter looking for gooks." "Yeah," the soldier in the wheelchair said, "some of those guys scratched themselves climbing in and out of their chopper and they got the Purple Heart; me I got to get my arm and leg blown off to get it." "How did you get wounded?" I asked. "Well, we was out on a patrol looking for VC. We never saw none, just old women and kids. But our captain wanted to look real good so he had the platoon sweeping the paddies and going through the hoochies to try and get a prisoner or a body. The sergeant he told me to go around back of one of the hoochies and see if I saw anybody. I told him there wasn't nobody back there, but he said for me to get my ass back there and look. I come to this little old fence and I started to push open a busted-up gate so I could get behind the hoochie and there was this goddamn noise and I got knocked down and then I passed out. They told me it was a frag grenade that some gook bastard had hooked to the gate—it really blew the shit out of me. They're fixing me up real good here, but I been thinkin' about it and I figure it was really all for nothin'. Hell, I never even seen no VC. Just went over to that stinkin' Nam and got my leg and arm blown off."

The young soldier sitting on the couch had been wanting to say something. He blurted out, "It's one thing to be in Nam huntin' Charlie and another to be there in some air-conditioned trailer. A lot of them guys don't have to sweat none. They fly around in them command choppers once in a while and then they go back to Saigon or somewhere and live it up. Nobody gave a shit what happened to us grunts. I mean they just didn't really care. Just so everything looked okay and none of the wheels chewed anybody's ass—that was all that mattered to 'em. I mean they kept givin' you all that fucking bullshit about helpin' the fucking gooks but the gooks ain't gonna do nothin'. The main thing was that the wheels look good. Shit, I lost my foot going into a fuckin' village that the sergeant kept trying to tell the captain was just one big fuckin' booby trap. But the captain, he was new, and the battalion commander wanted the village checked and we had to go charging in there so the captain wouldn't look bad. Now I ain't got no foot, mister, and what for? I'll tell you why, because the Army don't give a shit about guys like me. I mean a grunt he don't mean nothin'. Nobody gives a shit what happens to him. I wish I'd gone AWOL."

After thinking about what Floyd and the two soldiers had said, I talked with some young officers who were in a room down the hall from my alcove. These three lieutenants had been wounded in Vietnam. One of them, a stocky blond-haired fellow, was propped up in bed with his hip and right leg in a cast. The cast was elevated by a pulleylike device attached to a metal frame over the bed. He had been the victim of a helicopter crash. As he described it, "It was a hot LZ and we had just finished unloading our animals [soldiers] and were starting to gain altitude when this VC machine gun opened up right into us. We went in and the chopper caught fire—some guy drug me out of the wreckage or I'd have burned up." In the next bed to him was a tall, dark-haired, muscular officer who looked as if he had probably been a good football player in his recent college days. His football days were obviously over, however, because the left sleeve of his blue government-issue pajamas hung empty. His amputated left arm had been shattered by a captured U.S. Bouncing Betty mine while he was on a search-and-clear mission near the demilitarized zone. He had been leading a platoon searching vainly for Vietcong to kill and add to the unit body count. "We were walking along this trail when I heard a 'pop' and then there was this explosion in front of me. I looked down and my left arm and chest were covered with blood; my left hand was just hanging by a few strips and I thought, jeez, what happened?"

The third young officer was sitting on the side of his bed. He

was slight and slender. Along the left side of his closely shaved
head there were two or three jagged pink scars. His head was
swollen and he had large white bandages over what had been
his eyes and over where his right ear had been. He was twenty-
four years old and blinded for life. He described his agony,
saying, "I was leading a search-and-destroy patrol down in the
delta when I got it. The 9th [division] was real big on body
counts and the battalion kept patrols out every day looking for
Charlie. Trouble was you never knew which 'Slope' was a VC
and which was a friendly. I couldn't see shootin' people unless
I was damn sure they were Cong. And about the only way you
could be sure of that was when they shot at you first. We'd
been out nearly all day and hadn't seen one likely suspect. I
knew if I went in without a body count or at least a prisoner I'd
be on the shitlist, so I kept the patrol out. We had just checked
this village and one of the old women said that morning they
had seen some guys with rifles in the woods beyond the village.
So I spread the platoon out and we started sweeping toward
the woods. I was up behind the point walking along a little trail
when the point man snagged a tripwire. All I remember was
hearing a blast from the right and that was all she wrote. They
told me later we walked into a U.S.-made Claymore mine that
was rigged alongside the trail. What still gets me, though, is
why the hell we had to be out there like a bunch of clay pi-
geons trying to up the body-count figures on some graph back
at U Sar V [U.S. Army Vietnam Headquarters]. I just don't believe we're ever going to have a chance of winning in Nam running around burning villages and killing ducks and chickens.
We've got to whip Charlie's main-force units and you can't do
that when they hear your choppers coming before you arrive to
fight. I haven't figured out what good I did in Nam—just got all
screwed up like this . . ." And his voice trailed off. "What did
it accomplish?"

Lying in bed I listened to the groans that came from the
other side of the wooden partition that separated my bed from
that of poor, retired Captain Smith, who was slowly dying of
cancer. I had thought how I would probably some day in the
not-too-distant future also be ending my life in the corner of

some Army or VA hospital. That after all was the way most lives ended—in pain in a hospital bed among strangers. So wasn't the most important thing to provide for one's family and live as well as one could while there was life? Were convictions and conscience more important than living life as comfortably as possible? These were the questions I had to answer if I were going to make a reasonable decision on my future.

Since June 12, 1966, I had been serving with the Joint Chiefs of Staff. I held a Top Secret and a Special Intelligence clearance which gave me access to nearly all the JCS documents I wanted to see. My duties included assignment to a highly classified job on an alternate emergency staff of the National Military Command Center. In my wallet I carried the blue-striped JCS identification card that gave me instant access to all parts of the restricted JCS area in the Pentagon. And in a corner of that wallet I carried the small slip of paper containing the name of my Special Intelligence contact officer in DIASO-2 of the Defense Intelligence Agency.

Daily I worked with members of the JCS Plans and Policy Division, J-5. I was also in frequent contact with the director of the Joint Staff and the office of the Chairman of the Joint Chiefs of Staff. And I maintained liaison with the Department of Defense Office of International Security Affairs (ISA). From what I read, saw, heard, and participated in, the principal policy of the Joint Chiefs of Staff was to use United States military power as the answer to every worldwide problem. The entire thrust and purpose of high military leaders seemed to be to expand our role in the Vietnam war, while extending other deployments and assistance agreements. They acted like executives charged with expanding the base of a business. I found no indication that these decision-makers were giving sufficient emphasis to the public interest or the lives of our sons. The only stockholders who seemed to profit from this growth were we professional military men. I was convinced this was wrong for the United States, and yet daily I was a part of it.

Whenever we met, old friends and colleagues always asked me if I had been to Vietnam. When I replied that I was on a fixed, stabilized JCS tour for three years and didn't evidence

any burning desire to be off to Vietnam, they always advised
me to get my ticket punched with a Vietnam tour if I wanted
to make colonel. Friends like Colonel Rex Blewett anxiously
volunteered to go to MACV Headquarters in Saigon. As Rex
told me in his office in the JCS Joint Secretariat one day in June
1966, "You've got to get over there first any way you can, then
maneuver around and get command of a unit. I've got to wran-
gle a brigade command or I won't have a prayer of making
BG."

Other old infantry friends like Colonel Jere Whittington,
who had not seen combat in World War II or Korea, quickly
volunteered. It was easier for Jere than for others to get a brigade command because he had graduated from West Point. He
came back from his first tour in Vietnam a lieutenant colonel
and then was promoted to colonel. I encountered him one afternoon in the hallway of the Pentagon and he told me he had
fixed things with the Colonel's Division so he could volunteer
for another tour in Vietnam. He would be taking command of a
brigade of the Americal Division. His immediate worry was
that recently initiated peace negotiations might bring an end to
the war or a reduction in combat action. This would mean that
he would have no chance to achieve any sort of a command
"name" for himself to help him gain brigadier's stars.

Not one of my officer friends or colleagues expressed the
slightest concern about the young Americans who were being
killed and maimed in these units that they were all so anxiously
volunteering to command. They knew they would serve about
six months in command and then be moved to a staff job to
finish out their one-year tour of duty in Vietnam. The more I
thought about it, the more convinced I became that it was
wrong for the Army Officer Corps, wrong for the nation—and
something I could not be a part of.

But I had orders to go to Vietnam and be a part of this mistake. For twenty years I had been trained to follow orders un-
questioningly. And if I did that now it was in my future best interests. Why not just say nothing, keep my convictions to
myself, and do my year? I could alibi my actions, as so many
others were doing, by hiding my desire for promotion behind a

façade of "duty." And if that also promoted my career, so be it. I would be innocent of anything except "duty." I had killed Asians before in making America "safe" from Communism, and what difference would one more time make? In Korea I had been disturbed by what I had seen, but I really hadn't known then whether that war was right for our country or not. I didn't have access to the facts. In the case of Vietnam I had been given access to many of the most secret facts and I was convinced it was a tragic error—could I still claim innocence for the lives lost by going ahead and being part of it chiefly to enhance my personal future?

I thought back to the days of 1947 when as a teen-age soldier I had seen members of the South Korean constabulary beat and torture helpless Korean refugees they claimed were Communists. This was during the time when the United States military governor helped make Syngman Rhee President of South Korea. A few years later I fought in Korea to maintain the same government in power. Could I, as a forty-year-old father, again be responsible for the death of American and Asian boys in order to perpetuate another even more corrupt and despotic South Vietnamese government? Particularly when I was convinced that the war had no legitimate connection with the national security of the United States?

I talked this over with my wife when she came to visit me at Walter Reed. We whispered in Spanish because in January of 1969 it was not politic for a regular officer to disagree with the war in Vietnam to which the new Chief of Staff, General Westmoreland, was so dedicated. She said that I should follow my conscience and not worry about the problems that my early retirement would bring.

A few nights before I was scheduled for discharge from the hospital, I started down the hall to the pay-phone to call my home. I came abreast of the young lieutenant who had been blinded by a mine. He had been feeling his way with an aluminum tapping rod. "Where you going?" I asked. "I'm on my way to the phone to call home," he replied. "So am I, how about if I help you get there?" "Thanks, but I've got to learn to do it myself," he answered. "Well, I'll walk along with you," I said.

When we reached the swinging doors which led out into the main corridor, I held them back while he tapped his way through. "Thanks, those swinging doors are a witch."

We continued in silence except for the "tap-tap" of his rod against the wall of the corridor. When we reached the coin-operated wall telephone, I guided him to it and he fumbled in the pocket of his robe for a dime. "Could you pick me out a dime please? I still have trouble telling a penny from a dime," he said, thrusting out a handful of coins. I picked out the dime and asked if he wanted me to dial the number for him. He said, "No, I think I can do it." He counted back from one to the operator hole on the dial phone. "Is that the operator slot?" he asked. I told him it was and he seemed pleased to have found it himself. I walked over to a nearby couch and sat down to wait for the phone. I was thumbing through a magazine when I heard the lieutenant tell the operator he wanted to call Columbus, Georgia, collect. Then he said, "Hi, how's my boy? Have you been helping your mommy like a big boy? Remember you're the man of the house while Daddy's away. Let me talk to your mommy."

The well-worn magazine I was looking at showed a side profile picture of General Westmoreland looking unusually gray and grim and every inch the picture-book general. I asked myself why this general, who had been so spectacularly wrong in his tactics in Vietnam, had been promoted to Chief of Staff where his misguided emphasis on image rather than substance would destroy what little was left of Army morale?

I was pondering this when I heard the lieutenant say, "But who will take care of the kids while you are working? I know we need the money but you can't just leave the kids with anybody. It looks like I will be here for another month yet." He told his wife how much he missed her and his children and then said in anguish, "But I don't know what I'm going to do when they finish with me. I'll get 100 percent disability, but that's only about four hundred dollars a month from what I hear. They've been telling me about some training I can get to learn to do things with my hands, 'cause it's for sure no one is going to be interested in hiring a blind biz-ad major." There was another silence while he listened to his wife and then, "But I don't want you to have to support us for the rest of our lives, honey. That's my job, but how in the name of God can I do it like I am now?" He listened to his wife again and said, "No, don't worry about me, I'm okay, it's just that I miss you so and things look so hopeless. Some days I think it would have been better if that damn mine had killed me. What the hell good am I? Don't cry, honey, I didn't mean that really. I love you but, O God, I feel so helpless—so damn useless. Please stop crying, honey. Maybe I better get off and call you back. I'm sorry I upset you, don't worry please, things will be okay when we can be together. It's just that I feel so alone and everything." He rubbed the back of his hand over the bandage where his eyes had been and then pushed it over the fuzz that covered the top of his swollen head.

Listening to him I felt a silent tear start down my cheek as I tried to fight back my emotion at seeing this young man in such desperate anguish. In my mind I heard Private First Class Dunaway saying, "Doesn't anyone care what happens to us anymore, sir?" I looked down at the picture of a grim Westmoreland. What the hell did he care? But what did I care? Wasn't I considering keeping my mouth shut and going to Vietnam too so I could make my future more secure? I would be equally guilty of assuring my future at the cost of the life or future of some other man like this one who was struggling, and trying to put some meaning back into four lives. He didn't know that he had given his eyesight to protect the reputations of some powerful men and provide a means for promotion and more comfortable retirement for others—but I did. Was wearing silver-plated lead eagles on my shoulders and having a few more thousand a month in retirement pay more important than the lives of young men like this? I decided that it was not. I would leave the Army no matter what the cost. Anything that might happen to me would be small and unimportant alongside what had happened to this young man and thousands of others. I wiped my eyes with my sleeve and walked over to where the lieutenant was feeling for his tapping rod. I put my hand on his shoulder and told him I'd be glad to walk back to the ward with him. "Thanks," he said. "But I've got to learn to do it on my own, sir."

I watched him shuffle off down the hall with his rod busily tapping against the wall. His bandaged head slumped forward on his chest and I felt another tear start to trickle down my nose. Would America ever wake up and stop permitting her sons to be maimed and killed by handsome gray-haired men in pursuit of power, or another star, or more defense spending for our homeland? When would this hypocrisy end?

Chapter 3

The Fight to
Leave

☆ ☆ ☆ ☆ ☆ ☆ ☆ ☆ ☆

At the end of January 1969 I was released from Walter Reed. I
spent my first weekend at home drafting a letter requesting
voluntary retirement. The following Monday morning I walked
through the dark, dingy main hallway of "Tempo A" in south-
west Washington where the Army's Infantry Officer Branch is
located, past the rows of vending machines and wall posters, to
a room with a large blue and silver replica of a Combat Infantry Badge over the door.

A pleasant receptionist asked who I'd like to see and if I
wanted to examine my records. I told her I wanted to see the
field-grade overseas-assignment officer and that I would like to
examine my records. She marked a card I had filled out and
then buzzed on the phone and said, "King, Edward L.
069711." In a few minutes a file clerk came into the room with

two thick folders. One of these contained the record of service of "069711" and the other contained copies of all my efficiency reports covering twenty years of service. My record was good. I had learned the lessons of conformity and ticket-punching reasonably well and, except for a couple of cases of trying too strongly to exercise the courage of my convictions, I had an excellent OEI (Officer Efficiency Index). Outwardly I had become a good Army organization man while growing to dislike myself for conforming.

Across the room sat two young captains. Each wore the red and gold shield of MACV on the right shoulder of his uniform to show that he had served in combat with that unit. Each wore the medals that had become standard fare for an officer's service in Vietnam—a Bronze Star, an Army Commendation Medal, National Defense Service Medal, and two Vietnam campaign ribbons, one with a silver clasp. Both wore the combat infantry badge and paratrooper wings. One, wearing a heavy West Point class ring conspicuously on his left ring finger, said, "Well, I've got to get a high-level staff on my record before I go to the Advanced Course and then on to get my master's degree. I figure the best place to do it is in Europe, because there I can get another command punch on my ticket before I come up for major."

The other captain replied, "Well, I'm here to volunteer for another hitch in Nam. Last time I got stuck as an adviser and didn't get to command a unit—I've got to get that on my record before I come up for major or I might not make it." The ring wearer replied, "I hear you can pick your assignment if you volunteer for a second tour, but I heard they were giving adviser duty equal weight with command now."

"Yeah, I heard that too, but did you see who got passed over on that last list to major—nearly all were guys who either hadn't been to Nam or had been advisers. My wife doesn't think much of the idea of another year alone with the kids, but I told her I gotta get that combat command on my record."

I glanced back at my efficiency reports and noted that my last report from a major general had rated me superior and recommended that I be promoted ahead of my contemporaries and sent to a senior service college. It sounded nice; at least four other generals had said the same thing over the past three years, but I had been around long enough to know that their ratings were only part of the process of getting ahead in the U.S. Army. A boyish-looking major came into the room and introduced himself as the overseas-assignment officer. After we sat down at his desk wedged between two filing cabinets, I asked about my orders to Vietnam. He first told me he had no idea what duty assignment I was going to in Vietnam, but when I said I was sure I must be filling a requisition of some sort, he confessed that I was probably going to either the J-3 or J-5 section of the headquarters of the Military Assistance Command in Saigon.

I told him that I had previously informed the branch that I was contemplating retirement and wondered why they hadn't at least checked with me before issuing overseas orders. He answered, "Well, Colonel, you old guys just have to face it, you have to go to war. There is a policy now which prohibits regular officers from resigning or retiring until they do a tour in Vietnam. So even if you put in a request for retirement I'll turn it down and send you to Vietnam." He smiled as he said, "Anything else you'd like to know, Colonel?" As he said this he picked up my record folder and held it vertically in front of him so there would be no chance that I could see the note he scribbled on the inside.

One thing about the U.S. Army in each war is that we create a new crop of arrogant officers who believe their war to be the only war, and a reason to forget all the rest as past history. For example, a review of the Philippine insurrection could have prevented many of our mistakes in Vietnam. It was understandable that young officers back from Vietnam wanted to act a little arrogant and superior. After all, for years they had been book soldiers and now they too were combat veterans. They would come to know the price of arrogance after a few more years of service, but the danger was that in the meantime they would orient the Army toward their own limited experience in Vietnam.

Seeing my jaw tighten, the major quickly shifted his tack.

"There's no reason for you to retire now, Colonel. If you get your ticket punched with a Vietnam tour you'll be in good shape to make full colonel next year. That's the main thing for you to do now—get on a Vietnam tour before you come up for full bull."

I thanked him and left. All I had learned was that there was evidently an unpublished policy which would deny me retirement until I had been to Vietnam. I had already submitted my request for retirement so I would find out in due time whether there was such an Army policy or not. While I was waiting I decided to explain to the Chief of Infantry why I was requesting retirement. I went to see Lieutenant Colonel Aubrey Norris, who was the deputy chief of the Infantry Branch and an old acquaintance from school days at Fort Benning. I asked him if he knew anything about a new policy denying resignation or retirement to regular officers. I told him that I had looked through all the regulations and couldn't find any reference to such a policy. He smiled. "Well, let's put it this way, Ed, it hasn't been published but the Chief of Staff approved it effective 1 October 1968. It's OPO [Office of Personnel Operations] policy to hold all regulars until they do a Vietnam tour. We're saying it's for an overriding military need—and in a way it is— they have to go to Vietnam."

My appointment with the Chief of Infantry came up the following week. Colonel George E. Newman was a short, stocky, graying man who continued to read some papers while I waited. After a minute or two, the colonel laid aside the papers and said, "Colonel Norris tells me you have some problems with your overseas orders."

"No, Colonel," I replied. "That is not why I have asked to see you. I have submitted a request for voluntary retirement and I wanted to tell you why I submitted the request before you routinely turned it down. I can no longer remain silent and support what is being done to the Army and the nation in Vietnam. I have lost confidence in the leadership of the Army and the Joint Chiefs of Staff. I am convinced that any further active service by me would be fraudulent to myself, and what I believe are the true best interests of the country."

When I had finished Colonel Newman said, "Well, I don't see any problem about you going to Vietnam, we'll just assign you in a noncombat job since you seem to have an objection to the war."

"But you don't understand, I'm opposed to our whole policy in Vietnam. I can no longer actively serve in the present-day U.S. Army in any capacity."

"But you have an excellent record, a lot of experience. We need that in Vietnam," he said. "If you love your country you will go."

"It's because I do love my country and my fellow citizens that I cannot be a part of what we are doing to our country in Vietnam," I replied. "In the first place I'm not going to be serving the country by performing 'duty' in some busywork, paper-shuffling job in Saigon. I can't go to Vietnam and be responsible for getting kids killed while I get promoted and decorated, and then later come back and say I was opposed to it all along. I've got to retire, Colonel."

"You know that when you get back from your year in Vietnam there will be a very good chance that you can go to an attaché job in South America. That's something you've been wanting to do, isn't it?"

"Yes, I've been told that by your assignment people," I replied. "I've wanted to go down there because I have always thought I could help in a small way to stop the erosion of United States prestige in South America. But I'm not about to be part of what we're doing in Vietnam. If that's what it takes to be an attaché in South America I don't want the job."

"And how about your friends that are going to be sent back to second tours in Vietnam this year. Doesn't that bother you?" he asked.[1]

"Sure it bothers me if some lieutenant colonels have to begin going back involuntarily to Vietnam. But what bothers me even more is why the Infantry Branch permitted hundreds of lieutenant colonels to retire in 1965, up to October of 1968, and

---

[1] No infantry lieutenant colonels were returned involuntarily to Vietnam in either 1969 or 1970.

yet now finds itself short of lieutenant colonels. It's like closing
the barn door after the horse is out."

This last remark brought blood to the colonel's face. "Well,
that's not the point," he said. "The point is that you are qualified for a Vietnam tour and what you think about it doesn't
make one damn bit of difference. I can assure you that you are
not going to retire until you pull a tour out there, and I'll personally see to that. You can just count on going because I'm
gonna turn your request for retirement down flat and I've
never been overruled on turning one down yet. Anything else
you want to ask?"

"Yes," I said, "I want you to know that I intend to fight your
decision in every way I can. What's the next channel I can
take?"

"You can submit a letter to the Secretary of the Army stating
your reasons for wanting to retire and requesting reconsideration. But I can tell you right now it won't do you any good, I'll
turn it down too."

So ended my talk with Colonel Newman. I would not see or
hear of him again until I would read in the October 21, 1970,
edition of *The New York Times* that he was again in Vietnam,
and had made the nation's front pages by ordering some enlisted soldiers of the 1st Cavalry Division to prepare a bogus
citation for a Silver Star medal for Brigadier General Eugene
Forrester. I was not surprised.

A few weeks later, in March 1969, I received a barely read-
able mimeographed form letter informing me that I was being
involuntarily retained on duty until August 1970, because a determination had been made that "my retention on active duty
was required by overriding military needs in my grade and
branch."

I decided that as a matter of principle I had to state my opposition to the Secretary of the Army. On March 28, 1969, I
wrote him that I wanted to retire because of:

> 1. My total disagreement with the policy which
> the United States Government is following in Viet-
> nam. I cannot any longer continue to blindly and un-

questioningly support the objectives of the United States in the tragic undeclared war which we are waging in South Vietnam. I can no longer remain silent and apolitical on an issue which I feel is threatening the very existence of not only the Army but our nation. It is my heartfelt belief that this poorly conceived military and political adventure is not only unrelated to the defense of the vital liberty of our nation, but by its very insidious mercenary nature is destroying the heart and soul of the national armed forces which have traditionally been the defenders of the vital liberty of this republic.

These national armed forces are being converted by this unrighteous and unnecessary war into mercenary military forces, which under the guise of obedience to civilian authority have become more concerned with personal promotion and aggrandizement than they have with the well-being and defense of the vital liberty of the nation. Today I hear most of my army colleagues—contemporaries and superiors alike—talk anxiously in terms of getting to Vietnam quickly in order to gain tax exemptions, increased pay, and allowances, to secure short-tour command of battalions and brigades there so they may be more rapidly promoted and decorated. They talk of everything except the lives of the poor or middle-class American boys who must be conscripted and sent there to be maimed or killed in order that we "professionals" may achieve these above-mentioned "incentives." Such "incentives" are, in my estimation, purely mercenary and are not worthy to be considered with the past tradition of the American Armed Forces. Nor is it in the historic tradition of the United States Army to get American boys killed in undeclared wars in which there is absolutely no chance of military victory even if it were politically permitted.

I do not in any way object to killing enemies of this

republic—I had killed several before I was twenty-three years old—and would not object to going to Vietnam or any other place in the world, if I were in any way convinced that my presence there or my dying there in any slight way contributed to the defense of the vital liberty of my fellow citizens and my country. I do not, however, want to in any way profit from the agony and useless death of any of my fellow citizens, either under the guise of "professionalism" or any other pretext. I object to and cannot in principle any longer countenance being responsible for getting more of my fellow citizens killed in a useless, needless war which does not have as its objective the defense of the vital liberty of the United States of America, but is rather an inept attempt to cover repeated political blunders by a stalemated, attritive military action; in which the only objective comes forth as the waste of the lives of American youth.

2. Total loss of confidence in the high civilian and military leadership of the Armed Forces of the United States and particularly with the lack of leadership evident in today's U.S. Army. Disillusionment with an Army leadership that consistently ignores the many far-reaching and potentially destructive problems in the fields of training, personnel, administration, planning, and operations. A leadership which has adopted as its watchword expediency and which cannot or will not confront or attempt to solve the crucial problems existent in the Army. In Vietnam we see the incredible spectacle of nearly 400,000 United States troops committed and the Army unable to tactically commit more than 65,000 to 85,000 to actual battle. A leadership which blindly refuses to face the fact that such an Army tactical organization is disastrously wasteful of manpower. A leadership which is not only lacking in imagination, but is timidly committed to military bureaucratic status-quoism and defense-

industry experimentation regardless of the consequences to the Army or the nation.

On the evening of March 27 my secretary typed up the letter. As we filed the copies, she said, "It's none of my business, sir, but wouldn't it be easier to go to Saigon and sit around the headquarters there, rather than put yourself through all the grief that this letter will bring?"

"I'll still have to go," I replied, "but at least it won't be as a fraud."

After mailing the letter to the Secretary of the Army I felt as if a great weight had been lifted from me. For the first time in many years I was free. A week passed with no response. Then one afternoon I answered the phone and a voice said, "This is Colonel Fife, Special Affairs and Review Division, DCSPER [Office of the Deputy Chief of Staff for Personnel]." I thought, Oh shit, here it comes. His voice, however, sounded friendly. "Listen, I've seen your letter and I wanted to tell you that I'm with you 100 percent. In fact, I'm gonna put in one like it." I felt a sense of relief but all I could manage to say was, "Thanks, what's happening with the letter?"

"It's really pissed them off, and right now it's down in JAG [Judge Advocate General of the Army] being reviewed to see if there is any way they can court-martial you. Watch your step," he cautioned. "They have already started running a security check on you and JCS Security Division has been asked for a recommendation of what security action to take against you. Be careful of any classified documents you may be signed for. I'd sign them over to someone else if it were me."

The last point was good advice, for one of the tried and true ways to "get" an officer is with a security violation. I recalled a time when I was serving in France as officer of the day and found the commanding general's security safe had been left unlocked. I was told to forget the whole episode. Three months later this same general had approved disciplinary action against a major who made the same mistake. I knew how the game was played so I signed over all the classified documents I was personally responsible for—and the next day found my desk had been forced open during the night.

A day later I had lunch with Jim Fife. We met in the Pentagon and went to one of the basement cafeterias. "Why did you
write your letter?" "I just figured I couldn't play their game
anymore," I replied. "What I've seen the past five years in this
building makes me sick," he said. "I've been here in the Army
Staff ever since the Vietnam build-up began, I've watched decision after decision made on the basis of the personal self-interest of the decision maker." He believed that it had been because of such organization men making policy that we failed
the trust of the nation in Vietnam. "There's always some ring-
knocking [West Point graduate] sonuvabitch trying to promote
himself—to hell with the Army, to hell with the country, just so
he gets his star."

"Hell," I said, "this war is just what they wanted. It's their
dream come true, and that's exactly why not one of them has
opened his mouth to protest what has been happening to the
Army. You think anyone on the Joint Chiefs wants to see this
war end—hell no—they would make it bigger if they could.
Then there would be still more promotions and more hero
medals."

I was busy for the next several weeks arranging to spend
$10,000 from military assistance funds on a trip for about
twenty Latin American generals and admirals. This was an annual affair that was supposed to acquaint them with our military bases; it was actually one week of cocktail parties, lunches,
and dinners paid for by United States taxpayers. The bases we
visited were usually in California, Nevada, Colorado, and Flor-
ida. I had arranged for an Air Force C-118 VIP airplane, put a
dozen cases of whiskey, wine, and beer aboard, and three Air
Force enlisted men to serve it.

On May 2, 1969, I was informed by a personnel officer that I
was being removed from my thirty-five months' duty with the
Joint Chiefs of Staff. I was told to report at once to the headquarters of the Military District of Washington. No explanation
was given for my removal nor was I given written orders directing my relief from JCS or my transfer. At the Military District a sergeant sent me to nearby Fort McNair. There I was assigned to a room alone on the second floor of the headquarters

building. That room measured exactly eighteen paces long and eleven paces wide. I know because I paced it from morning to night for the next three months, until every mark on the floor was familiar. Just before reporting there I had attended a farewell staff luncheon for Sol Linowitz, who was leaving his post as United States Ambassador to the Organization of American States. It had been my good fortune to serve for two years as the military representative on his advisory staff. This had been one of the pleasant aspects of my JCS job, because I had enjoyed working for this intelligent, extremely human man. It was ironic that on the very same day I was being removed from my duty he was to thank me for my work and predict that I would be of further help to the Army in Latin America.

Even though I had no orders, I was officially finished with my service in the Joint Chiefs of Staff. I left with a great sense of relief at no longer serving with a body of men who tragically believe that war is peace and that the United States should constantly be at that kind of peace. On May 6 I reentered Walter Reed for minor exploratory surgery. After a few days of convalescent leave I returned to my room at Fort McNair.

It was there that I was to endure a professional ostracism and humiliation that surprised me—given my twenty-three years of service. I knew the post commander well and I was the ranking lieutenant colonel assigned to the post headquarters, yet I was not given any duty assignment. My only duty was to arrive every morning at 7:30 A.M. and sit in the small room with the peeling paint until 5:00 P.M. This unusual situation was quickly noted by the officers and enlisted men in the building and I became the object of much speculative gossip. I had not yet received any official acknowledgment from the Secretary of the Army that he had even received my appeal for reconsideration of my request for retirement.

I did receive a letter from Colonel George W. Putnam, the Chief of Officer Personnel, demanding that I submit to a psychiatric examination. Although Colonel Putnam had never met me, he stated in this open official letter that there were "grave doubts" about my integrity despite the fact that there were efficiency report ratings covering nineteen years of my ser-

vice—all attesting to my integrity—on file downstairs from his
office.[2] I protested that such an examination was not required
by Army regulations governing retirement. I was ordered to
submit. On the day I was forced to take this psychiatric examination, I went by the Pentagon to be awarded the Legion of
Merit medal for "exceptionally meritorious service" while serving in the Joint Chiefs of Staff. The citation that accompanied
the medal lauded my integrity and dedication to duty, yet I had
to refuse a cup of coffee after the ceremony so I wouldn't be
late to the forced appointment with the Army psychiatrist. He
found me sane and rational, but angry!

At the end of May I finally received a letter from the adjutant general informing me that the Secretary of the Army had
received my March request and was taking it under consideration. Since I was experiencing some of the effects of his "consideration" in my isolation at Fort McNair, I couldn't help but
be apprehensive about the outcome. The orders I had finally
been given had indicated that I could be held without duties at
Fort McNair for up to one year.

The boredom and frustration of the empty days were becoming difficult to bear. At first I had thought I would spend my
time looking for a civilian job, but that proved impossible because I had no idea when I would be available for work. Then I
had tried reading, but sitting all day reading, without hearing
another voice, also quickly became tiresome. And there was the
problem of lunch. The first week I went to the officers' club at
the end of a row of large government-owned brick houses occupied by various generals and admirals who worked in the
Pentagon. I walked by the large two-story houses that I knew
came equipped with crystal, china, and two or three enlisted
servants. The big roomy houses always went to the old generals
whose families had grown up and left, while the younger
officers with growing families crowded into high-rent apart-

---

[2] Colonel Putnam was shortly after promoted to brigadier general and then
major general in Vietnam, where he gained prominence by restricting news
coverage in the 1st Cavalry Division and assigning escorts to spy on reporters.
He now serves as Chief of Personnel Operations in the Department of the
Army.

ments and townhouses out in Virginia. The old men could afford to buy or rent suitable houses; the younger ones couldn't. Yet the ones who could least afford civilian prices lived off the posts and the generals who made the most money got the larger, cheaper on-post houses.

I stopped walking to the club for lunch after two long-time officer acquaintances got up and hurried away from a table when I started to join them. Rumors about me were apparently getting around. After the incident at lunch I had considered calling the Infantry Branch and telling Colonel Newman that I would go to Vietnam. I asked myself, why in the hell go through all this when it is only going to mean even more heartache? I had thought, hell, call them and say you've reconsidered and you'll go. That way you can stick around and go to South America and retire with more money. But my conscience told me that I hadn't made a mistake and that I could not again be responsible for more Dunaways and the poor blind and crippled kids at Walter Reed. I decided to stick it out, but it still hurt very much to take the Army's "treatment."

I knew that I must find some way to combat the boredom. It was while I was grieving over my feelings of rejection that an idea came. I had been wondering what had happened to the Army, and I thought about what I would say if someone asked me how to correct things. What better way to use my time than putting down my thoughts on ways to improve the Army?

Unexpectedly, near the end of June, I was notified by letter that my request for reconsideration had been approved and I could voluntarily retire on August 1, 1969. I was informed that my voluntary retirement had been approved in the "best interests of the Army," because "the conclusion could only be drawn that [I] had suffered a complete reversal of the previously highly rated attitude and motivation reflected during [my] career." I regretted that never once during the period of official consideration of my request had any senior officer wanted to discuss my reasons for insisting on retiring. The Army leadership was apparently not interested in understanding. Their only interest had been in trying to force compliance through fear of court-martial and when that failed resorting to sheer vindictiveness to "get even." Such was the low state to which the Army leadership had fallen by 1969.

The ostracism and official hostility went on even though I was to retire. On July 31, 1969, I went to my small room for the last time. I had been saddened at the prospect of my last day of duty, but heartened that some good had come from my battle. The *Army Times* had headlined the day previously that fifteen hundred other regular officers who had also been forced to remain on active duty would be released. So my struggle against the Army bureaucracy had at least accomplished something.

At five o'clock I gathered up my papers and typewriter, walked to the officers' sign-out roster, and signed myself off active duty in the U.S. Army. No one said good-bye. As I walked from the headquarters building toward my car I passed a young black soldier who threw me a snappy salute which I returned. I stopped and said, "Come back here, soldier." He turned, surprised, and walked back to me with a questioning look on his face. I said, "I never got to give a dollar for my first salute [an old Army tradition], but I'd like to give you one for my last salute." I handed him a dollar and turned quickly away as I felt a lump forming in my throat.

A few days later I was in Spain and in my bitterness I thought I'd never return to my own country again. Before I left I mailed a thirty-two-page letter of ideas on ways to improve the Army to Secretary of the Army Stanley Resor. There was no response from him. Then shortly afterward I heard of the scandal over the activities of General Turner and Sergeant Major Wooldridge; this was followed by the reports of the tragedy at MyLai. As I had said in my letter to Secretary Resor, the Army was on the wrong road and in trouble. One night I began to write the outline of this book. I decided that it wasn't the time to be running away and dropping out. The United States needed all her sons and daughters at home. I told the Spanish corporation I was working for that I was leaving. I had to go back and fight for what I believed.

PART II

Chapter 4

What Has Happened to the Army?

☆ ☆ ☆ ☆ ☆ ☆ ☆ ☆ ☆

What has happened to the Army? How has it deteriorated to the sorry state it is in? What are the underlying causes of the deterioration? And what are the cures? These were the questions I had asked myself as I paced up and down the length of my "office" at Fort McNair. And in Spain I struggled with the same questions. I tried to analyze the steps that the Army had taken over the past twenty years and to determine when the Army had started down the wrong road.

I thought back to the days of the Korean War. Some of the seeds of the Army's current problems had been planted then, but it was difficult to pick a precise point from which the Army's decline could be traced. It seemed to me that the decline set in after the war in Korea. On August 17, 1953, Army Chief of Staff General Matthew B. Ridgway summed up the

Army's mission as: "It [the Army] must win in war." Yet the
no-win end of the war in Korea, in June 1953 had already made
this World War II mission obsolete. This concept of using
ground-combat troops to chastise and contain Communist expansion, rather than defeat it, was the forerunner of a similar
reaction in Vietnam. The idea of containment rather than victory dictated that the Army should reconstruct its classic con-
ception of "closing with and destroying the enemy" to bring
victory in battle. But the rank and file of the Army weren't told
that the Army was no longer supposed to win. They would continue to believe in winning victories while General Staff planners were preparing and preaching a doctrine of "limited
brushfire" war that postulated containment—not victory—as
its objective. Thus were sown the seeds for frustration and failure in Vietnam.

But the confusion of objectives was not the only problem to
face the Army after Korea. World War II had been a war of civilians in uniform. After World War II the American public
had been told that future wars would be fought with machines
and technology—not manpower—just as today the public is
being told about the coming automated battlefield. After each
episode of infantry bloodletting the public is quickly promised
that future wars will be fought by machines. This strategy helps
to soften the recollections of the fruitless killing and dying in
man-to-man combat in some far-off jungle or barren hillside.
But it does not prepare the citizen for the next round of ground
combat. It does not prepare him because it tells him it will not
happen again. Yet professional soldiers do not seriously plan on
using machines for a major ground-combat role. They know
that machines do not work very well and are terribly expensive
to produce and maintain. Men are much more efficient, and are
cheaper and easier to obtain through systems like the draft. To
rely principally on machines means that an army must lose
much of its traditional character and drastically change its fundamental doctrines and tactics. Thus it might very well become
less "professional" in the context of World War II thinking.
And we must remember that all of our Army leadership has
considered the Army in this context for the past twenty-five

years. So despite the frequent illusionary images of automated warfare, the guts of the U.S. Army has remained combat manpower and its fundamental strategies and tactics have revolved about this ingredient.

Even though the concept projected after World War II was for less infantry slaughter, the war in Korea was a small-scale replica of World Wars I and II. The major difference was that the citizen soldiers were now led by professional career officers at nearly all grades above captain. Most of these officers had entered the Army during or immediately after World War II. They had decided prior to or during the Korean War to make the Army their lifetime career. Most were typical of their generation and contemporary American society, which means they were highly competitive in their pursuit of advancement and job security. Unlike many of the World War II officers who had served because the nation was fighting a war for national survival, these men were working at their chosen career and wanted to get ahead. The best way to do so was to go to war and command the sons of their fellow citizens in combat operations. In 1950–52 hundreds of career officers anxiously volunteered to go to Korea to serve in the limited war. They volunteered for a variety of reasons, chief among which was to get credit for combat command, or in Army parlance—get another punch on their promotion ticket. Company, battalion, regimental, and division commands were regularly rotated at six- to eight-month intervals to provide more career officers with an opportunity to obtain combat-command credit on their personnel records. Such credit was an essential ticket to future promotion.

Every officer knew that promotions would be slow and few after the war in Korea ended. One had to get all the tickets one could while the war lasted. Another such ticket was combat decorations. These combat medals were extra pluses in selection for promotion. Some officers received them for extraordinary valor; others were awarded them by friends or senior officers who wanted to help them in their careers. No officer was awarded a combat medal for being cautious or for attempting to avoid exposing his men to unnecessary risks. To the contrary, medals were awarded the commander who ruthlessly committed his men to battle—any battle—just so long as it made the unit appear aggressive. Officers from general to captain relentlessly pursued the promotions and medals with the same single-mindedness of purpose that they would display again in Vietnam. None wanted to fall behind in the race to the "top" of the Army.

The high value placed on combat commands resulted inevitably in a great deal of intrigue and scheming to secure them. In both Korea and Vietnam, the ability to command frequently took second place to who one knew and whether one had graduated from the U.S. Military Academy. Quality and stability of command fell victim to the frequent rotation of aspiring command candidates and the ones who paid with their lives for this inexperienced leadership were the GI's in the draft-filled ranks. If commanders were to make their reputations as combat leaders within the short periods of their commands it was necessary that there be continuing combat operations. This was no problem in Korea in 1950 and early spring of 1951 as the North Korean and Chinese armies repeatedly pressed down the peninsula.[1] By the late summer of 1951 it had become more difficult for senior officers to maintain combat on a sufficient scale to establish reputations for later promotion. To fill the need for steady combat operations U.S. Eighth Army Headquarters devised a plan of limited-objective attacks within the framework of a so-called active defense. This not only satisfied a requirement for keeping the troops "sharp" with combat action, but also provided the rationale by which career officers could continue to gain combat-command credit and decorations. It all blended together very nicely; the Army could help to contain Communist expansion, defend the "free world," and at the same time enhance career opportunities. This experience conditioned the thinking of a generation of career Army officers. If

---

[1] It was during the winter of 1951 that the U.S. Eighth Army conducted Operation Killer, which had as its objective killing the enemy rather than seizing terrain. Daily body counts of enemy soldiers killed were kept by Eighth Army Headquarters. Units and soldiers with high-kill ratios were rewarded. This same practice has been more ruthlessly computerized and applied in Vietnam.

you had a war—any war—you could fulfill your patriotic duty to serve your country on far-off battlefields and at the same time promote your career. It was a most attractive prospect for any man who contemplated an Army career. All that was needed was a war.

By the time the Vietnam situation came along, career objectives had largely superseded the desire for selfless service to the nation as a motivation for many career officers. And by the same token the officer's concern for the welfare and lives of his fellow citizens in uniform had diminished. A preview of this diminishing concern was to be seen in Operation Smack, conducted as an experiment in air-tank-artillery-infantry coordination on January 25, 1953, in Korea. This ill-conceived Army "exercise" was conducted only a few scant months before the war in Korea was to end, and during a period when the President of the United States had called for the absolute minimum of United States casualties. The purpose of the exercise was not to defend the security of the United States, but to "test" Air Force bombing techniques and Army tactics. Drafted citizen soldiers of the U.S. 7th Infantry Division were used as guinea pigs.

On the day before the test United States taxpayers provided 136,000 pounds of bombs, 10,000 artillery rounds, and 14 napalm tanks to be dropped on the small Chinese-held "test objective" called Spud Hill. On January 25 an additional 224,000 pounds of bombs, 8 more napalm tanks (only one of which hit the target), 12,000 rounds of artillery, 100,000 rounds of 40-millimeter and 50-caliber ammunition, 2,000 rounds of 90-millimeter tank shells, 4,500 rounds of mortar ammunition, 125,000 rounds of 30-caliber ammunition and 650 hand grenades were fired at the hill.[2] Seventy-seven American soldiers were killed or wounded, while a large group of visiting Army and Air Force generals and their staffs stood comfortably on a nearby hill, monitoring the exercise with the help of carefully printed three-color scenarios. While they watched through

---

[2] Walter G. Hermes, *United States Army in the Korean War, Truce Tent and Fighting Front,* Chief of Military History, Washington, D.C., 1966, pp. 386–88.

their BC-scopes a young draftee was shot through the head and killed trying to work his way to a position to fire a flamethrower into a Chinese trench. A young lieutenant was hit a second time by grenade fragments and forced down from the hill—minus one eye.

Despite the terrific bombardment, Spud Hill was not taken from the Chinese. They lost fewer than sixty men defending the hill and expended about a tenth of the ammunition that we did in trying to capture it. In *Truce Tent and Fighting Front* the Office of the Chief of Military History probably best sums up the impact of the test exercise: "All in all, Operation Smack was a fiasco. Yet since the entire exercise was on a small scale insofar as the number of infantrymen and tanks engaged was concerned, it might well have been chalked up to experience and quietly passed over, but for a zealous member of the press." As a result of the story the "zealous member" filed in American newspapers, the Army found itself embroiled in a full-blown scandal and faced with indignant public protest. Quick appearances before the friendly Armed Services Committee of the Congress and vague explanations by Army spokesmen served to squelch the public outcry. But these actions did not explain away what it boded for the future of the Army when its officers were willing to stand by and watch men die or be maimed to "test" theories and tactics which would justify more sophisticated weapons. Nor was any explanation given as to why a member of the press had to point out an Army mistake before it would be admitted and any action taken to rectify the matter. Sixteen years later in Vietnam another zealous member of the press had to force the Army to act on another covered-up mistake, or MyLai might also have been "chalked up to experience and quietly passed over." The seed that was planted by Operation Smack was to bear bitter fruit for the Army in Vietnam.

Although the cause of many of the Army's problems can be traced back to Korea, the actual deterioration of the Army started after that war. As I thought back over the years it seemed to me that the breakdown began in 1955 and 1956. It was during this period that officers like General Ridgway, who placed the best interests of his soldiers above all else except the interests of the nation, began to leave active service or lose influence within the Army. The day of the Army organization man dawned with the advent of military technocrats such as Maxwell Taylor and John Medaris. These officers were part of the "Airborne Club"—which has traditionally been action-oriented rather than analytically inclined. They accepted the precepts of modernization and constant corporate growth that were dominant in American industry. For the first time loyalty to the Army began to take on more importance in an officer's career than dedication to the country and the public good. Actions were taken to promote the Army's modernization and expansion of roles and missions which were not necessarily in the best interests of the American people. These parochial Army interests were concealed behind the façade of national defense. As the ambitions of its technocrat managers increased so did the parochial needs of the Army—and so did the overall costs of national defense. The only dam to this ever-expanding flood of corporate military growth was Dwight D. Eisenhower, the soldier in the White House who was influenced by austere old troop leaders like General Fox Conners, and who tolerated few of the grandiose schemes of "Modern Army" managers.

But even President Eisenhower was a disciple of big business and did not initially see the danger of an expanding military-industrial complex. He supported the first modest modernization measures. During General Taylor's tenure as Chief of Staff, service with troops became less important for officers than speaking a foreign language and holding at least one advanced degree. The pursuit of the good staff life, rather than troop command, became the goal of nearly every aspiring young career officer. The Army officer became a professional advocate of change. Anything new and modern was automatically better while anything that smacked of tradition and the past was considered only in the context of how it could be changed. Few of those making the changes ever paused to consider that they might be wrong in participating in the euphoria of turning over the past which was sweeping the Army. There was only room in the Modern Army for those who had a driving desire to propel themselves constantly onward. and upward. Every promotion list was a measure of conforming dynamism. It was unacceptable to be content with a position or a rank, transcending change; upward movement was the order of the day.

The Army even changed the democratic olive-drab uniform that it had worn through three wars. At General Taylor's insistence, it cast aside its publican officer's hat with a plain hard-brown leather bill and a flat unimposing crown and in its place adopted a gaudy high-crowned Wehrmacht style replete with gold-braided "scrambled eggs" on the bill. At the same time it cast aside the traditional Eisenhower jacket and adopted a greenish-gray uniform. These changes were part of the image-building that the Army organization men were copying from Madison Avenue. They did not stop to consider the possibility that an army built on the basis of a showy image would fight in much the same manner.

But it was not enough to change the uniform. General Taylor and his airborne-ranger managers would also reorganize the Army tactical formations. Officers like Colonel Frank Izenour at the Infantry School would develop a new Army tactical concept. This force was designed to "survive on the atomic battlefield of the future" that General Taylor thought he foresaw so clearly. To survive on General Taylor's atomic battlefield it was considered necessary to restructure the Army combat division. This divisional structure had evolved from the square division of World War I down through the triangular division and then to the regimental combat-team formations of World War II and Korea. A lot of combat experience had gone into this evolution. But in 1956 most of this hard-earned combat experience was to be cast aside by officers like Izenour (who had seen his principal combat at the ill-fated Anzio Beachhead in Italy) in the name of battlefield mobility. The battle-tested regimental combat-team formation was exchanged for the "Pentomic organization," known in the Army as the Reorganized Combat Infantry Division or ROCID—and referred to as "RANCID" by the first classes of young combat officers that studied it at the Infantry School. Under this ill-conceived doctrine the standard Army infantry division shrank from a force of three regiments containing three battalions with five companies each to a Pentomic force of five battle groups of four companies each.

I was a student in the first advanced class at Infantry School which was taught—or forced to learn—this new tactical formation. The purpose of the advanced course was to train first lieutenants or captains to function as colonel battle-group commanders in the event of national mobilization. The more those of us with combat experience studied the ROCID structure, the more convinced we became that it would not work in combat. We frequently argued with our instructors—some of whom were not in favor of the new formation either, but were good team men who did their best to defend the system. I recall one student officer standing in class and saying, "What have we gained with this formation? Before we could deploy two companies forward to fight and hold a reserve to counterattack, now we have no reserve and must rely on some other battle group for help. What if they can't provide it? What then?" "You pray," replied the instructor. I once asked, "Under present promotion policies it takes about eighteen years to go from captain to colonel. In this battle group there are only two command levels—company commander [captain] and battle-group commander [colonel]. Don't you think this is going to produce some pretty unqualified battle-group commanders when they have to wait eighteen years between chances to command?" The instructor answered, "Well, yes, we considered what you are saying, and we recognize it is not desirable, but it's just the price we have to pay to have combat mobility on the atomic battlefield." Reason did not enter into a discussion of the Pentomic division.

Other problems were created by this weak tactical formation. To make this hybrid structure fit into the Army of new green uniforms, it was necessary to modify drastically the traditional regimental structure that is the backbone of every major army in the world. The regimental tradition in our Army went back to the Revolutionary War. The soldier who looked at his regimental colors during World Wars I and II or in Korea was looking at a flag that symbolized battles covering the history of our country. Perhaps no other symbol exemplifies the tradition of military service like the regiment. The British Army has always been built around the history of its regiments. The Soviet Army is the same. But in 1956 the U.S. Army was to cast aside most of this tradition and form battle groups loosely related to theoretical shadow regiments that existed only on paper. This was a serious mistake. It caused a decline in the combat esprit of the infantrymen who have traditionally cared little for their divisions, but would often lay down their lives for the honor of their regiments. (Significantly, Vietnam is the first war we have fought in which the traditional Army regimental organizations have not been the principal combat elements.) An American soldier can readily identify with the traditions of a regiment like the 19th U.S. Infantry nicknamed the "Rock of Chickamauga." He can feel that he is following in the footsteps of heroic soldiers like General Thomas, who led the regiment in the bloody 1863 Civil War battle. It is hard to generate this association and esprit for a present-day battalion referred to as the 2/19 Infantry.

Fortunately for the Army, it was not called on to fight a war during the time it was organized in the Pentomic formations. The only action in which the Pentomic Army participated was the Lebanon crisis and that was nothing more than an exercise which gave the Army a chance to prove it could move troops more rapidly than the Marines. There was no legitimate need to move over 10,000 Army troops to Lebanon. But such a movement enhanced the Army's position in the fight for mobility funds, and promoted the careers of major generals William C. Westmoreland and Paul D. Adams, who played key roles in the unnecessary build-up. By the time the Army found its war in Vietnam, the technocrats had, at the insistence of the few remaining troop commanders, abandoned the Pentomic formation and returned the Army more than halfway back to the same structure they had cast aside in 1956.

To go along with the new uniforms and Pentomic organization, the Army managers next devised "new" doctrines and roles for the Modern Army. If it were going to compete with the Air Force and Navy for an equitable share of the money pie, the Army had not only to go modern, it had to develop some feasible role as an international "peacekeeper." The Air Force Strategic Air Command was flying high around the world and in the Congress as the airborne sheriff who represented "Power for Peace" and enforced Pax Americana with atomic bombs. It was hard to compete with an Air Force that had "Peace Is Our Profession" as a motto and a worldwide net of bases, or with a Navy which projected "Peace" from the decks of its aircraft carriers anchored in touristic world danger spots like Hong Kong. The Army managers saw there was a plentiful supply of defense dollars and numerous three- and four-star billets wrapped up in the Madison Avenue-packaged image of the armed forces as "peace" forces. But how to get their share? They had a dressed-up, Pentomic Army with no place to go. They needed a war, but a war would be atomic and that was the Air Force's baby. What was really needed was a little war—a flexible one—in which the response could be graduated to include Pentomic troops, before the peacekeepers in the Air Force blew the world apart.

The answer was counterinsurgency and limited brushfire war in underdeveloped world areas, and flexible response short of atomic war to Soviet aggression in Europe. It was a clever package. Army planners had seized on the fact that the United States had fought a politically dictated no-win war in Korea and had then covered the no-win aspect by calling it a "limited" war. To postulate this kind of war as a future mission of the Army would be to catch the political leaders in a trap of their own making. It looked like a winner once Eisenhower left the Presidency. Throughout the late 1950s the Army completed its new image. The doctrine of small limited wars was perfected in the Army General Staff and command-school system of the Army. According to this doctrine there would be no large conventional wars in the future—nuclear weapons ruled these out—except in Europe.

Since the Army wanted to keep its 200,000-man European force intact, the concept of flexible response was incorporated into Army doctrine. Under this concept, localized Soviet probes and hostilities were envisioned to test the resolve of the

NATO forces. Rather than letting the SAC airborne sheriff strike back with massive atomic attack against these low-level probes, the Pentomic Army in Europe would be armed with a variety of sophisticated low-yield atomic nuclear weapons. These weapons could gradually, along with ground attack, be applied to the intruding Soviets until a point was reached where the Soviets ceased their unprofitable aggression. Little, if any, thought was given to the growing Soviet nuclear capability, or to the possibility that if the Soviets decided to move they might not restrict their attack to localized probes of NATO when they had sufficient force to overrun the area in a non-nuclear conventional war. These details were pushed aside in the rush to hammer out a doctrine that would give the Pentomic divisions an international role and subsequently justify the expensive weapons and machines that were considered necessary for those divisions.

But it was in the limited-war role in the underdeveloped countries that the Army saw its brightest prospects. The State Department under Secretary John Foster Dulles had concluded a web of security treaties with many underdeveloped countries. These countries would quite possibly need United States assistance and it was in this role that the Army could outplay the Air Force. The limited-war doctrine foresaw Army forces entering underdeveloped nations to help contain Communist aggression or block wars of liberation against friendly free-world governments. These peacekeeping efforts would be short-lived, carefully controlled military actions sharply restricted to achieving specific, limited tactical objectives within narrowly defined geographic areas. With surgical precision the Army would enter the restricted geographic area to assist United States-trained local forces in containing and repelling Communist aggression. No clear distinction was drawn between a war of national liberation and a civil war, except that the war of liberation would be externally inspired and supported.

The key to limited brushfire capability was rapid worldwide mobility for the new Pentomic forces. The Army had formed the XVIII Airborne Corps at Fort Bragg, North Carolina, which contained two Pentomic airborne divisions. This corps, dubbed "Freedom's Fire Brigade" by its commander, Lieutenant General William C. Westmoreland, was constantly on stand-by status, ready to move to any part of the world to put out a Communist brushfire aggression. The Army was now almost able to compete with the Air Force in the international peacekeeping mission. There was one problem: the Freedom's Fire Brigade had to travel in Air Force firetrucks and depend on Air Force tactical fighters to hose down the brushfire while they moved in to save our free-world friends. The Air Force was understandably reluctant to help the Army compete for the world peacekeeping role that they had occupied unchallenged since the inception of SAC. The Army turned to its friends in Congress, stressing the advantages of limited war over massive retaliation and of course their need for more airlift. The Army fought the bitter airlift battle through the halls of Congress, within the Department of Defense, and in the Joint Chiefs of Staff, where the Navy and Marines were quite willing to join in shooting down the high-flying Air Force. The Air Force, seeing that the piloted bomber was becoming obsolete in a world of missiles, and looking with increasing suspicion on the "tactical" missiles being developed for the Army by Dr. von Braun and General Medaris, agreed to buy more transport aircraft if the Army would get out of missile development.

This was a compromise of convenience by both sides. The Air Force realized that it would need a place to assign excess pilots as the B-47 bombers were phased out in the 1960s. Procurement of additional transports, from the C-130 to the C-5A, would enable these pilots to continue collecting flight pay. The Army agreed to pass control of all long-range missiles to the Air Force, while retaining control of tactical battlefield missiles of less than 1,500-mile range. There still remained the problem of how the Army could control its own airborne fire support. All Army planners were concerned over their dependence on Air Force fighter planes. This problem was solved by first establishing the helicopter as a necessary mobility vehicle for the Pentomic divisions, and then quietly experimenting with arming them for fire-support roles. Thus was born the "Sky Cavalry" concept which was to be used to flesh out the limited-war doctrine.

But there was still a flaw in the Army doctrine. If "aggression against freedom" did not reach the level of a brushfire war, how could the Army justify its involvement? Army planners answered this question by adding yet another dimension to the way that United States ground forces could be committed to battle. They adopted the concept of counterinsurgency as a corollary to limited war. This concept was developed by a small group of airborne-ranger officers under the command of men like Colonel William Yarborough at Fort Bragg, North Carolina. It was conceived in the new Army doctrine as the intervening step between sending in a few military advisers and bringing in the Pentomic divisions.

With the inclusion of counterinsurgency, the new Army doctrine was complete. First, there were the military assistance advisory groups that had been pioneered in Greece and Turkey in 1947–48 and whose techniques had been polished in the Korean Military Advisory Group (KMAG) during the Korean War. By the late 1950s the Army was participating in advisory groups all over the world. There was an advisory group anywhere it was possible for aggression to break out (and in some places, like Rio, Paris, and Rome, where aggression was not so likely but living was pleasant). These Army groups would be the nucleus around which a larger Army involvement could be developed.

When an expanded Army presence became possible these groups would first be augmented by additional "technicians and specialists" to work with the local army. Green Berets would be introduced to advise the local forces and begin clandestine United States combat operations. In this way the initial Army commitment would be short of open combat, but could provide the basis for further commitment of Army forces. As the Army's counterinsurgency combat role grew, the rationale for sending in the Pentomic divisions would become more compelling.

This three-part advisory-counterinsurgency-limited-war doctrine gave the Army a way to ensure a role for itself in the world of the 1960s and 1970s. With its new doctrine it was sure of getting a piece of the international action, and a healthy slice of the defense budget. And if this wasn't enough good fortune, President Kennedy was to embrace wholeheartedly the Army's doctrine and appoint General Maxwell Taylor Chairman of the Joint Chiefs of Staff. The young President saw the Army doctrine as a low-profile way to mix tangible military force with United States diplomacy in underdeveloped areas of the world. In accepting this doctrine he opened the door to a larger United States role in the war in Southeast Asia. The Joint Chiefs of Staff had missed a chance to fight there in 1954, when President Eisenhower opposed the introduction of U.S. combat troops. They were not going to miss a second opportunity under Presidents Kennedy and Johnson. The Army doctrine of counterinsurgency and limited brushfire war was the vehicle by which the United States was taken into Vietnam.

By this time, Army leaders had actually begun to believe in the image they had created of the new Modern Army. They gave little thought to the fact that the Army was committing the lives of its soldiers, its prestige, and reputation in support of a doctrine which had not been thoroughly tested. The road down into the quagmire of a civil war in Vietnam was open and the Army managers rushed happily along that road, picking up commands and promotions on the way. In 1962–63 Vietnam appeared tailor-made for application of the new Army doctrines, as well as a place to gain "experience" for the modern Army. The U.S. military advisory group had been in Vietnam since 1955. It had been commanded by some of America's best-known generals, men like "Hanging Sam" Williams and "Iron Mike" O'Daniels, who had formed and shaped the Army of the Republic of Vietnam (ARVN) in the image and likeness of the U.S. Army. They called the ARVN "the finest little army in Asia." [3] Yet by late 1962 and early 1963 it was proving unequal

---

[3] In June 1950 the U.S. KMAG commander called the South Korean Army "the best damn army outside the United States." A week later it collapsed under North Korean attack.

to fighting the kind of war that the Vietcong and increasing numbers of North Vietnamese troops were pressing upon it.

The military advisory group had served its purpose. It was time to put some steel into the ARVN by introducing the counterinsurgency phase of the new Army doctrine. With the President's approval, thousands of green, young infantry officers began moving out with the combat companies, battalions, and brigades of the ARVN. Theoretically, they were advisers, but in actual practice they were there to command—and to fight. Most had never seen combat, but they were eager to make points for promotion. Since they did not speak Vietnamese these young Americans had some initial trouble advising combat-experienced South Vietnamese officers on new methods of command and battle tactics. But the Americans were brave and more eager to be killed than the ARVN officers, who fought more to survive than to die or excel in their careers.

While these American "advisers" were trying to lead the ARVN in the "Follow Me" tradition of the U.S. Army Infantry School, the Green Berets were quietly moving their elite airborne-ranger-trained men out into the brush to take up the fighting required to counter a civil war that was mistakenly being called an insurgency. Bright, ruthless staff technocrats like Brigadier General William E. DePuy (whose permanent rank was lieutenant colonel although he rose to the temporary rank of major general while serving an extended period in Vietnam) had plans for every eventuality and ready answers to every question about the Army's objectives in Vietnam. This was the war of the future and the way to high rank for these uncommonly self-assured organization men and their patron, General Westmoreland. They brooked no interference or doubts. Those who questioned the wisdom of the new doctrine, or what the Army was about in Vietnam, were sent home to military oblivion or early retirement. In Saigon the saying was, "DePuy eats colonels for breakfast." These arrogant military technocrats had all the answers then and they still believe they have all the answers. But they were wrong—and it would take the Army and the nation six bloody years to find out how wrong. And by that time they would be out of Vietnam and safely ensconced in high positions in Washington.[4]

In mid-1964 it became apparent that United States advisers and Green Beret forces were no match for the growing number of North Vietnamese troops entering South Vietnam. The advisers had learned quickly and the airborne-ranger special-forces troops fought well, but for some unfathomable reason the ARVN could not cope with its armed countrymen.

The Army manager/leaders tried to put the best face possible on the situation. North Vietnamese conscripts were reported as "regulars," while South Vietnamese conscripts were called "citizen soldiers." Despite their rhetoric the North Vietnamese and Vietcong dedication to combat was fast overtaking the carefully nurtured image of the ARVN as a "fine little army." It was in fact in imminent danger of complete collapse despite nine years of U.S. Army advice and equipment. A defeat of the South Vietnamese would have been a major defeat for the Army's doctrine of low-profile counterinsurgency as the way to defeat wars of liberation. Ambassador Taylor was not going to sit idly by and watch his doctrine discredited. He pressed hard for the introduction of American ground troops.

But for years the American public had been told that infantry ground wars were passé, especially in Asia. How could the Army admit it needed infantry troops in Vietnam and not puncture the image of the new Modern Army it had created? The answer was to commit a helicopter-borne, air-mobile division to Vietnam. The 1st Cavalry Division designation was hastily given to the 11 Airborne test division and—with President Johnson's personal blessing—the division was rushed to Vietnam.[5] This gave the American people the impression that machines were going to do most of the fighting and it gave the Army a chance to combat-test their air-mobile concepts. The

---

[4] Westmoreland as Chief of Staff, Bruce Palmer as Vice Chief of Staff, and DePuy as Assistant Vice Chief of Staff are today shaping the future of the Army they led to destruction in Vietnam.

[5] About 1962, the 11th Airborne Division had been converted to a test division for "Sky Cavalry" tactics. By 1964 these tests were well along but still far from conclusive.

prospects looked bright. With the helicopter mobility of the Cavalry Division backed up by Air Force and Navy tactical airborne firepower, it was felt that the Army would quickly teach the North Vietnamese the high cost of killing American advisers and elite Green Beret troops. And the air-mobile division would help prop up the ARVN until more Army ground troops could be sent to Vietnam.

So the 1st Cavalry Division proved to be essentially a forerunner of a full-scale brushfire-war build-up. The green troops of the division learned quickly and fought bravely. In their initial engagements in the A Shau Valley the troops were committed to battle piecemeal and suffered fairly heavy casualties. A captured North Vietnamese after-battle report stated that the American troops had poor fire discipline, were easily frightened at night, tended to bunch up when brought under fire, and could be best attacked when they were dismounting from their helicopters. This same report indicated that U.S. forces used incredible amounts of artillery and air fire support, but were lax on posting flank guards and sentries.

Despite the firepower and mobility of the airborne division, it was not able to protect the scattered special-forces camps and prop up the sagging ARVN. Department of State and Defense reports began to enlarge upon the estimated number of enemy "regulars" that were "pouring into South Vietnam." The stage was set for the third phase of the Army's doctrine. The brushfire was now in full flame, but in 1965 it was not being called a limited war by the Army organization men. It was thought of as all-out war and the Army excitedly built up to the proper fighting level by shipping standard infantry divisions into Vietnam. The Army had already maneuvered in the Joint Chiefs of Staff to have the Military Assistance Command Vietnam (MACV) designated as a subunified command under a four-star Army general. This move (1) gave the Army overall command in Vietnam; (2) placed the MACV commander under only nominal command of the Navy admiral who commanded the Pacific Command; and (3) meant that the Army MACV commander could end-run the Pacific Command and go straight to General Wheeler in the Joint Chiefs of Staff on vital issues. This command arrangement also meant that the Army would get the lion's share of the layers of high-rank jobs being created in Vietnam.

The military leaders understood the purpose of this United States combat involvement in terms of "winning the war." And they were joined in this belief by President Johnson, who wanted to limit the war—but also wanted to win it. The President, like his generals, was a member of the World War II generation that talked about limited wars, but nonetheless expected to win every war in which the flag was committed. This dichotomy of rhetoric and true purpose continued to lurk below the surface of the expanding war of 1965–66. Sooner or later it would surface and then there would be all hell to pay. But, for the moment, all the lessons of Korea and General MacArthur were forgotten.

For the Army these were heady years. The lieutenant colonels and colonels of World War II, and the lieutenants, captains, and majors of Korea, smelled the smoke of battle and welcomed the opportunity of fighting in this war as generals or senior colonels. For those who had dreamed of commanding a battalion, brigade, or division in combat, it was a fulfillment of their fantasies. There was something in this war for everyone. The Army managers devised a system of career incentives which rotated the precious combat commands. The technical-service officers argued that the young men being drafted (while the automated-war ideas had been quietly filed away) could not be expected to go to war without the comforts of their society. And to provide those comforts required numerous logistical commands and bases, which of course required hundreds of technical-service officers to command and staff. The Army went to war first class—austerity was a forgotten word—and this took huge amounts of supplies and equipment.

To prove that "nothing was too good for our boys" the Army assigned at least 60 percent of its manpower in Vietnam to command and support duties. The small number of "boys" in combat units had to use unbelievable amounts of ammunition to hold off an enemy who was numerically inferior overall, but who usually had more combat manpower available for any one encounter. But the Army managers were undaunted by the poor combat ratio. They were busy supervising the accumulation and distribution of tons of supplies and equipment that they were confident would bury the enemy under sheer bulk and thereby win the war. They kept countless records and reports—and this administrative work necessitated the establishment of countless numbers of headquarters. Corps and logistical headquarters mushroomed throughout South Vietnam and with them the number of good, safe noncombatant career-developing jobs also increased.

The rush of Army units to Vietnam continued well into the fall of 1967. Friends who served in MACV Headquarters during those hectic days have told me how they worked around the clock putting together long "laundry lists" (copied from field manuals) of all the Army units they could think of that might conceivably be needed in Vietnam. Those lists, after a superficial review by the Department of the Army, became the rationale by which President Johnson sent Westy hundreds of thousands of troops to "nail the coonskin on the wall." Many of those units were not needed in Vietnam. Some of the engineer battalions ended up constructing swimming pools, tennis courts, noncommissioned officer and officer clubs for the thousands of noncombatant command and support personnel engaged in busywork in rear-area bases.

Yet those were days of high optimism for members of the airborne club. There were a few nagging doubts as the merciless artillery and airborne firepower failed to bring the Vietcong and their northern allies to their knees. But the doubters were few. The dichotomy of winning the no-win limited war that Army doctrine had postulated began to be faintly discernible. But winning had become all-important. It was inconceivable to any branch of the armed services that American troops should be asked to take the field in another championship game—and not be allowed to win it. Their undefeated varsity record was on the line. The "big team" coach leaders from Annapolis and West Point had to win.

The Wheelers, Moorers, Westmorelands, DePuys, Ewells, and Pattons remained supremely confident that if they killed enough people things would turn their way in Vietnam. The only problem was the number of limits in this limited brushfire war. And so the game plan was modified; the bombing would have to be stepped up, Haiphong blockaded, Cambodia and Laos invaded, and an end-run amphibious landing made above the demilitarized zone. Such a plan gave each of the services a way to excel while helping to win the game.

But the civilian leadership still believed what the military had so confidently told them at the beginning of the "limited" war, namely, that it could be cheaply and quickly won with a limited commitment of American resources. The President and his advisers had been told that six good U.S. Army divisions could do the job in Vietnam. Yet by 1967 there were the equivalent of nearly ten Army divisions in Vietnam and the situation was still deteriorating. Furthermore, as the supposedly limited war took on more and more of the characteristics of a small-scale replica of World War II, the United States political leadership became increasingly concerned that Vietnam might trigger World War III. This concern caused them to look with anxiety on military plans to widen the war. Yet the armed forces had forecast correctly that once they were in the war it would be possible to tow the Administration in their wake as they steadily increased their presence.

Things continued to go the Joint Chiefs of Staff's way until the Tet Offensive of 1968. Despite the presence of nearly 1,000,000 ARVN troops and 525,000 Americans, the Vietcong were able to seize 37 of 44 provincial capitals and send the United States ambassador fleeing for his life from the American embassy in Saigon. The highly mobile but woefully under-manned Army combat units were not able to protect the huge noncombatant support-base complex—and fight the North Vietnamese as well. But the Army's answer to the crushing Tet Offensive was to ask Washington for more men instead of re-assigning part of the tail-heavy support force to combat units to fight the enemy. General Westmoreland requested that an additional 206,000 soldiers be sent to Vietnam.

The Tet Offensive shattered the reputation of some technocrat-generals like Westmoreland, and revealed the falseness of the Army's counterinsurgency and limited-war doctrine. Political leaders began to realize that the doctrine had been from the beginning a mercenary expedient to assure Army participation in international affairs and a way to obtain the money to go with it—without any meaningful adjustment in worldwide force structures (Europe and the Middle East) or any relationship to contemporary political priorities. The political leadership began to draw back from the abyss toward which the limited-war doctrine had been carrying them. The displeasure of the Joint Chiefs of Staff and the armed services was immediate and predictable. They would continue to insist on the United States winning the Vietnamese civil war, but except for the Cambodian invasion their protests would be of little avail. The war remains, like Korea in 1953, reduced in military activity but costly in lives. It will in all probability eventually evolve into a Korean-type situation with around 40,000 American servicemen remaining indefinitely in Vietnam as a residual base force. Such a force has been planned since 1969.

By creating a doctrine that required a mission, the Army leadership had deluded two Presidents and brought the nation and the Army to the brink of ruin. It failed the trust of the nation. And that was what bothered me the most as I began trying to fathom what had gone wrong. In failing the nation's trust the Army had shown weaknesses which if not eliminated would almost certainly return to haunt us. How had the Army let an erroneous doctrine, false pride, and parochial ambition lead it to the failure of Vietnam? Why had Army civilian and military leaders failed to recognize the danger or, when they had recognized it, remained silent? These questions had to be answered if the Army was to be effectively reformed so that these mistakes would not be repeated.

Chapter 5

The Failure of
Leadership

☆ ☆ ☆ ☆ ☆ ☆ ☆ ☆ ☆

Perhaps the Army let itself become trapped in Vietnam because of pervasive ethical laxness at all levels over the preced-
ing fifteen years. This moral laxness created a new breed of
Army officer. The tone of the Army became one of subterfuge,
public deception, and promotion of personal self-interest. A
system evolved which rewarded only those members who practiced conformity, and actually encouraged officers to hide mistakes and place the blame on scapegoats. It bred a false Army
pride. General Westmoreland is quoted in the November 1970
issue of *Harpers Magazine* as saying, "The armed services were
not about to go to the Commander-in-Chief and say that we
were not up to carrying out his instructions—as a matter of
service pride." Yet it is the sworn responsibility of the chiefs of
the United States armed services to inform the Commander in

Chief of their true military capabilities and to advise him truthfully on the feasibility of military courses of action. Failure to do so in an effort to protect "service pride" may have contributed to the deaths of nearly 50,000 Americans in Vietnam.

This growing ethical laxness among Army officers has been accompanied by a sense of being in an adversary relationship to those "outside" the Army system. Those on the "outside" are frequently viewed as "the enemy" by those "in" the Army. In the minds of many officers there is the incontrovertible conviction that theirs is the ultimate patriotism. Consequently they are able to rationalize all their acts as patriotic, no matter how self-serving. It is easy for these ultimate patriots, well intentioned as they may be, to act in a repressive or vindictive manner toward people who do not agree with their definition of patriotism and what they believe best for the country. It is for this reason that many high-command levels inside the Army operate along lines more reminiscent of the Mafia than the traditional U.S. Army.

The Army structure is permeated with fear. Only lip service is paid to the concepts of justice, equality, and constitutionally guaranteed freedoms for members. Seldom is an enlightened, concerned attempt made to understand or redress grievances. Any deviation from the rules, any basic criticism of the system, is swiftly and ruthlessly punished. Reprisals can come in many forms: the "efficiency" report, secret security investigations which Army members have no way to refute, official character assassination, professional ostracism and humiliation, rigged boards which hand down unfair judgments, trumped-up courtmartial charges and trials, forced psychiatric examinations intended to discredit, and official orders that banish nonconformers to undesirable overseas stations where families are not permitted and there is an above-average chance they may be killed. Fear of such reprisals keeps many good officers and noncommissioned officers gagged, and forecloses the possibility of critical self-examination of Army policy. This frees the organization men to get away with almost anything, enables the Army to wear a uniform face for the public and the Congress, but it is a mask of strict and sterile convention—no healthy consensus is allowed to emerge.

Enforced conformity and fear of career reprisal are not new phenomenons in the Army, but they have steadily worsened. I had seen their effects in Korea, but they became startlingly apparent to me at Fort Riley, Kansas, where I was stationed after returning from Korea. The post was an infantry training center for replacements to Korea. They came to the training companies bewildered and homesick, a cross section of middle America. There were hardy farm boys from the Great Plains and skinny slum kids from Chicago, Detroit, and St. Louis. Most were young—nineteen or twenty—and scared to death. They came off the troop trains like dirty, tired animals to be greeted by a blaring band and by a field-grade officer who had been ordered down to the railroad siding to make a welcoming speech. No one really cared very much about what happened to them. They were so many warm bodies to be transformed into unquestioning machines that would kill or be killed in Korea in three or four months. Among their number would inevitably be numerous dumbshits. These were boys with low IQs from poor or underprivileged backgrounds; they hardly knew who or where they were—the mental walking wounded of American society—and a high proportion of them would become physically maimed and crippled in Korea. When they left the post after eight weeks of training and indoctrination, they would wear the same blank puzzled looks they had worn when they arrived. They could not fully understand or cope with the everyday world in which they had been born. The Army sloughed off any sense of responsibility for them; it had not created them, but it had to use them. Those of us in the training center could do nothing, or were not willing to try, because we were expected to qualify at least 90 percent of the recruits for overseas shipment. For a company commander not to do so meant to risk relief from command and a low efficiency report resulting in being passed over for promotion.

So we ground them out, certified kids as "POR qualified" (prepared overseas replacement) when we knew damn well they would be lucky to survive the first day of combat. Each time a group of these pitiful "loners" would leave the company, I would remember the kid I received as a replacement rifleman one evening in Korea. He had arrived at the reserve area late in the evening. I had been sitting in front of my pup tent writing a letter. The platoon sergeant walked with him. The soldier was thin, dusty, and dirty from the trip up to the battalion area in the back of a truck. He was obviously scared. I rose and he saluted sloppily as he looked at me with small questioning eyes. I returned his salute and motioned for him and the platoon sergeant to be seated on two nearby ammo boxes. The platoon sergeant told me the rifleman was a "new man" just in from the "States." The boy said he was from Iowa and had been trained at Camp Breckinridge, Kentucky. We talked for a short while and I realized he was a dumbshit, probably a fine kid but without the mental capacity to understand what was going on. We were moving back into combat the next morning, so I decided to put him in the second rifle squad, which was led by Arlie Cope. Corporal Cope had over twenty-two years of Army service and was a damn good soldier.

But he liked to drink large amounts of whiskey and when he did so he liked to fight. This had gotten him broken from master sergeant twice. I had picked him up in Japan as a private when no one else in the company would take him because he was a "D.R. [delinquency report] getter." When we got to Korea I had told him, "No drinking in the field; if I catch you boozing, you're out, but if you keep your nose clean I'll do all I can to help get your stripes back." He was a great combat leader for the young kids who made up the platoon (and a help for me, too, because at twenty-two I had a lot to learn). They looked up to him as a father figure and he looked after them like a mother hen. So I sent this thin, tired, scraggly young soldier over to Cope's squad. Before he went I told him, "Tomorrow we go back up to fight; you be careful and listen to Corporal Cope. He knows the ropes. Watch the men in your squad. Do things like they do—they are all veterans and they know how to stay alive. That's the way you learn." "Do you think I'll be okay, sir?" he asked. "I just got married before I left home and I really want to get back," he said, with a kind of desperate honesty. "You'll be okay if you keep your eyes open and think. Be careful and do exactly what Cope says. He'll take care of you." He saluted as sloppily as before, still looking at me questioningly, and walked with the platoon sergeant to where the second squad was camped.

Later I asked Cope his impressions of the new man. "Well, he's kinda a dumbshit, but if I can keep him alive for a couple of weeks he'll probably make it okay." Cope told me he had put the man with Private First Class Smith, the most experienced rifleman in the squad. I thought no more about the young soldier. The next day we moved back into the front line and that night we came under Chinese attack. After a night of artillery and small-arms fire we managed to drive the enemy off. In the early daylight hours of the following morning I began counting up the toll of the night's fighting. Each squad brought its dead back to the platoon CP (command post) from which the bodies were carried down to a two-and-a-half-ton truck that would haul them to the rear. As I leaned against a sandbag bunker I saw four shadowy figures coming out of the morning haze. They carried an olive drab GI blanket that sagged in the center and had a large dark stain on it. As they came to the bunker Private First Class Smith said, "Where do you want the bodies, sir?" "Who is it?" I asked. "The new man, sir." "What the hell happened to him?" I muttered. "Well, you remember about 0300 when the Chinks got in between us and the third squad? Well, I seen about four of 'em moving up that little gulley just down about fifty yards to the right of our trench. The new guy had a grenade launcher on his M-1, so I told him to take a rifle grenade and pop it down on 'em." "Why didn't you shoot it?" I asked. "I was going to, once he got the grenade on the launcher, but about that time three or four other Chinks come up out of the brush in front and started running right at us, so I cut down on them. While I was firing at them, Danny, the new guy, slipped over to the far end of the trench and I guess he figured to fire on the Chinks in the gulley. All I know is that I heard this big fucking blast and he was down in the trench. The fragments went everywhere. I figured a Chink bullet had hit the grenade before he could fire it. But this morning I picked up what was left of his rifle and it had a clip of AP [armor piercing] rounds in the chamber. One round was missing so he musta fired a live round instead of a crimped cartridge. I'm really sorry, sir, but there just wasn't nothin' I could do."

I told them to leave the body of the new man (no one knew his last name; "Danny" was all they had called him besides the "new guy"). "You did your best," I said to Smith. "It isn't your fault. The blame lies way back in the States, so don't feel so bad over it." He looked at the ground as he said, "But that ain't gonna help him none." "I know, but don't take it on yourself," I answered. After they left, I reached down and pulled the blanket up around what was left of the chest and torso of this young soldier who had ridden up scared but alive the day before and now was going back on the same truck—dead—a decapitated mass of mangled bloody pulp. Someone in his training unit had either forgotten to teach him that it took a special type of cartridge to fire a rifle grenade, or he had not been mentally able to comprehend and remember this fact. He was no longer one of America's walking mental wounded—he had served his purpose. I wondered what I could say in the letter I would have to write to the young girl in Iowa who was anxiously waiting to hear from her new husband.

At Fort Riley I not only saw the poor misfits and hapless dumbshits being sent to the slaughter, I also saw the treatment given those who had managed in some way to survive and return. A continuous board of officers convened by order of the commanding general to consider the elimination of soldiers under provisions of Army Regulations 368 and 369 (today called 208 and 209 boards). These boards reviewed the cases of soldiers considered unsuitable or undesirable for further service. I sat for a time as a member of one of these marathon boards. Our instructions were to eliminate as many soldiers who appeared before us as possible. The proceedings were cut and dried. The soldier saluted and was told to take a seat—in the center of a bare room—facing five officers seated at a long table. The president of the board was an Adjutant General Corps colonel who I knew had never seen a day of combat, but who played the role of the gruff combat veteran. He would ask the soldier if he liked the Army. The answer was invariably negative. It was impossible to expect any other answer from men who had been harassed as much as most of these soldiers had before they finally arrived at the board hearing. These were men who in many cases had survived combat only to be assigned to endless police details, picking up cigarette butts and papers all over Fort Riley, or to permanent KP and mop details. They weren't considered smart enough to do anything else. They had served their purpose in Korea and the Army didn't know what else to do with them.

But because of their combat service, they believed they had finally earned a place in the Army and in the country which had been ignoring them since the day they entered kindergarten. So they rebelled in the only way that was open to them. They went home without leave. They got drunk in town and were picked up and beaten by the MP's before being given a "DR." The DR reflected unfavorably on the commander of the company to which the soldier was assigned. It also reflected unfavorably on the battalion and regimental commanders because they could be accused of harboring troublemakers in their commands. The post commanding general would be subject to criticism by the Army commander in Chicago if the post had a high DR rate. All of this could result in these various commanders receiving less than superior efficiency reports. The solution was to get rid of the troublemakers by slipping them onto another levy of replacements for Korea. But some of the soldiers had only a year or less of service remaining and could not be returned to Korea.[1] Company commanders were instructed to start building 368 or 369 case eliminations on those who could not be returned to battle.

During the case-building period, the poor dumbshit became the target of "close supervision" by his company officers and

---

[1] During Vietnam this regulation was changed so that soldiers with as little as six months remaining service could be sent to Southeast Asia.

NCO's. Each time he made a mistake (and he frequently did) someone was on his back. To escape this harassment, he usually ran away, got drunk on post (since he was denied a pass to town where he might get a DR), or became insubordinate to one of the officers or NCO's who were riding him. Any of these offenses made him subject to punishment under the Uniform Code of Military Justice (UCMJ). If the punishment was nonjudicial under Article 15 UCMJ, the soldier was moved to another company, ostensibly to give him a chance, under a different commander, but actually to make the case record appear more fair. When a soldier had received three or more Article 15 punishments his commander submitted papers requesting that the man be considered for a general or bad-conduct discharge under Army Regulations 368 or 369. If the soldier had become insubordinate or committed some other more serious offense, he would be tried by a court-martial, usually found guilty, fined, and dismissed from the service with a dishonorable discharge.

When a soldier came up for his elimination-board hearing, a few antagonistic questions would often be asked to provoke the soldier into displaying an "uncooperative attitude" which would prejudice his case. After being questioned by members of the board, the president would ask if the defendent had anything further he wanted to say. This would sometimes produce another angry statement that could also be used to justify a general discharge. The soldier would then be told in a parade-ground voice by the AG colonel that he was "dismissed." He had to rise, stand at attention, salute, and leave the room. The colonel would then ask if everyone was ready to vote. Each member would mark "yes" or "no" on a small piece of paper and pass it to the lowest-ranking officer who would count the votes. "Yes" meant to eliminate the soldier; "no" signified he should be retained on active duty. Neither I nor my colleagues had the guts to mark many "no" votes. So a large number of young Americans, who already had every strike in society's book against them, were thrown out of the Army with a less than honorable discharge. This added one more stumbling block toward their ever earning a living or making a place for themselves and their families in American society. We felt smugly righteous about our actions. We were removing undesirable people from "our" Army—we were making it "better." They shouldn't have been in the Army anyway, so by eliminating them we were just correcting an initial mistake. Never mind that these "undesirables" might have risked their lives for us and the country some months earlier. As the AG colonel used to say, "They were now negative personnel assets which could not be converted to a positive asset for the Army."

And there were the blacks and the Puerto Ricans—the most unfortunate were the black Puerto Ricans. Most of these soldiers were assigned menial tasks. The Puerto Ricans were considered of little value for anything other than KP details, latrine guards, barracks' firemen to stoke the coal-fired furnaces, or to serve as "aggressors" on training exercises. They didn't speak English very well, if at all. This had been no particular problem while they were fighting in Korea in the segregated all-Puerto Rican 65th Infantry Regiment. But when they returned to their own country they too became negative assets to the Army. So many of them also found their way before the 368 and 369 boards. Most understood practically nothing of what was said there, but they soon found themselves being discharged as undesirables. One of the board members remarked one day, "There's no place in the Army for all these damn spics and niggers; we don't need them now." I sat there and said nothing. I too wanted to be successful and to get ahead in the Army. It is one of the shames with which I live that I was too selfish for my own future to speak up for fellow Americans. I did ask that I be relieved from the board at once and my request was granted. But I had figured, Hell, it isn't my fight. Why get into it?

Then in 1954 I went to Germany to serve in the United States Seventh Army. If anything, the policies of U.S. Army leaders in Europe were more hypocritical than in the United States. There was never-ending talk about high "combat-readiness" (which didn't exist), but the real concern was in looking good to higher headquarters. For example, most Army company and battery commanders in Germany maintain two sets of unit equipment. One set is for use in field maneuvers and the other set—usually accumulated by begging, stealing, trading, or scrounging—is kept for the numerous command inspections that consume a good portion of the Army's time in Europe. The primary event of each year was not scoring high on combat-readiness tests. On the contrary, it was passing the annual Seventh Army Command Maintenance Inspection (CMI). Failure to pass the CMI meant relief from command and a low efficiency rating for officers, so unit commanders and their NCO's would stop at nothing to look good on this inspection.

Supply sergeants would trade equipment to units standing inspection. Lost or mislaid items would be stolen or borrowed from other units in nocturnal foragings nicknamed "midnight requisitions." The day the inspection team arrived was one of apprehension for all members of the unit, who had been working night and day for at least a week trying to get ready for this most important event. Training was put aside so the unit could devote full time to removing the inspection equipment from its sealed and bolted repository, polishing it, and lining up displays in accordance with the rigid display rules. The inspectors checked every item listed on the unit property book. Wrenches that were listed as being one and one half inches in length, but measured only one and one quarter inches resulted in a "gig" on the inspection report. Since much of the equipment was borrowed from units that were inspected later, it was not infrequent for an inspector to unknowingly measure or handle the same item several times.

The apprehension that preceded the inspection was minimal compared to that which followed while the unit waited for the results. If the inspection report was favorable there would be letters of commendation from all levels of the chain of command. Unit officers could count on good efficiency reports and the NCO's could expect promotions. If the report was unsatisfactory the supply sergeant would be demoted, the first sergeant transferred, and the company commander relieved from command and given an efficiency report indicating negligent supervision. If one or more units in a battalion were found de-ficient or unsatisfactory, the battalion commander could also expect early orders to the Seventh Army staff.

Racial Bitterness

When the units were not busy with "Mickey Mouse" inspections, they trained by running about German forests—or as the GI's called it—playing "bang-bang, you're dead." If any German trees or property were damaged during field training a unit claims' officer disbursed United States taxpayers' money to the German farmers, soothing them for minor damages committed by those sent to Germany to defend them.[2] When not engaged in these activities, unit commanders took care of "disciplinary problems." In Germany there were always plenty of these. Soldiers who brought in DR's from the local Army military police unit were frequently either victims of discrimination by individual MP's or involved in altercations with German cabdrivers, bartenders, and prostitutes. But the DR's were reported through channels to Seventh Army and this caused unit commanders "problems," so troublemakers who received delinquency reports had to go. Pressure was placed on commanders to eliminate these soldiers through the trusty 368 and 369 boards or by court-martial. I remember Colonel (now General) William B. Rosson telling an assembled group of company commanders and first sergeants of the 39th Infantry Regiment, "I've been sent down here to straighten this regiment out [it had the highest DR rate in the Seventh Army at the time] and I intend to do it. If I don't I'll be relieved, but before I am, I can promise you that everyone in this room will have walked out of the front gate ahead of me. Are there any questions?"

There were no questions; the message was clear. We were to get rid of soldiers who brought in DR's or damaged good German-American relations. Maintaining German-American relations was the paramount concern, while the rights of the United States soldier were secondary. Thus a black soldier in

---

[2] The Army paid $4,216,671 in FY 1970 and $5,622,532 through May 28 of FY 1971 to satisfy maneuver damage claims filed by West German nationals.

the company I commanded could say in reply to charges of
raping a German woman, "I beat her up afterwards, but I
didn't rape her, Captain. She was willin' and didn't say nothin'
until I told her it wasn't no good and I wasn't payin'. Then she
starts hollerin' her head off for the *polizei* and they turned me
over to the MP's, but it wasn't no damn rape, no sir." I believed him. So did the officer who served as his defense counsel.
But there had been two previous rapes by GI's in Nürnberg
and Bamberg and the German government was demanding
punishment from senior Army generals in Heidelberg. So a
young soldier from the black ghetto of Detroit, who had gone
to town to drink in an all-black *gasthaus* and tried to satisfy a
biological urge with one of the girls who frequented the place,
had to be tried by general court-martial. He was found guilty
and sentenced to confinement for six years at hard labor, for-
feiture of all pay and allowances, and a dishonorable discharge.

His court-martial eliminated the possibility of any additional
unfavorable publicity which might damage the careers of senior officers, or myself. And it ensured a continuing good relationship between the senior Army generals in Heidelberg and
the wealthy German civilians and politicians who invited them
to hunt on their private game preserves. Our generals coveted
their status as military proconsuls and enjoyed being treated
with deference by powerful West German figures. A young
black soldier couldn't be allowed to interfere with good relations. Besides, if the Army didn't put him in jail the Detroit police might. And who really cared one way or the other?

Each day I became a little more disillusioned. One Monday
morning as I entered my company orderly room I noticed a tall
American Indian corporal, who had a Mexican-American sur-
name, among the usual group of soldiers waiting to see me. I
was surprised to see him among the regular Monday morning
line-up of weekend DR winners. I asked the first sergeant what
the corporal had done. "He got drunk Saturday night and
damn near tore the EM Club apart. You know how them Indi-
ans are when they get a little booze in 'em, Captain." I had the
man sent in to my office. "What the hell happened to you?" I
asked him. "Just two weeks ago you were before the board for

consideration for promotion to sergeant, and now you pull a stunt like this. What the hell is your problem?" He looked at me sullenly. "No problem, sir, I just made a mistake. I got drunk and some smart-ass made a remark and I cleaned the place out." "What the hell could anyone say that would cause you to do over two hundred dollars worth of damage to the EM Club?" I asked, looking at the report of the incident. "It wasn't nothin' important, Captain, I'm ready to take my medicine. I'd just rather not talk about it." "Well, we're sure as hell gonna talk about it right now," I snapped back. "You can bet your ass that as soon as the colonel gets into his office and reads the weekend duty report, he's gonna have me up there on the double to start explaining. He's gonna chew my ass up one side and down the other because of you, and if I'm gonna have to get an ass-chewing first thing Monday morning on your account, you are sure as hell gonna tell me why you ripped up the damn club. Now cut the bullshit. I can't help you if you're gonna give me a bunch of crap."

He looked at me apologetically. "I'm really sorry, sir. I didn't mean to cause you no trouble. It's just that I was so damn disappointed about not making sergeant [I had not known he had not been approved for promotion; he was a fine soldier and I had figured him a cinch to be selected] that I went over to the club to have a coupla beers. Two sergeants there, they got to tellin' me that we didn't need no spic sergeants in this battalion. They said it was bad enough I was a crazy Indian, but being a greaser besides was just too much. Well, I just got mad, sir. You don't know what it's like to come from Colorado and all the time have people laughing at you because your mother was Indian and your old man came from Mexico. That's why I joined the Army. I thought things would be different. I thought in here if you worked you could get ahead. But it's the same old shit in here just like it was outside, Captain. I was the most qualified guy who went before that board, sir. I know all the guys who got picked and I can soldier rings around 'em any day. How come I didn't get picked, Captain? How come I got the shit? And now you'll have to bust me." He was near to tears. At that moment I wished I was more than twenty-five years old and had the experience of age to counsel him, but all I could say was, "Don't worry about me busting you. I think you're a damn good soldier. Let me talk to the colonel. Maybe I can get you off with just paying for the damages."

After he left I stared out the window a few minutes before signaling the first sergeant to start sending in the rest of the weekend disciplinary line-up. Then my phone rang. It was the battalion commander. "King, what in the hell is this about one of your men tearing up the EM Club? You better get right up here. I want to talk to you about this. We can't have trouble-makers like that in this battalion." I replied, "Yes, sir, I'm on my way now." As I walked out through the orderly room those waiting to see the "old man" looked quickly at the floor.

On another Monday morning I had come into the orderly room to see a very frightened yet pretty young German girl sitting on the couch in my office. Next to her sat a ruddy-faced hausfrau who was staring determinedly at my desk. I went into my office, saying, "*Guten Tag*," and then asked, "How can I help you?" The older woman smiled and told her daughter something in a torrent of German. The daughter looked at her mother and then embarrassedly at me. "My mother has come with me to talk with you about my fiancé, William Jones. My mother doesn't want me to marry him," she added. "She thinks he has not been telling us the truth, because it has taken so long for him to get permission to marry. She doesn't believe that he has requested permission."

"Tell your mother that he has requested permission to marry, but it just takes a very long time for these things to be settled through our channels." The country woman smiled when she heard this but she resumed a worried look as she again spoke rapidly to her daughter. "My mother is worried about how I will live in America. She has heard that there are problems for black men in America. She asks if what she has heard is true." I thought for several seconds before I began to try to answer the woman's question. I was an American, Jones was an American, but he was a black American and she had come to ask me if there were unfair treatment of black men in America. Hell, I thought, not only is there unfair treatment of black men in America, there is unfair treatment of them in the American Army in Germany. That was why Jones's request to marry was taking so long to process.

The Army was not anxious to have many more black soldiers with white wives. They caused problems of assignment. They could not be assigned to bases in the South unless they could live on the base. And it was difficult for them to find off-base housing in other parts of the country. So requests like Jones's were being buried in red tape in the hope that the soldier would go back to the United States at the end of his tour, leaving the girl behind. Many soldiers had done so and that was why the mother was so concerned—that and the fact that the girl was unusually thick around the waist. I decided I could not lie so I said, "I don't know what you have heard about conditions in America, but Negro Americans are not always treated the same way as other Americans. This is particularly true in the part of the United States that Private First Class Jones comes from. It could cause some problems for your daughter and her husband; they may find many people against them for being married. It is something that she and Private First Class Jones must work out for themselves."

The daughter's face had fallen as I said this; then she turned to her mother and told her in German what I had said. The mother looked at me gravely. "You should both go and talk with our chaplain about this and I will give Private First Class Jones time to go too if he wants," I finished. "But why are some Americans treated different from others?" asked the girl. "I don't know," I replied. "But yours is the land of the free. All men are equal. It says so in your books. I know—I have read them," said the girl. "You are here in Germany to keep us free from the Russians, and surely you have the same freedom in your country." The old woman said something to the daughter. "My mother says she understands what you have said: she remembers that before in Germany some people were treated different from others." "Oh, but we're not as bad as that," I said smiling, and trying to make light of the remark. "There is not much difference, it seems to me," replied the German girl.

They rose and I walked with them to the door of the barracks. *"Danke,"* said the old woman. The girl said nothing. I watched them walk across the parade ground of the barracks that had once housed a German SS battalion and was now the home of a battalion of United States infantry.

I went back to my office and told the first sergeant to send Jones to see me. He arrived a few minutes later. A thin soldier of medium height, he had never been in any trouble and was a rather quiet young man. He stood and looked at me with round black eyes that shone with both concern and indignation. He had heard from the company gossip that his girl and her mother were down talking to the "old man." He must have been waiting for me to send for him because he wore freshly pressed fatigues. "Your girl and her mother were just in to see me, Private First Class Jones," I began stiffly.

"They shouldn't have come, sir. I tried to talk her old lady out of it, but she was dead set on coming. She thinks I'm lying about wanting to marry Helga, but I'm not, Captain, you know that. You saw my request for permission to marry four months ago."

"That's what I told her, Jones."

"Well what did she say to that?"

"She seemed happy to hear it, but she is worried about her daughter, what's going to happen to her in the States."

"Did you tell her how it is in the States?" he asked.

"Not exactly," I answered. "I just said there could be problems."

His face took on a hard look. "Yeah, like being married to a nigger."

"I recommended she go talk with the chaplain and told her you could go along if you wanted to," I said, trying to change the subject.

"Man she ain't gonna get no help from that damn preacher. He's the one that held up my request for a month. He's a Southern Baptist, and he ain't about to ever approve my gettin' married, no sir. Ain't no use talkin' to him. All he wants is to see me get shipped out."

"Look, Jones," I said, "what you do off-duty is your business so long as you don't get in any trouble. I don't want to get involved in your business, but I want to help you if you need help. That's part of my job. You want me to check and see what's happened to your marriage application?" I was brushing him off—we both knew it.

"No, that's okay, Captain. Thanks anyway for offering. Ain't nothing anybody can do. I'll just have to go back to the States and reenlist and come back and start trying to get permission over again in some other outfit."

"I recommended approval, that's all I can do," I said lamely.

"I know you did, Captain. Ain't your fault. Guess that's just the way the Army is, but it beats going back to work in Mississippi anyway."

After he left I knew that once again I had failed to discharge my responsibility to a fellow citizen. I had taken the Army's side against one of its soldiers. It seemed that this was becoming all too frequently necessary.

Once when I was assigned as OD (officer of the day) I experienced an example of the pent-up hatred felt by black soldiers as a result of discrimination in promotion, job assignments, and overall unfair treatment. I had gone to the BOQ (bachelor officer quarters) to change clothes before setting out on my rounds. As I entered the building I heard loud talking and laughter from a recreation room at the end of the corridor. I walked past the rows of doors to see what was going on. A crowd of officers, accompanied by some of their German girl friends, were standing around a large table which had been covered with a blanket to form a dice table. Several of the dice throwers were in T-shirts and were busily quaffing beer while waiting for their turn with the dice. I knew that gambling in a government building was illegal, but this weekend dice game was a ritual in the BOQ. As officer of the day it was technically my duty to enforce the prohibition against gambling. But a number of the dice throwers were senior officers and it did not seriously occur to me that I should stop them.

Instead I went to my room, changed into "pinks and greens" (officer semidress uniform prior to 1956), pulled on a heavy green trench coat, and before I left the room placed a .45-caliber automatic pistol in the pocket of the coat. It was the OD's job to make several rounds of all the off-post *gasthäuser* and dives frequented by soldiers of the regiment. I was supposed to see that soldiers were conducting themselves in accord with Army regulations on dress and deportment. The real purpose of the checks was to catch troublemakers before the MP's did and cut down on the number of DR's that the regiment had been getting from an unfriendly local MP company.

I was not required to carry a weapon, but only a few nights before a lieutenant on "courtesy patrol" to enforce the same dress and conduct standards had been attacked in a local black *gasthaus* by a group of soldiers. He had been savagely beaten, and was cut severely about the face with razor blades inserted into pieces of wood and held between the fingers of one of his assailants. The officer had been unarmed and unable to fight off the group that attacked him. As a result of the slashing and beating he was still in a coma and in danger of losing an eye.

I did not want the same thing to happen to me. After about two hours of going into one dive after another throughout the city, I came around midnight to a place known in the GI slang as the "Bloody Bucket." It was a black *gasthaus,* meaning that it was patronized by black soldiers only. White GI's entered at their peril. (There were a larger number of white *gasthäuser* where a black soldier took his life in his hands by entering.) I went in through the heavy wooden door and found myself in a large noisy room, filled with rough-hewn tables and a heavy wooden bar along one side. It was typical of dozens of neighborhood *gasthäuser* all over Germany with its high wood-beamed ceiling and rough-plastered walls. The room was thick with smoke and the sound of a blaring phonograph.

As I walked in wearing the black and white armband with the letters "OD" conspicuous on my left overcoat sleeve, a black soldier turned and whispered to another. Several unfriendly black faces and pairs of hard black eyes stared at me. I stood quietly by the door for a moment and then walked toward the bar. At a nearby table there were four young soldiers who had removed their Ike jackets and their shirts and sat drinking beer in their T-shirts. This was a uniform violation that would net each of them a DR when the local MP's checked the bar on their nightly round.

I stepped next to the table and said in a low voice, "Better put your shirts and jackets on, soldiers." They looked at me sullenly and made no move to obey, so I spoke in a little harder tone. "I said, put on your shirts and jackets, the MP's will be through here in a little while and they'll give every one of you a DR if they catch you like that." One soldier rose and began to put on his shirt. Another tall soldier jumped up and said, "Don't put on your shirt, man, you don't have to do what he says." Then he said, "Captain, your word don't carry no weight in here. We're off-duty and you better get your ass out of here while you can still walk." It had become a direct challenge. I didn't dare back down. I looked straight at the tall soldier and said quietly, "I gave you an order, soldier. Now put on that shirt and jacket and save both of us a lot of trouble." He replied, "I ain't gonna obey your fuckin' order, you sonuvabitch." Several other soldiers had crowded around him. "You drunk, man, you don't know what you're saying," they said, trying to get him to sit down. "We don't have to obey them fuckers when we're off-duty. They don't own us. Fuck 'em! Fuck 'em!" he shouted, looking at me with a hatred I had never seen before. I stood there looking steadily at him and the group of soldiers who had gathered around him. My hand tightly gripped the butt of the pistol in my pocket. "This is your last chance. Either you put on that shirt and jacket or I'm taking you in."

All of them looked at me with angry eyes and the tall soldier's knuckles tightened as he gripped the back of a heavy wooden chair. I figured he was going to swing it like a club. I slid my finger to the safety catch of the pistol and switched it to the fire position. I stared back at them and tensely waited. Then he took his hands from the chair, picked up his shirt and tie, and began putting them on. The rest also began putting on their shirts while continuing to stare at me with looks of hate. A German girl who had tried to calm things earlier started to talk, just as the *gasthaus* owner came inside with my jeep driver, who was carrying a large monkey wrench. As I eased the safety

catch back on the pistol, I noticed that the tall black soldier's
Ike jacket had a 25th Infantry Division patch sewn to the right
shoulder—we had probably fought together in Korea two years
before and now I was facing him with a loaded pistol in my
pocket. If I reported his conduct to his commander, he would
be court-martialed, and, on the basis of my testimony and that
of other witnesses in the *gasthaus*, probably convicted and confined at hard labor. This would solve nothing and ruin his life.
If I didn't report him I was derelict in performing my duty by,
in effect, tolerating insubordination. As I rode back to the barracks I tried to decide what was the right thing to do. I had his
name and unit and I was still angry. But I decided I could not
in all fairness report him for protesting my demand that he
abide by regulations I was unwilling to enforce on the officers
in the BOQ.

One of the reasons for these problems was that although
official segregation and discrimination in the Army had ended
some years before, covert discrimination had continued—and
continues at the time of this writing.[3] Blacks and Puerto Ricans
were segregated in Germany in 1955–57 by such devices as
forming Puerto Rican-only platoons. If there were not enough
Puerto Ricans to fully man such a platoon it was rounded out
with blacks. Companies were given quotas of black soldiers.
The average unit was not allowed to have more than 30 percent of its total strength in black soldiers. Nearly all headquarters' units had fewer than this number. Manual-labor units such
as truck companies, quartermaster companies, and ammuni-
tion-supply units frequently contained nearer 50 percent black
or Puerto Rican soldiers. Such discrimination was not lost on
the individual black or Puerto Rican soldier. He acutely felt his
second-class status. He still feels that same discrimination
today.

Upon assuming command of a company with over 40 percent black and Puerto Rican soldiers, one of my first actions

---

[3] A black-citizen group has recently concluded an investigation into racial
conditions in Army units in Germany and has alleged that MP's in a unit in
Mannheim, Germany, are members of the KKK and that Army units have been
forming black platoons to enforce segregation.

was to disband an all-Puerto Rican platoon and assign these soldiers throughout the company. Some of the black soldiers were qualified to be noncommissioned officers and I submitted their names on a recommended-promotion list. I was privately told that the regiment had over its percentage quota of black NCO's and instructed to withdraw some of their names.

Because of these covert policies the minority soldier has become increasingly frustrated. It was not until 1970, after numerous articles in the national news media had indicated a high degree of racial unrest in United States forces in Germany, that the Pentagon ordered a task force to investigate allegations of racial crisis. The task-force report published in December 1970 indicated that "black frustration and anger" had reached a volatile level among United States troops in Europe. The task-force report further stated, "We did not anticipate finding such acute frustration and volatile anger as we found among the blacks, nor did we expect to find a somewhat lower level of frustration fairly evidenced by young whites." The task force certainly should not have been surprised by this anger. It grows out of discrimination and years of unconcerned leadership. To my knowledge it has been reflected in constant barracks and *gasthaus* fights between black and white soldiers in nearly all Army units in Germany since 1954.

The black soldier has learned that there is a certain remorse of conscience over unfair practices which permits him to escape with some minor infractions that a white soldier could not. This creates bitterness among both white and black. The whites are resentful because they see this as favoritism to the blacks; the blacks see such treatment as condescending.

A sincere effort to develop a more equitable policy is just beginning. Up until 1971 anyone in the chain of command who questioned racial policies was quickly silenced. This was what happened when Major Lavell Merritt, an articulate black officer, charged the services with being "the strongest citadels of racism on the face of the earth." His cry for "truth and integrity in the system" was answered by removal from his job, assignment to a room at Fort McNair, and, finally, involuntary retirement.

Selfishness at the Top

Top Army leaders have for too long demanded unquestioning loyalty up the chain of command and reflected little, if any, concerned loyalty back down that chain to the men and women of the Army. Communication has broken down. The top leadership has been content to play "Pentagon politics" in order to promote their personal careers and parochial Army objectives. They have told the rank and file to "Do like I say, not like I do." They have forgotten that personal example is a prime requisite of good leadership. Among the rank and file this has created a growing bitterness that is starting to boil over in Europe and Vietnam in acts of open refusal to fight, contempt for senior officers and noncommissioned officers, insubordination, and "fragging." Among the younger officers doubts about the system are growing daily.

There is a broad difference between the leadership of Colonel "Paddy" Flint, who died leading his regiment into battle among the hedgerows of France with his motto of AAA-O ("Anything-anytime-anywhere-bar nothing") chalked on GI's helmets, and the leadership exercised by the colonel who "led" his troops into Cambodia in a helicopter circling at an altitude above rifle range. His troops went into combat with the motto UUUU ("We are the unwilling, led by the unqualified, doing the unnecessary, for the ungrateful") chalked on their helmets.

The war in Vietnam is not the cause of the deep malaise which besets the U.S. Army. But the futility of Vietnam has been the catalyst that has brought the long-dormant disillusionment and frustration of the rank and file into open conflict with the hypocrisy of its leadership. This has set in motion a chain of events that can end only with profound changes in the Army, or its eventual demise as the servant of a free people. The rank and file are not going to continue to tolerate the abuses of privilege and the exploitation they have endured silently for years. They are not likely to again risk their lives so senior officers can live in plush villas in Saigon, Seoul, or Heidelberg and qualify for another "star" by circling in helicopters over battlefields where GI's are being killed or maimed. They are not going to fight again for brigade or division commanders who live in comfortable air-conditioned command trailers and take evening dips in Esther Williams swimming pools, while soldiers sweat in tents or holes in the ground. Nor are they impressed by commanders who go "gook hunting" (chasing Vietnamese civilians from a helicopter and killing them with M-16 rifle fire or hand grenades) and then have themselves awarded combat decorations for doing so. The American soldier doesn't believe that rank is entitled to such abuse of privilege. He is not going to tolerate much longer today's heel-clicking and "yes sir-ing" busywork. This has never been in the tradition of the American soldier and smacks of Prussian militarism. The military service of all citizens should have equal value. Some, because they can lead and train others, are allowed to wear insignia of rank, receive higher pay, and certain privileges as a reward for these extra efforts. But Army customs which demean the service of one citizen in favor of another should not continue under the guise of "discipline."

It is difficult to imagine the bitterness that permeates the lower enlisted and officer ranks of the Army. Letters regularly appear in the unofficial but widely read *Army Times* newspaper similar to one in the April 8, 1971, edition from a "Major's Wife" that said, "Does anyone really appreciate or care what the military and their families are going through in this clown show of a pull-out from Vietnam? When are we going to end our silent stand and speak out?" Her letter was answered the following week by "RA Lieutenant Colonel" who said, "I ask God's blessing on her for telling it like it is, but she hides behind a cloak of anonymity for the same reasons we all do: (1) the hazarding of a career for the sake of expediency is a hard principle; (2) Duty, Honor, Country—no meals, rents, or college education purchase; and (3) there continues the faint, fond, albeit admittedly diminishing hope that some will be appointed to high places and still care enough to practice the old axiom of loyalty down begets loyalty up." This "RA Lieutenant Colonel's" letter is representative of those officers who have remained silent because like other men they have mortgages to

pay, children to send to college, and higher-paid retirement to
anticipate if they "go along."

Thousands of young Americans, and a few older ones, have
refused to serve in today's Army because they do not believe in
what that Army is doing. One example is Specialist/5 Bill
Thompson, a black veteran of Korea, who was decorated on his
first tour in Vietnam, but chose a court-martial rather than
serve there again. Other examples are the skyrocketing AWOL
and desertion rates. In 1967 over 27,000 soldiers deserted from
the Army; in 1968 the figure rose to 39,234; in 1969 to 56,608;
and in 1970 to 65,643. During this time General Westmoreland
stated that these figures were "not alarming" compared to
World War II rates. What he did not mention, of course, was
that the Army in World War II had nearly ten million men,
while the peak figure during Vietnam was about three million.
And at the time the Army Chief of Staff was not alarmed by the
matter, the Army General Staff was putting out urgent mes-
sages (over General Westmoreland's signature) directing that
all possible measures be taken to reduce the serious rise in the
number of soldiers refusing to serve. During 1969 the situation
became so bad in the Sixth Army that some of those who failed
to report to California for shipment to Vietnam were charged
against other continental Army areas. In this way it was possible to keep the total number of AWOL's and deserters from
Vietnam service concealed from the public. In addition the
Sixth Army would have looked statistically bad to have consistently reported such large numbers of AWOL's and desertions.

Most Americans have not been aware of this gradual deterioration of Army morale. They, like the civilian and military leaders, have assumed that frequent pay raises would produce
satisfied soldiers. This has not been true. Money is not the principal motivation of a soldier. A man who is strongly motivated
to earn money does not become a soldier. The soldier's life has
appealed to the man who desires to render service and who
craves public approval and recognition. A concerned civilian
leadership that accurately informed itself about conditions in
the Army and tried to provide the soldier with an environment
in which he would receive just and equal treatment could raise

morale. Demanding conformity to hypocrisy and rewarding that conformity with higher pay will continue to be ineffective. For many young officers service to the nation, and their subordinates, dedication to justice, individual dignity, and self-respect would be more appealing attributes of military life than service to their own careers first and to the existing system second. Only mercenaries lay down their lives for money. Free men have always been willing to die for a principle, *if* they believe in the fairness and sincerity of their leaders and the justness of their cause.

It has been no secret, in Vietnam or Korea, that some officers have been willing to send soldiers out to die for questionable missions. The poorly conducted attacks on "Hamburger Hill" are one example. From May 10 to May 20, 1969, battalions of the 101st Airborne Division, commanded by Major General Melvin Zais, made ten frontal attacks against this 3,000-foot hill. After the hill was finally captured on the tenth frontal assault, the troops were immediately withdrawn. A MACV spokesman in Saigon said they had been withdrawn because "there's no tactical reason to stay there." Had there been any overriding tactical reason to take the hill in the first place? General Zais called the succession of bloody assaults a "gallant victory." Senator Edward Kennedy called the battle "a senseless and irresponsible action," and said it was "a stiff sacrifice for a false sense of military pride." Senator Stephen Young called the piecemeal attacks "a very tragic incident in the unpopular, undeclared war we are waging." According to Senator Young, "The most that can be said for the general who ordered these continuing frontal assaults despite heavy losses is that he exerted maximum pressure. In other words, maximum offensive strategy." The cost of this strategy was sixty soldiers killed, twenty-five missing and presumed dead, and 308 wounded.

General Zais was quoted after the battle as saying, "I don't consider them [the casualties] high at all." At the time of this writing General Zais is the J-3 Director of Operations on the Joint Staff of the Joint Chiefs of Staff, one of the most important posts in the Pentagon. In 1968, a few months before Major General Zais returned voluntarily to his second command tour in Vietnam to assume command of the 101st Airborne Division, I had an opportunity to hear him state one of his reasons for going back. This happened at a dinner which Major General Yarborough, then Chief of Army Intelligence, hosted for General Corona of the Mexican Army. General Zais and I were the other persons present at this intimate dinner. General Zais had been invited because he and General Corona had been classmates at the U.S. Army Command and General Staff College. I was along to act as interpreter and to write a report for Army Intelligence on the Mexican general's comments. As the evening at the Shoreham Hotel progressed over good food and excellent French wine, the conversation turned to Vietnam. General Zais said, "Well, I'll be going back to Vietnam in a few months." "But you've only been back a little over a year, Mel. Why go back so soon? After all, you just remarried," General Yarborough said, surprised. General Zais's answer was "Johnny Johnson [General Harold K. Johnson, Army Chief of Staff at the time] has offered me command of the 101 [101st Airborne Division], Bill, and you know if I'm ever going to make a third star I need to have command of a division. It's an opportunity I can't pass up. There's nothing I'd rather command than a combat division."

On August 1, 1971, barely three months after Hamburger Hill, Major General Zais saw his "opportunity" realized when he put on the third star of a lieutenant general. This is yet another example of how fine men can delude themselves into thinking that what they do to help themselves also serves the country. I have known General Zais for several years and he is a brave and honorable man. I'm sure he felt that he was doing what was right in attacking Hamburger Hill. The point is that he was doing it in part out of necessity to hold a divisional command to qualify for a third star. "Letters from Hamburger Hill" that appeared in the November 1969 issue of *Harpers Magazine* show vividly the bitter resentment of enlisted men who made the attacks.

But, at best, the motivation of officers who "lead" either wholly or in part to promote their own careers is questionable. The war in Korea had quite a few such officers; Vietnam has had even more. The Army policy of frequently rotating troop commands to give some career officers a better chance for promotion has encouraged too many commanders to think more of their own advancement than of the welfare of their men. In *The New York Times*, October 12, 1970, edition, Ron Perez, a former combat medic awarded a Silver Star for valor in Vietnam is quoted as saying, "They wasted a lot of guys. Killed for no reason. Top officers were always trying to establish reputations and got guys killed." Another soldier is quoted in writer Jim Bishop's newspaper column: "The military leaders of our forces have a personal stake in fighting this war. They get promoted faster, have young, beautiful mistresses, and are treated like Roman emperors. War is their job, their life style."

This mistaken career-incentive policy has encouraged commanders like Colonel (now Brigadier General) George S. Patton, III, son of the famed World War II general, to ruthlessly commit his troops to battle so he could "see the arms and legs fly." In his eagerness to create a battlefield image as a "Blood and Guts" commander worthy of his father's glory, Colonel Patton demanded a high body count of his 11th Armored Cavalry Regiment. As one officer who served in Vietnam under his command told me, "It didn't matter what kind of bodies they were, just so they were gook and lots of 'em." Colonel Patton mailed Christmas cards to his friends in 1967 which featured a picture of a stack of bleeding Vietnamese bodies on one side and on the other the words "Peace on Earth, Colonel and Mrs. George S. Patton, III." Other West Pointers like Lieutenant Colonel (now Brigadier General) Henry "Gunfighter" Emerson, who served repeated tours in Vietnam, built their reputations for rapid promotion by running up a high body count and shooting the fleeing foe from their command helicopters.

This policy of rotating commands and making service in Vietnam mandatory for promotion (and until December 15, 1969, for resignation or retirement of regular officers) was the cause of ill-fated officers like Brigadier General William Bond volunteering for service in Southeast Asia. I knew Bill Bond well. I had worked with him frequently while he was assigned to the International and Civil Affairs Office of the Army General

Staff. I remember the day his name appeared on the recommended list for promotion to brigadier general. I stuck my head in the door to his office and said, "Congratulations. It's good to see a non-ring knocker [a non-West Pointer] get ahead." [4] He looked up with his boyish grin and said, "Thanks, Ed, no one was more surprised than me. I had kind of given up hope."

I next saw Bond in late 1968 when we discussed the Hemisphere Army Commanders' Conference that the U.S. Army was hosting in the United States. We had talked about how he would spend the $200,000 that the Army had allocated to entertain the chiefs of all the Latin American armies and their wives during the week they would be in the United States. Then the conversation turned to the subject most soldiers usually end up discussing—what our next assignments would be. He had said, "Ed, you should go down to Brazil as the Army Attaché when Art Moura comes out." "That would be nice," I had replied, "but I haven't been to Vietnam and I guess you have to go there before you are allowed to do anything else." "Yes," he replied, "I've got to get back over there myself just as soon as I get promoted, or I won't have a chance of ever making a second star."

A little over a year later I was to read in the newspaper that Brigadier General William Bond had been killed by an unknown sniper's bullet while leaving his helicopter to inspect a troop-landing zone that had been reported cleared of all enemy troops two hours before he landed. He is the only Army general officer to date to die from direct small-arms fire during the war (three others have died in helicopter crashes). General Bond was a fine officer and man; he died victim of a system (and possibly of an American bullet fired by a disgruntled GI) which has

---

[4] Another colonel, who had been passed over for promotion on the same list said, "I just can't understand it. Over 80 percent of the nearly three hundred officers considered for that list were non-West Pointers and yet out of the fifty-six officers selected, only Bill Bond and eighteen others were non-West Pointers." I made the downward-knocking motion with the ring finger of my left hand. Among non-Academy officers this symbolizes the "ring knockers" of the WPPA (West Point Protective Association). He smiled faintly and said, "Yeah, I guess there's no fighting them or joining them."

established gung-ho combat-command tours as the only way to attain the "stars" that he was fighting to earn.

Others like Brigadier General (now Major General) Edward De Saussure have attained stars despite failure during their combat-command tour. De Saussure was relieved from command of the 196th Infantry Brigade after its disastrous performance in Tay Ninh in 1967. Because he was a WPPA member, rather than being shipped back to the United States, he was moved to a divisional artillery element, later moved to a staff job in Saigon, and quietly promoted to major general. The victims of his combat leadership had by that time already started moldering in their new graves. Surviving officers who understood the magnitude of the fiasco remained silent either because of fear of career reprisal or self-implication.

Almost half of the Army generals who served in Vietnam during 1969 came home with medals for bravery in combat. Only about one in ten of the GI's who do most of the actual fighting received similar awards. *The New York Times,* October 20, 1970, indicates that fifty-seven Army generals returned from service in Vietnam during 1969. Of this number, twenty-six, or nearly half, received the Silver Star, Distinguished Flying Cross, or Bronze Star for valor. After the Medal of Honor and Distinguished Service Cross these are the highest awards for valor in combat that the Army can confer. The *Times* article also stated that 345,000 soldiers of all enlisted ranks had returned from Vietnam during 1969. Of this number, 30,002, or less than one-tenth, received Silver Stars, Distinguished Flying Crosses, or Bronze Stars for combat valor. Of the fifty-seven generals who returned, fifty received Distinguished Service Medals for their tours in Vietnam. This award is known among career officers as the "generals' good conduct ribbon." It is handed out almost automatically each time a general leaves a high-level assignment.

One of my duties in the Joint Chiefs of Staff was to write up a citation and recommendation for award for each general or flag officer who was reassigned from duty with the United States Delegation to the Inter-American Defense Board. I had a master citation which I had drawn up. Each time a general or admiral received orders to leave the delegation, I would get the master copy out of the file cabinet and fill in the dates he had been assigned and his name and rank in the blank spaces and give it to the secretary to be typed in sufficient copies. These then went to an "awards board" in the JCS where they were always approved, and in a few weeks the medal engraved with the general's name would come back accompanied by a copy of the same master citation that I had dreamed up. Reading these same citations at the six award ceremonies I conducted always embarrassed me, but it never seemed to bother the generals or admirals who had heard it before and would hear it on their award when they left. So I kept using the same citation for the three years I was in the job. And I imagine it is still in use today.

Another example of the almost automatic award of decorations to senior Army officers is the award of the Silver Star and Distinguished Flying Cross to Brigadier General Eugene P. Forrester (West Point, 1948) on October 15, 1970, in Vietnam. After the general had accepted the two awards (later rescinded after they were publicized by the news media), six enlisted men said the "facts" on which the awards were based were ones they had invented in response to orders. The chief of staff of the division (my old acquaintance Colonel George Newman), who ordered the enlisted men to prepare the false citations, said that he "directed the preparation of the citation and award of the combat decorations because it was a routine customary farewell gesture to generals being transferred from the division." To substantiate the bogus citation, "eyewitness" certificates were signed by the general's aide and by his helicopter copilot. If these two junior officers had not signed these false certificates they would have left themselves open to the wrath of the division chief of staff (not to mention the general) for failing to "play the game." This would have undoubtedly resulted in their being relieved from their rather choice assignments and given a lowered efficiency-report rating that would have damaged their future careers. Here we have a clear indication of how the self-interest of senior Army leaders can corrupt junior members of the Army. This "playing the game" has helped undermine Army integrity and left it ripe for the cover-up, murder, and torture that has occurred in Vietnam.

Generals are not the only recipients of unearned combat medals. Many infantry battalion commanders—usually lieutenant colonels—have pocketed their Silver Star, Bronze Star, and Air Medals received as part of what the GI's call the "battalion commanders package" when they departed for a staff job in Saigon (where they also get either an Army Commendation Medal or the Joint Services Commendation Medal) after performing their six months command tour. As I have said, all soldiers like medals but they are particularly cherished by generals and future generals from West Point. These combat decorations (along with a West Point diploma) are the mandatory tickets one must have to achieve high rank in the U.S. Army.[5] Of course all senior officers cannot perform the valorous acts in combat (particularly circling in a helicopter 2,000 feet above the reality of what is happening in combat on the ground) that a combat GI performs and accepts as routine daily fare while under fire.[6] So the military establishment has made the award of combat decorations a little less difficult for senior officers to achieve. The anxiety to "get the right promotion tickets punched" has caused many junior officers to try and meet the misplaced standards of commanders like Julian J. Ewell (nicknamed the "Butcher of the Delta" when he commanded the 9th Division) who made the body count the criteria of successful command ability. In all fairness it must be remembered that such commanders were only operating by the

---

[5] In Vietnam each major Army unit has had teams of "award specialists" to rhetorically embellish routine combat actions to justify the award of combat medals to officers and noncommissioned officers. The result of this competition has been that units with the most ambitious commanders and best writers have awarded undeservedly large numbers of combat medals. This has produced a "you write me up for a medal and I'll write you up" philosophy.

[6] It has been this helicopter-borne insulation and isolation from the reality of the ground combat, combined with an attitude of conditioned unconcern, that has allowed so many senior Army officers to be misled about what was happening in Vietnam.

body-count ground rules that had been established by General
Westmoreland as the mark of an effective commander. They
were good organization men; if the system demanded a high
body count as the way to professional success, these officers
produced such a body count.

But one of the tragic results of the erroneous importance attached to the computerized kill-ratio graphs meticulously
maintained in MACV headquarters were cases like that of
twenty-two-year-old First Lieutenant James B. Duffy, a platoon leader in the 9th Division. Lieutenant Duffy was found
guilty of first-degree murder of a prisoner. The court-martial
changed its verdict and found him guilty of involuntary man-
slaughter after he claimed he was following orders not to take
prisoners in order to keep the body count high. Lieutenant
John Krueger, another platoon leader in the same company as
Lieutenant Duffy, testified that in the unit it was accepted
practice not to take prisoners. He also testified that "unless a
monthly quota of twenty-five kills was reached, platoons might
not get essential parts for radios and armored-personnel carriers, and might be kept in the field for longer than normal periods." When asked if rumors that other prisoners of war had
been executed in the 9th Division were true, he answered, "Individuals around here are pretty reliable. Can you tell me, for
example, how a VC major can fall a thousand feet from a helicopter when he has been tied by his hands and feet and
strapped in?" Asked if he had received any instruction regarding prisoners of war since arriving in Vietnam, Lieutenant
Krueger said, "Somebody asked about this at a briefing when I
got in the country—the reply was a laugh!"

It was no laughing matter to the many Vietnamese who were
indiscriminately killed in order to run up unit body counts. It
should not have been a laughing matter to the U.S. Army. This
mistaken emphasis on killing as one of the criteria for "professional" advancement has done much to destroy the moral fiber
of the Army.

Many Army leaders are now claiming they were aware of
grave problems and failures of the civilian leaders from the earliest days of the Vietnam War. Yet all of these Army leaders

formerly publicly supported the war. Men like General Harold K. Johnson may have been privately troubled by what was happening to the Army, but they supported the civilian defense leadership.

If Army leaders were aware that things were not going right in the war and were concerned about what was being done to the Army, why didn't they speak out and voice their concerns *before* so many soldiers died? Lower-ranking officers are alibiing their failure to question policies and tactics that were inimical to the best interests of the country and the Army by claiming they didn't have "sufficient information" to make a judgment. Most officers rationalize their acquiescence in the corruption and destruction of the Army by saying, "But I'm only the construction worker. I must build what the political architect tells me to build. So how can I be blamed if the job turns out badly?" They seem unable to realize that if a construction worker finds that the architect has placed the cornerstone in such a way that the building will fall down in a year or two, the construction worker owes it to the public to bring this to the architect's attention at once and in forcible terms until the stone is placed right.

Too many officers equate their jobs with that of a corporate executive in General Motors or IBM. To them the welfare of the corporation (Army) is success in terms of gaining new weapons and accomplishing Army objectives. They substitute this for corporate profit-making. They forget that the Army is not a profit-making organization. The corporate product of the Army is not profit but "victory" produced through death. The officer corps has been satisfied to hide behind duty and the old adage of "Mine not to reason why, mine but to do or die" as a rationale for lack of concern for what was happening to the men of the Army in Vietnam. In return for more rapid promotions, increased high-command slots, larger forces, more weapons systems, and other benefits of wartime activity, the officer corps closed its conscience to any question of what it was doing in the name of freedom. It accepted the mind of the institution and ignored its own responsibilities to the American people and the men of the Army. By so doing it broke the long-standing public trust in the integrity of the officer corps. This trust will be difficult to restore.

Officers must again face their responsibility to truthfully inform their fellow Americans on all military matters and to adhere to their principles without regard for what that will do to their careers. They will not do this so long as they are required to serve an organizational system which stresses personal achievement and careerism as the objectives of service. The way to instill honesty and morality in the officer corps is to stop rewarding those who ignore such virtues. An Army which punishes criticism of policies that serve the Army over the nation cannot be the framework for beneficial or honest service.

Injustice

One of the more famous of the antiwar Army court-martial cases occurred in the Sixth Army headquarters at the Presidio of San Francisco. Robert Sherrill has vividly described the trial in his book *Military Justice Is to Justice What Military Music Is to Music.* In 1968 General "Wolf" Larsen allowed charges of mutiny to be brought against twenty-seven dumbshits who were being held in the Presidio stockade on a variety of minor charges. The dumbshits had protested what they claimed was maltreatment by guards (a GI guard had shot and killed a prisoner a few days before the demonstration), overcrowding (which an Army investigating team confirmed after the trial), unsanitary conditions (also confirmed after the trial), and poor food. An Army court-martial found twenty-three of the soldiers guilty and convicted them of nonviolent mutiny. Defense lawyer Paul Halvonik called the entire legal episode "a classic example of Army overkill." This was the same opinion that several Sixth Army staff officers had harbored regarding the original charge of mutiny. Their objections had been overruled when Army investigators came up with a supposed link between the young prisoners and peace groups who were smuggling in guidance and encouragement from the "outside." In accordance with Army practice and the spirit engendered by the mistaken trial of Captain Howard Levy, General Larsen decided that these twenty-seven young soldiers from poor backgrounds and with low IQ's should be made examples of Army discipline.

This was what the Army had been doing for years to maladjusted soldiers. So there was no motivation for General Larsen to consider any other course. It was also an opportunity to strike a blow at the peaceniks who had expressed sympathy for the lot of the prisoners.

The subsequent reversal by a higher court of review of most of the mutiny convictions is indicative not only of the Army's "legal overkill," but the lack of sound command judgment that permitted such inflated charges to be made in the first place. At the Presidio, court-martial was used in lieu of concerned leadership. An attempt was made to enforce conformity by confinement and trial, rather than gaining compliance through enlightened leadership.

Conformity by confinement has also been used in the Army's "correctional custody facilities." On November 11, 1970, eight soldiers (four of whom had served in Vietnam) at Fort Benning, Georgia, filed a lawsuit against their commanding officer alleging that they had been confined in "a correctional custody facility where cruel and unusual punishment is inflicted." According to the soldiers the facility amounted to a maximum-security prison in which they were forced to perform at least sixteen hours of hard labor daily. They also charged "protracted incommunicado detention, unusual verbal abuse, inadequate and unsanitary toilet facilities and in some cases beatings with rubber hoses."

These soldiers were in the custody facility for minor infractions of discipline that did not merit a trial by court-martial. Some were confined for offenses such as missing bed check or a formation. Such infractions fall under the provisions of the nonjudicatory punishment of Article 15 of the Uniform Code of Military Justice. This punishment is not intended to take the form of confinement in a specially constructed detention facility. If any form of confinement is involved, it is usually carried out in the soldiers' barracks. But the Army does operate Article 15 correctional facilities—or "eight-ball" units—at posts like

Fort Dix and Fort Hood, where they are called Special Processing Battalions. These are the places where the Army stashes away its frustrated black or Puerto Rican soldiers, low-IQ white soldiers, and other misfits and mental walking-wounded cases that never should have been in the Army to begin with. The Army position is that it is limited in what it can do to make these young men satisfactory soldiers and better citizens. Frequently educational readjustment programs are started with much ballyhoo, but they inevitably disappear or become ineffective. Either the Army must establish effective, long-term programs to help its dumbshits adjust to Army life, or the Army should not be forced to accept them for military service.

What should not be continued is the current practice of attempting to use force to solve social-adjustment problems of soldiers who often do not understand varying Army standards. These soldiers should not be harassed to the point of committing some major infraction for which they can then be court-martialed and gotten rid of. The fact that for years this *has* been the Army response to the needs of many of its soldiers is a striking testimonial to the lack of leadership and vindictive sadism that has existed in the modern Army.

The Army hierarchy is consumed with the idea of punishment. The desire to punish is so strongly ingrained in Army philosophy that its offshoots are often ridiculous—and tragic. For example, when I served as commander of a company at Fort Carson, Colorado, one of the sergeants received a traffic ticket from the Colorado Highway Patrol. He had exceeded the posted speed limit along a stretch of highway between Fort Carson and Pueblo, Colorado, that is heavily patrolled on weekends to catch unwary GI drivers. The sergeant had paid his fine and dismissed the matter from his mind. Because he was a member of the Army a copy of his traffic ticket was forwarded to the Fort Carson provost marshal. The provost marshal in turn filed a DR on the sergeant and sent it through channels. It eventually came to me with directions to investigate the matter and take "appropriate disciplinary action." Additionally, the sergeant was ordered to appear before the provost marshal, and I accompanied him. His driving permit on post was withdrawn and he was ordered to attend after-duty instruction in safe driving. All of this was ordered *before* any form of investigation had been conducted.

He was quite upset about losing his on-post driver's permit, because it meant that he had to hitchhike eighteen miles to work from his home in North Colorado Springs. Since he was due at work at 6:30 A.M. it was practically impossible for him to arrive on time. His only solution was to move into barracks and live on post during the time his driver's permit was suspended. This left his family stranded because his wife did not drive. I explained these facts to the provost marshal and pointed out that the man had already paid a fine to the state of Colorado for the offense for which he was now being punished. The provost marshal tongue-lashed both the sergeant and me and absolutely refused to reinstate the sergeant's post driving "privilege." I appealed his decision to the regimental commander, who thought that a noncommissioned officer who brought a DR on the regimental record should be "busted one grade to teach him a lesson." I refused to reduce the sergeant and he was transferred to another company where he was later reduced one grade "without prejudice." Because of the sudden reduction in his salary the poor man was unable to pay his debts. This resulted in a letter of indebtedness from a local loan company. This letter was passed through the same channels as the DR and the ex-sergeant was marked as a troublemaker. He was punished for "failure to pay his just debts." The next step was to get rid of him, so he was placed on a levy of NCO's being sent to Korea. This removed a troublemaker from the regiment, but for the ex-sergeant it meant another year away from his family. It also meant that on a corporal's salary he couldn't maintain a home for his family, support himself in Korea, and pay the bills he had incurred as a sergeant. More letters of indebtedness pursued him to Korea and a year later he was eliminated from the Army as an undesirable.

Caste System

There is a pattern of group conformity that has become the expected life style of NCO's and officers. The NCO usually tends to come from a rural background with little formal education (high school or less). He often has a folksy vocabulary and is expected to be reasonably willing and respectful to senior officers. He may be permitted the latitude of being a little smart-alecky with junior officers. Among the NCO's he is expected to be "one of the boys." Neither he nor his family will be tolerated if they put on airs or try to appear superior to other NCO's and their families. It's quite acceptable to live well and drive a new car—most NCO's "moonlight" to augment their salaries. Probably most important for the senior NCO among his peer group is that he be a staunch right-wing conservative and conform to the policies and standards of the Army. Private criticism of officers and complaining about policies and decisions that he doesn't agree with is okay, but the NCO is expected to enforce unquestioning compliance on the other enlisted men.

A tradition has been established in the NCO corps that only southern white NCO's rise to the super-grade NCO ranks. Officer boards considering NCO promotions have been psychologically influenced by this tradition, as well as by the inferior-status syndrome which nearly all officers apply to soldiers from minority, racial, or ethnic groups. Catholic and Jewish white soldiers have felt the sting of discrimination as a result of these superiority attitudes but not to the extent that minority racial groups have. Black, Puerto Rican, or Mexican-American soldiers must perform twice as well as a white soldier if they are to be recognized and promoted to NCO rank.

I recall sitting on a promotion board in Europe in 1961 which was considering NCO's for promotion to master sergeant (pay grade E-8). Out of the five NCO's interviewed, the most qualified was a Puerto Rican sergeant with twenty-three years' service including World War II service as an officer. The promotion went to a white sergeant from the South who had less experience, less service, and less education. While we were discussing the selection, one of the board members, a quartermaster major, agreed the Puerto Rican sergeant was well qualified. But he said, "He's Puerto Rican and he won't command the respect of his men. I've seen lots of good Puerto Rican sergeants but they are not E-8 material." A signal corps major agreed, saying, "They are just lazy by nature. You know, do it tomorrow. They just can't measure up to be master sergeants. Sergeants first class, yes, but master sergeants, no." I had argued that the job we were considering the men for was administrative and education was important. But the quartermaster major said, "Education has nothing to do with it. What matters is getting men to cooperate and work together and the Puerto Rican sergeant won't be able to cut it." "How do you know?" I asked. "Because that's the way they are," he replied.

In the eyes of the career NCO the lower-ranking enlisted men fall into two categories: the draftees and the regular Army enlistees. The draftee is a "civilian" to be tolerated and used. The enlistee is expected to try harder, and if he does he is given some advantages over the draftee. If the enlistee shows promise of wanting to make the Army a career he will be helped. For example, I remember Sergeant Johnson, the platoon sergeant of the first regular Army company I served in, telling me, "Kid, you might make NCO someday. I'm gonna teach you a few things about being one." He ordered me to meet him at the leveled strip we used for a parade ground on a barren hillside in Kaesong, Korea. As we stood there one evening after duty hours he said, "You see that big tree down there, I'm gonna go sit under it. I want you to give me commands and I want to see the leaves on that damn tree rustle every time you sound off." We did this over and over and he would say, "Sound off like you had a pair. I can't hear a fucking thing you are saying," even though I would be shouting my lungs out. In later years I never had any problem giving commands to battalion-sized units—he taught me well. When I would ask him why he had served for so many years in the Army he would answer, "It beats hoeing cotton in that gawd-damn Georgia sun." He was a tough "old Army" man who drank a can of beer every morning as soon as he arose from his bunk. This was followed by a glass of medicinal alcohol that he and the cook got by the bottle from the company medic and strained through a loaf of white bread before they poured it out to drink. Shortly after I had been promoted to staff sergeant I asked Sergeant Johnson what

I should do about an older draftee who had told me, "I'm not taking no orders from no goddamn eighteen-year-old sergeant." His answer was, "You catch that sonuvabitch when he least expects you and you cold-cock the bastard with whatever you can get your hands on." Most of these old Army NCO's have finished their service, but the stories of their methods and traditions still survive in the NCO corps.

The NCO looks fondly back on the days of Sergeant Johnson when force reigned supreme. Those methods do not work today but the NCO has been provided no alternative techniques. He has been left in limbo by the policies of Army leaders. The NCO has had to abrogate much of his disciplinary function to the commissioned officer who holds the court-martial power, which is really about the only enforcing power that the Army has left itself.

The problems of a conforming life style are not unique to the NCO corps. The officer faces the same problems. He too has traditionally come from a rural area or small town and has a white conservative background. The pattern of success for the Army officer has been even more stereotyped than that of the NCO. The successful Army organization man will have graduated from West Point and developed a close circle of friends among his classmates. Over the years he must also gradually develop an appreciation for good living and passable social graces. The key to his rise to success is how well he is able to get along with the various rating officers who write his efficiency reports over the years.

It is in this endeavor that the officer's wife plays an important role. He must be pleasant and agreeable to almost every whim of his rater. His wife must be equally pleasant to the wife of his rater if he is not to risk incurring some unknown displeasure. There is an Army saying that "a wife can't necessarily make you, but she can sure as hell break you." A young officer's wife must play the role of being sweet and properly respectful to older ladies. It helps if she is attractive, but she must be careful not to appear to flirt with senior officers because this is a sure way to incur the wrath of their wives. The majority of officers' wives also come from middle-class small-town or rural backgrounds. They are usually as conservative as their husbands in dress and outlook. They, like the officers, are expected to conform to the Army system and be good Army wives.

There is no question but that the Army families suffer from the same strains that afflict the rest of American society. The adjustments to frequent prolonged separations, ruthless competition, and keeping up with the Joneses take their toll of Army families. It is difficult to say how many are affected by the pressures for promotion and career success, but my guess would be that the number is greater than anyone suspects. You can catch a glimpse of these problems on Friday or Saturday night at any officers' club. The Friday night "happy hour" is a case study of the stresses that the Army system imposes on its members. A particularly good example is Fort Leavenworth, Kansas, where the supposedly brightest officers come to study. Almost every officer on the faculty or in the student body fancies himself as a potential general. On Saturday night at the officers' club one-up gamesmanship is played to a smiling science. From a vantage seat at the end of the basement bar it is possible to see a kaleidoscope of human emotion and motivations. There are the bright young majors and their wives "on the way up" and the older colonels and their still-hopeful wives wondering where things went wrong—why he failed in his quest for a star. Too frequently he is trying to drown his feelings of remorse and inadequacy in a martini glass and she attempts to project false gaiety while also downing drink after drink. Many of those who are drinking away their frustrations on Saturday night at the club are present at the chapel on Sunday morning to hear the chaplain confirm the sanctity of what they do in freedom's name.

Elitist Control

The Army's top managers are as discriminatory toward the officer corps as toward the enlisted men. But they must be a good deal more circumspect in controlling the officers. Favoritism excludes all but a small preordained group of officers from entry into the controlling levels of the Army high command.

This favoritism must be exercised in such a way that the majority of the officer corps will accept it and yet still work their hearts out to serve the purposes of the high command. This has been accomplished by indoctrinating all members of the officer corps from the time of their commissioning to accept the myth of superiority of an elitist group from West Point. This conditioning has been combined with a program of career incentives that keep all officers busy struggling to achieve various competitive levels of success. Few stop to realize that the program favors the elitist group that controls the Army. At each level the West Point managers weed out increasing numbers of those officers who are no longer useful. Only the most cooperative and best indoctrinated non-West Pointers are permitted to progress to the general officer ranks. Few of them are allowed to go beyond the grade of major general.

Ward Just in his book *Military Men* says, "There is no doubt that a sort of West Point Protective Association exists in the Army." The WPPA does exist and it is constantly at work to protect and promote classmates from West Point at the expense of the rest of the officer corps. Defense Secretary Melvin Laird has stated the goals of service life:

1. Attract people with ability, dedication, and capacity for growth.

2. Provide opportunity for all service people to rise to as high a level of responsibility as his talent and diligence will take him.

3. Make military and civilian service a model of equal opportunity for all regardless of race, creed, or national origin.

During 1969, when the secretary was stating his goals, the Army Command Information Fact Sheet of March 28 stated, "Of 520 U.S. Army generals on active duty as of 1 February, 1969, 154 are graduates of ROTC. This includes three lieutenant generals: William B. Rosson, Fred C. Weyand and William R. Peers." A check of the official Army Register for that year shows that the remaining 366 general officers on active duty were graduates of West Point. Graduates of the military academy comprised less than 4 percent of the total active duty officer corps. Yet they were able to furnish 366 of the 520 general officers on duty. And of the sixteen four-star generals included among the 520 total only two were not West Pointers and neither of these two was serving in high-command policy-making assignments.[7] The Army's officer corps has long been a closed shop in which the graduate of West Point regularly gets his "ticket punched" by other old-boy alumni, as he moves along with his classmates into the top jobs of the Army. It is unrealistic to expect that officers who owe their careers to such a system of favoritism and discrimination are going to understand or reform the racism and discrimination applied to the rank and file.

The civilian leaders of the Army cannot continue to condone the practice which permits a small minority clique of West Point classmates to dominate the top command levels of the Army. Only active civilian surveillance and intervention can change this deeply entrenched favoritism. Just as the black or Puerto Rican soldier senses a difference in what he can hope to achieve in the Army so does the non-West Point officer. Army rhetoric loudly proclaims equal opportunity for all and implies strict adherence to Secretary Laird's goals. But twenty years of service life teaches that there is little substance to the rhetoric. A non-West Point officer's daily life is replete with constant reminders of his inferior status. For example, when I reported to Camp Stoneman, California, after volunteering for active duty in July 1950, I had never received any training as an officer, having been commissioned directly from enlisted status. The 1950 West Point June graduating class had been sent from their four years of Academy military training to attend basic courses in their branch of service before being sent to Korea. When I asked a major commanding the overseas replacement battalion if I shouldn't receive some training as an officer before going to lead troops in combat in Korea, he told me that since I had been a platoon sergeant in 1947 I wouldn't have any trouble "picking up what was going on in Korea."

---

[7] General Weyand was serving as General Abrams's deputy and General Rosson was serving as deputy Army commander in the U.S. Army Pacific. In the past sixty-nine years only two non-West Pointers, General George C. Marshall (1939–45) and General George H. Decker (1961–63) have served as Army Chief of Staff.

When I persisted by saying that after being out of the Army for over two years, I didn't really feel prepared to assume the responsibility for the lives of a platoon of soldiers, he promised to look into the matter. I then walked back to the replacement-company orderly room, where a young clerk told me, "Man, you've really got the major upset. He called and said to get you on orders and out of here. You'll be flying out tonight as a special courier." I was to learn to be an officer by on-the-job training. But despite their training the West Point class of 1950 did not fare well in Korea. Some were like Lieutenant Joe Trent, who admonished his platoon to fire at anything that moved and was shot by one of his men while he was checking positions in darkness. Another lined up his platoon and attempted to assault a hill defended by a machine gun. Over twenty men were mowed down in the first minutes of the attack. He survived to go on to Vietnam and become a colonel, leading more soldiers into combat from a helicopter.

Assignment after graduation from the Infantry Officer Advanced Course was another example of the favoritism shown to officers from West Point. Prior to graduation the chief of the Infantry Branch traditionally visits Fort Benning and announces the assignments of officers in the advanced class. The chief first told us how much time and effort had gone into selecting our next assignments. We had waited anxiously as the assignments were read. Those whose names began with the letters A through F were assigned mostly to troop units; G through M were assigned to Reserve or National Guard duty, and so went our carefully thought-out assignments. The exceptions were the West Point graduates in the class. Nearly all were assigned to graduate studies at civilian colleges, or to instructor duties at Fort Benning. None were ordered to the less desirable Reserve or National Guard adviser assignments, or to training centers like Fort Polk, Louisiana—those dead-end career assignments were all given to non-West Point officers. Non-West Pointers who applied for graduate schooling (which most of the West Pointers selected to attend had not done) were told to wait till the next year.

By the time a non-West Pointer reaches major he has begun

to prepare himself unconsciously to accept the fact that he will probably be fortunate to make colonel. While the West Point officer almost automatically gets his ticket punched with good assignments, the rest of the officer corps must scurry around desperately trying to avoid the dead-end jobs that so often fall to their lot. This growing feeling of inferiority and resignation to a limited-career opportunity is exactly the result that the system is designed to produce in the mind of the non-West Point officer. Events like the Founder's Day Dinner serve to reinforce the non-West Point officer's feeling of being isolated. Each year on Army posts about the world, West Point alumni new and old gather to relive the memories of their days at the institution on the Hudson (referred to by non-West Pointers as South Hudson Institute of Technology or SHIT). An alumni meeting of officers from a civilian college, such as the University of California, would not have the use of Army aircraft, buses, and sedans that are provided to transport "old grads" to the annual Founder's Day celebration. They would be lucky if they could obtain permission to use the officers' club, since some of their alumni woula be enlisted men.

The result of this covert, yet effective, discrimination by an elitist few against the majority of the Army officer corps has made possible the continuation of the shortsighted leadership that has characterized the Army high command over the past fifteen years. The 1969 edition of the Army Register gives a clear indication of the extent of the West Point stranglehold on the top command of the Army. Of twenty-four principal Army commanders and staff officers (including the Army Chief of Staff) twenty-two were graduates of West Point. The Chief of Staff was from the class of 1933; thirteen of the other principal Army leaders were either from his class or at the academy during the time he was in attendance there. These classmates learned on the plains above the Hudson not to ask questions and to stick together. Captain Robert Johnson, a Vietnam veteran and 1965 graduate of West Point, has said, "We were taught to cover up everything that reflects unfavorably on the Army and particularly West Point." Lieutenant Louis Font, a 1968 honor graduate, says, "The code we were taught was first

Duty, Honor, West Point; then Duty, Honor, Army; and then
Duty, Honor, Country third. I didn't learn to think at the
Academy. I was always asked to know the contents of an essay
and never asked what I thought about it."[8]

Having been trained as cadets to cover up or not face unpleasant facts, it should come as no surprise that these same
men should continue the practice throughout their Army careers.[9] West Point classmates protect and help each other as
they climb up through the Army hierarchy. And it is because of
dominant WPPA mentality that cover-ups like MyLai can
occur. Top Army managers have over the past fifteen or so
years become increasingly inclined to avoid responsibility for
any failure. They have been trained that to admit failure in
anything is tantamount to acknowledging that they cannot be a
"success" in their career. There has been no freedom to make
an error or fail in the modern Army. Since these men have been
human they have made errors and have been guilty of numerous failures. But they have not had to face their mistakes because the system has permitted them to blame their failures on
subordinates. Between the wars in Korea and Vietnam it was
easy to cover up mistakes. The nation had little interest in what
went on in the Army and the technocrats could easily cover up
such glaring errors in judgment as the Pentomic concept. But

---

[8] From cadet days conformity and unquestioning compliance with all existing rules is constantly demanded. When cadet David H. Vaught questioned the
requirement for compulsory chapel attendance, he was threatened with a
court-martial. His room and personal possessions were repeatedly searched and
he was made to march with a rifle for over eighty hours during the three weeks
before he graduated from the Military Academy. Major General Samuel Koster, then the West Point superintendent, called upon the 1969 graduating class
to look at those who were "troublemakers" in the class and see what happened
to them in the Army. In Lieutenant Vaught's case this meant continued harassment after graduation. He was denied an office on the Junior Officers Council
of Fort Bragg, North Carolina, after being duly elected. His promotion to first
lieutenant was delayed and he finally resigned from the Army in disgust in
1971.

[9] For example, after *Army Times Family Magazine* published an article I
wrote that was critical of Army leadership, Major General William A. Knowl-
ton, the superintendent of West Point, wrote the editor and canceled his sub-
scription to the newspaper because it had published the article.

when covered-up mistakes, examples of poor judgment, and attempts to mislead the public began to accumulate in Vietnam the press and the public started asking serious questions. The initial rosy estimates of victory being "just around the corner" and "light at the end of the tunnel" started to haunt the West Pointers who had made them. Men like Westmoreland, who had made their whole careers on such imagery and well-intentioned subterfuge, could not break the habits of a lifetime.

Their response to the Green Beret murder cases was predictable—they covered them up. MyLai should have been the turning point in this policy of deliberate subterfuge, but it was not. The desire for competitive career "success" is so deeply ingrained in the minds of the entire Army officer corps that they will go along with almost any policy the top West Point managers say is necessary to achieve success. And if what he does turns out to be wrong the officer will answer, "But 'they' told me to do it," while the West Point managers will cover up and deny responsibility. What happened at MyLai did not constitute for the "professional" officer or noncommissioned officer the same sort of tragedy that it represented to the American public. It must be remembered that most of the career officers and NCO's were not serving in Vietnam only because of patriotic motives. All were certainly motivated by patriotic feelings of keeping America secure from Communism, but in many cases the desire to further their careers was equally strong. The overt appeal of Army propaganda from the earliest days of the war was the theme of gaining career benefits by serving in Vietnam. Official Army publications like the Command Information Fact Sheet enjoined all commanders to make sure their NCO's were "fully aware" of the extra pay, more rapid promotions, tax exemptions, and increased savings deposits that were available to those who "volunteered" for service in Vietnam. It also directed commanders to inform their NCO's and enlisted soldiers of the liberal leave policies in effect for those who served second or third tours in Southeast Asia.

It was this policy that caused many poor young soldiers like Private First Class John Robinson of New York City to die while trying to gain increased career incentives. His young widow explained his feelings in an Associated Press interview of July 9, 1970. "His decision to extend his tour of Army duty and volunteer for a second trip to Vietnam wasn't because he believed what this country was doing there was right. Rather, he sought a chance for extra pay and higher rank." It should not have come as a surprise to the American public that career soldiers serving in Vietnam principally either to earn a better living for their families, or to qualify for another promotion, could callously disregard the lives of both their fellow GI's and "gooks," both of whom represented a means to an end. Such are the ways of soldiers who are misled into fighting for mercenary material goals.

MyLai represented to the average professional soldier nothing more than being caught in a cover-up of something which he knew had been going on for a long time on a smaller scale. The tried-and-true Army way of producing a scapegoat is to form an investigating group to look into the matter. This method not only permits a scapegoat to eventually be produced; it also allows for time to pass and the matter to be lost to public interest. Until the Calley case, it had never failed to work and it may succeed even in Lieutenant Calley's case if it turns out he is the only officer judged guilty of what happened at MyLai.

It is important the right man be appointed to head such an investigative group. It was not accidental that Lieutenant General Ray Peers was selected to head the MyLai investigation. He had many qualities to recommend him to the top West Point managers. First he was a graduate of the University of California, Los Angeles, who had been commissioned under the Thomason Act of the Seventy-fourth Congress. It was obvious that the investigation was a career hot potato that would finish whoever headed it. If he found a scapegoat he would be a traitor to the Army and if he reported a whitewash he would fall victim to the press and the Congress. No high-ranking West Pointer wanted to lay his career on the line for such a cause, and no member of the WPPA was going to force one of their own to do so. And Ray Peers was at that time one of three non-West Pointers who held the rank of lieutenant general and thereby presented a possible threat as a future Chief of Staff. After General George Decker, the WPPA was determined never to permit another nongraduate to become Chief of Staff. Here was an opportunity not only to keep a West Point club member from having to sacrifice his career ambitions, but also to eliminate a possible (though unlikely) contender for Chief of Staff. And General Peers had other qualities to recommend him for the hot potato. He was a tough and determined man, he had an outstanding combat record, and a reputation in the Army for being straightforward and speaking his mind. Junior officers liked him because he was inclined to listen to what they had to say and treat them with consideration. He was not one of the godlike officers that have come to be the standard among Army general officers. Ray Peers is a loyal man and he is Army through and through. There was the assurance that he would look out for the Army's interest as best he could.

Stung by Presidential, congressional, and public criticism, the Secretary of the Army ordered a thorough investigation. He could have hardly expected what he received. The West Pointers had not suspected that one of their own who was Commandant of the Academy and being groomed for future high position, possibly Chief of Staff, would be involved.[10] The President's insistence that senior officers not be spared made it impossible for the Army to charge only enlisted men and low-ranking reserve officers. And although General Peers had been accepted by the WPPA as reliable and "one of the boys" (otherwise he would not have become a lieutenant general), he was, unlike the well-indoctrinated West Pointers, the product

[10] There is some reason to believe that General Westmoreland may have learned of Major General Koster's problem over MyLai since it has been reported that he visited Ducpho, Vietnam, on April 20, 1968. Ducpho was the headquarters of the 11th Brigade, which conducted the MyLai attack. Also it is unlikely that Koster would not have informed fellow West Pointer Westmoreland about an incident which had such far-reaching implications for Westmoreland. It is not in the WPPA tradition for classmates to leave another in ignorance so he can't protect himself. They do not leave each other out on a limb.

of a liberal college education. He had been trained to think for himself, so he could name Major General Koster as derelict in his performance of duty at MyLai.

With the report of the Peers Commission the Army system took over. There was first the Article 32 investigation, which as every officer knows usually results in whatever findings and recommendations the commander desires. The top Army commanders did not want to see fellow-graduate Koster brought to trial. And General Mark Clark at The Citadel was not likely to sit back and let Citadel graduate Brigadier General Young be tried as the scapegoat. To court-martial a few sergeants and non-West Point officers like Calley, Medina, and Henderson was one thing, but to try a West Point general was an entirely different matter. The WPPA was not about to stand still and permit that to happen, even if it meant letting all the other officers escape trial. As I had predicted to writer Seymour Hersh in May 1970, the Army did not bring any of the general officers to trial. Koster was administratively censured and reduced one grade to brigadier general, and both he and Brigadier General Young were relieved of their Distinguished Service Medals. This, in the words of Congressman Samuel S. Stratton, constituted no more than a "slap on the wrist" and he demanded a trial by courts-martial to determine whether they had deliberately covered up the happenings at MyLai in an attempt to keep the Army from looking bad. If this were true, said Stratton, it was not an "administrative shortcoming" as the Army alleged but a crime. Stratton said, "The decision to drop the charges against Koster represented a victory for the WPPA, a mythical association within the Army, which puts the welfare of West Point classmates over the welfare of the nation and the fundamental right of the American people to know the facts: never mind what happens to the Army or the country, just make sure we keep our paid-up members out of embarrassment and hot water."

In dismissing a trial for Koster, the Army stated, "In determining that a trial by courts-martial would not be appropriate for these offenses, General Seaman [West Point, 1934, who had commanded the 1st Division in Vietnam in 1967 and had his

generalship called 'poor' by Radio Hanoi] considered the long
and honorable career of General Koster [twenty-eight years
service], the fact that the offenses did not involve, and the evidence did not show, any intentional abrogation of responsibilities on the part of General Koster." Congressman Stratton
charged, "Eight of the twenty-five formal findings and conclu-
sions of the subcommittee [of the House Armed Services Com-
mittee] go directly to the culpability of General Koster." But as
usual the Army managers were to have their way. At the time
of this writing the trials of Captain Medina, the reserve officer
who commanded the company at MyLai, and Colonel Henderson, the regular officer who rose from the ranks, earning a
bachelor and master's degree through off-duty study, were just
starting.

Even the offering up of scapegoats and covering up of mismanagement is not going to keep the Army from having eventually to face the question of its internal responsibilities as established by the Nuremberg and Tokyo war-crimes trials. For
years the elitist leaders have avoided facing the implications of
these post-World War II trials. Vietnam and MyLai have made
further evasions impossible. The Army system is going to have
to be reconciled with the principles of command responsibility
established by these trials. Telford Taylor in his book *Nuremberg and Vietnam: An American Tragedy* has covered in excellent detail a question I raised in the May 30, 1970, issue of *New
Republic*. That is whether or not American military leaders are
responsible for the atrocities committed by troops under their
command even when they are not aware of these atrocities. As
Taylor points out, the United States Supreme Court decision of
1946 which justified the hanging of Japanese General To-
mayuki Yamashita would seem to indicate our own officers' culpability.[11] Under this decision General Yamashita was hung be-

---

[11] Mr. Justice Murphy in a penetrating and prophetic dissent from the 1946
Supreme Court decision wrote, "In the sober afterglow will come the realization of the boundless and dangerous implications of the procedure sanctioned
today. . . . No one in a position of command in an army, from sergeant to general, can escape those implications. Indeed, the fate of some future President of
the United States and his chiefs of staff and military advisers may well have
been sealed by this decision."

cause he failed to control the troops under his command who committed atrocities on helpless prisoners of war, even though he claimed to have had no knowledge of the atrocities. General MacArthur wrote, "This officer, of proven field merit, entrusted with high command involving authority adequate to responsibility, has failed the irrevocable standard; has failed in his duty to his troops, to his country, to his enemy, to mankind; has failed utterly his soldier faith." Under General MacArthur's reasoning, did his West Point fellow-graduate General Westmoreland fail any less in his duty to his troops, his country, or his enemy?

Chapter 6

Disorganization

☆ ☆ ☆ ☆ ☆ ☆ ☆ ☆ ☆

If the Army's mission is no longer "To win in war," then what is its future purpose? This is the question that is frustrating Army managers today. In the early 1960s the Army had a doctrine requiring a mission—it found the mission in Vietnam. In the 1970s the Army is again looking for a role and a mission. The older generals see a traditional mission in armored, tactical nuclear warfare on the plains of Europe. Younger and middle-grade officers think in terms of preparing to serve as advisers in underdeveloped countries, where mobile Army light-infantry units could be used to defeat further Communist-inspired "Wars of National Liberation." A small number of officers see the future Army as less involved in military actions and more involved in solving domestic social problems while helping maintain domestic law and order.

False Mission

There is no agreement within the Army on its future role. Army managers publicly say the civilian leadership should tell them what this role is. Yet they know that such clear-cut civilian guidance is not likely and that in all probability they will by default be able to decide the Army's role and missions.

But one might ask what *is* the role of the Army today? What national security missions are the United States taxpayers financing through the Army's costly manpower and equipment? The nearest answer that can be given is that the Army is preparing to perform several missions. But I do not believe that all of these missions are essential to the combat defense of the United States. Some, such as that in Korea, are peripheral missions more rooted in Army parochialism than in a legitimate desire to defend the country. The Army's principal mission force for the past twenty years has been its troops in Central Europe. Equipping and manning the four and one-third divisions in West Germany and the three and two-thirds backup divisions in the United States is the Army's major justification for Army manpower and equipment levels, including the new tanks, helicopters, and personnel carriers.[1]

Yet Army technocrats know very well that there is only a slight possibility that the presently organized Army could successfully engage in conventional warfare against the Soviet Army. They have long counted on low-yield tactical nuclear weapons to offset the Soviet advantage in combat manpower and conventional firepower. But United States use of even low-yield nuclear weapons would almost surely escalate quickly to an all-out nuclear war. In a war of massive nuclear retaliation the role of the Army in Europe is not significant. So behind the façade of a conventional war mission in Central Europe, what does the Army really believe its mission is?

---

[1] The Tri-Cap Division that the Army is "testing" at Fort Hood combines requirements for new tanks and helicopters in a new Army division especially tailored for combat in Europe. This division structure will no doubt be approved to justify procurement of new weapons systems like the Main Battle Tank and Cheyenne helicopter.

It is this question that brings the ideas of the younger company- and field-grade officers into sharp conflict with the generals. Duty in Europe doesn't offer younger officers the same plush jobs and familiar World War II tactics and terrain that it provides for senior officers. Orienting the Army to an unlikely conventional-war mission in Europe is not appealing to these younger men. If they are going to develop their careers and march in the footsteps of officers like George S. Patton III, Henry Emerson, William DePuy, and others who shot up from lieutenant colonel to win general's stars in Vietnam, there must be a war. To the younger career officers the idea of low-intensity wars, which combine the Army adviser role with mobile U.S. light-infantry brigades, seems far more attractive than standing guard on the Rhine. They can visualize themselves in some far-off African jungle, or high rugged Andean mountain range, advising and leading United States-trained local troops in defeating the "Communists," or commanding the fast-moving helicopter-borne U.S. infantry brigades that may be sent to help. This is heady stuff—and it is the same old counterinsurgency doctrine dressed up in a new suit. The new suit is called "low-intensity war" and its foundation is the Military Assistance Officers Program (MAOP).

The MAOP concept goes far beyond previous involvement of Army advisers in the internal affairs of an underdeveloped country. This program would expand on the role advisers played in bringing South Vietnamese military decisions into line with United States policy objectives. The MAOP officer would be on the ground in the country and would become directly involved in the local political situation in order to shape its course. His job would be to make friends among local military officers who are interested in maintaining a political situation favorable to United States interests. To help in this, the Army will continue to authorize foreign officers on duty in the United States to use U.S. Army hospitals, commissaries, post exchanges, and so forth, despite the fact that these privileges are not reciprocated and the foreign officers are drawing substantial living allowances while in the United States. The MAOP officer would probably advise the United States ambassador of his findings, but he would have direct contact with his service

and through it the Joint Chiefs of Staff. His on-the-spot evaluation of the degree of threat to the internal security of the country could be used by the Army General Staff to strengthen the
case for sending in U.S. Army brigades. The Army's rationale in
pursuing these objectives is that involvement in any subsequent
low-intensity war would not bring the political problems that
have arisen in connection with Vietnam but that U.S. forces
could build on the experience and training of the veterans of
Vietnam.

In my opinion, it is the low-intensity-war mission toward
which middle-grade Army planners will try to turn the Army.
The European conventional-war mission will provide enough
money to finance the quiet training and preparation needed for
this new version of the now discredited counterinsurgency and
limited-brushfire-war concepts. Low-intensity war will become
the mission buzz-word to give the Army a component under
the Nixon Doctrine. It would also provide a trained force to re-
press any domestic civilian upheaval in the United States.

Paunchy Organization

The U.S. Army is badly organized for combat.

With or without a suitable strategic or tactical mission, any
army which allocates over 60 percent of its manpower to other
than the combat mission of firing on the enemy is not going to
win in any war. This is another uncounted cost of the modern
Army concept of going "first class" into battle. The officers of
the technical services have devised doctrines and concepts
which have required constantly expanded supply and logistic
forces to support ever-shrinking combat elements. It is this
technical-service concept supported by the officers involved in
research and development that has caused the present Army
"combat slice" to fall to around 40 percent for nearly all units.
The Soviet Army's combat slice has also decreased, but still remains at 60 percent even though it too has been modernized.
The North Vietnamese Army, which is patterned somewhat
after the Red Chinese Army, is not modern but it has been able
to hold its own against American and South Vietnamese ar-

mies by husbanding its combat force for important strikes. Through skillful application of the principles of war, such as surprise and mass, North Vietnamese have been able to pull off such coups as the Tet Offensive despite overall allied superiority. In contrast, allied forces have flitted and crashed about the countryside in blunderbuss "sweeps" and search and destroy missions.

In Vietnam, as in Korea, the United States has relied on artillery and airborne firepower to turn the tide. Over half a million North Vietnamese soldiers have probably been killed or wounded in this fashion. Little consideration has been given to the fact that greater use of artillery and airborne bombing has caused untold thousands of civilian casualties whereas increased deployment of combat infantrymen would have resulted in more selective use of firepower. Congress has been so impressed with the Army's argument that "nothing is too good for our boys" and the "American soldier comes from an affluent society and expects to take that affluence with him onto the battlefield," that it has provided more dollars for less defense in terms of fewer combat soldiers. The result has been that the total strength of the Army has increased yet the percentage of combat manpower has steadily declined. Vietnam has conclusively proven that it does cost a great deal more to go first class in battle. But has this really been good for "our boys"? The worst thing that can happen to the "boys" is to be killed. The likelihood of this occurring increases with the probability of being outnumbered and individually gunned down by a more numerous combat enemy. To date, U.S. artillery and airborne firepower has been able to balance out the fact that U.S. infantrymen have consistently been outnumbered by infantrymen of the other side who are up front, pulling a trigger, trying to kill them.

But what if the GI ever has to fight a first-rate modern army like his own, one which has as much or more artillery and airborne firepower—and gets a 25 percent better combat slice from its available manpower? In other words what if he has to face the Soviet Army? How good will his chances of survival be if his supporting firepower is neutralized or overcome and he is forced to fight the Soviets on the basis of infantrymen firing at each other? In such a situation the side that has the most men firing is going to win and the men on the other side are going to be killed or wounded. Providing an affluent rear-area battlefield environment at the expense of combat muscle—which is what the U.S. Army has been doing for the past fifteen years —is certainly no help.

How is the Army's organization for combat faulty? The failure begins in the Army Tables of Organization and Equipment (TOE) which are the official manpower-authorization documents. For example they show that there are about 16,000 soldiers in an Army division—11,000 of these are officers and noncommissioned officers, 5,000 are privates. A close informed reading of these tables will also show that fewer than one half of the 16,000-man division (about 7,650 soldiers) are assigned the mission of firing on the enemy.[2] The remaining 8,350 are engaged in administrative command and logistic-support duties. Two sustaining increments of 16,000 men each are required to support each combat division under present Army organization. One of these elements is called the Initial Support Increment (ISI) which provides support when a division first goes into combat. The Sustaining Support Increment (SSI) provides the long-term support needed after sixty days of battle. These three elements—Division plus ISI plus SSI—make up what is called the Division Force Equivalent (DFE) of 48,000 men. Broken down to basic combat terms this means that of the 48,000 American soldiers required to man and support a U.S. Army division, less than 10,000 finally deliver fire on the enemy.

Or, to look at the allocations in another way, the 1972 United States Defense Budget shows that the Army expects to have a June 1972 active-duty end-strength of 942,000 men and women to man a combat force of thirteen and one-third divisions. In terms of manpower utilization this figures out to:

---

[2] For example, each infantry maneuver battalion in the division contains forty officers and 492 noncommissioned officers, but only twenty-three of these officers and ninety-six noncommissioned officers are assigned as combat troop leaders.

a. 16,000 men × 13⅓ divisions = 213,000 men to man 13⅓ combat divisions.
b. 16,000 × 2 = 32,000 men to support each division, or 421,000 men to sustain 13⅓ divisions.
c. 213,000 + 421,000 = 634,000 soldiers to man and sustain 13⅓ divisions under current lavish Army TOE's.

These figures reveal a discrepancy in totals of 308,000:

942,000 men projected as the 1972 end strength
− 634,000 men required to man and sustain 13⅓
      divisions
———————
308,000 soldiers not in combat divisions.

Where will the 308,000 soldiers be assigned? In testimony before the House Armed Services Committee, Secretary Laird indicated that 82,720 soldiers would be involved in "Other Mission Forces" (intelligence and security, communications, research and development, support to other nations) and in "Command Functions." This still leaves 225,000 soldiers unaccounted for.

The situation in Europe is especially revealing. The U.S. Seventh Army has been stationed in West Germany for twenty years. Its four and one-third divisions are the combat heart of the United States defense of Western Europe. These divisions are normally manned at 90 percent of their full combat strength, although there were times during the Vietnam build-up when they were stripped so far below that percentage that they were incapable of combat.[3] Nevertheless, about 170,000 soldiers (accompanied by 200,000 dependents) are being maintained in Central Europe at the taxpayers' expense. Less than 40,000 of these soldiers are assigned to fire at an enemy. This is very little combat return for the nearly $14 billion annually it costs the taxpayer to support general-purpose forces in Europe

———————

[3] At 90 percent strength these divisions contain a total of around 59,000 soldiers and require an additional 88,100 soldiers to sustain them and their dependents. Another 22,900 soldiers are serving in Seventh Army headquarter command and support functions.

and the backup divisions in the United States for reinforcement purposes. It seems even less satisfactory when one considers that in fiscal year 1970 the United States incurred a reported adverse balance of payments on overseas-troop deployments of $2 billion, of which $1.1 billion was spent in the Federal Republic of Germany.

Why has the Army organized itself in such a way as to require over 100,000 men to command and supply such a modest combat force? According to Army doctrine a corps headquarters "normally" commands two *or more* divisions in combat. In World War II combat in Europe each corps commanded an *average* of four divisions and the U.S. Seventh Army commanded three corps. But during the following twenty years of peacetime the Seventh Army and two corps headquarters in West Germany have commanded no more than five under-strength divisions. This has happened because (1) the Army has grown top-heavy through bureaucratic inertia and faulty organization; (2) senior officers prefer living in Europe to living on isolated Army bases in the United States; (3) the civilian leadership has abdicated control over military policies. In its relentless search for command billets and increased opportunities for promotion, the Army has let itself become paunchy and soft in its organization for combat. With its layers of headquarters, logistic- and area-support commands, special activities, and so on, the Army in Europe has become more concerned with comfortable living than flexible response to aggression.

An example of the Army's paunch under its present post-exchange-style organization can be found in Exercise Reforger II conducted in the late summer of 1970. After nearly ten months of planning, more than a dozen Army units from Fort Riley, Kansas, were airlifted to West Germany to temporarily reinforce Army forces participating in a NATO maneuver. The purpose of the airlift was to demonstrate United States ability to rapidly reinforce combat elements in Central Europe. Of the dozen or so units flown across the Atlantic, only two were combat-infantry brigades, the rest were command and support troops. And it took a week, at a cost of $4,927,000, to airlift this modest force of 11,400 soldiers to Europe.

Only a fraction of these vastly increased command and support forces are required by the new Army technology. Some are needed to maintain the oversophisticated weapons the Army has burdened itself with. Most are merely the baggage that go along with sending the Army first class. They provide the manpower for the proliferation of headquarters' commands which do little more than pass orders to lower command levels and provide slots for general officers and their retinues.

For example, in Europe the Army has a separate command called Theater Army Support Command (TASCOM) which is supposed to supervise and control all logistic and maintenance activities. But the Army has also created two additional Corps Support Commands (COSCOMS) of about 17,000 men each, which duplicate the control that TASCOM was created to accomplish. This kind of organization is an important reason why the present U.S. Army is a dragon with a huge tail and tiny teeth.

The overall implication is clear—today's U.S. Army is far too expensive in relation to its actual combat potential. It does not have to be this way. Army manager/leaders have chosen to ignore the obvious implications of faulty organization in favor of continuing to create more high-rank commands. They have strenuously resisted the few attempts that have been made to critically evaluate the Army's organizational structure. They have covered up the serious imbalance between combat forces and administrative-support forces by lumping so-called combat-support elements with "combat" forces while listing other logistic-support forces as "support." Using such a definition, General Westmoreland could testify to the House Armed Services Committee in his 1971 Army Posture Statement that in Europe the ratio of combat troops to support troops was approximately 60 percent combat and 40 percent support. At the time the general made this statement the ratio of Army troops in Europe assigned to combat units was no more than 42 percent combat to 58 percent support, and even this is an exaggerated figure since less than half of these are expected actually to fire on the enemy. It is this type of Army self-delusion and pub-

lic deception that has misled the American people and made
reform impossible.

Irrational Deployment

If the organization of the Army is unsatisfactory and costly
both in terms of manpower and money, the problems created
by its deployment are even worse. Let us look again at forces in
Europe. U.S. Army combat units—in consort with other NATO
armies—are supposed to be able to fight a conventional war
against Soviet and satellite Warsaw Pact troops. If the U.S.
Seventh Army were efficiently organized and commanded,
could it do what it is supposed to do? The answer is probably
no.

This answer is partly prompted by the geographic location
and sheer combat advantage enjoyed by their adversary: over
175 Soviet and East European divisions could be thrown into
battle against twenty-two NATO divisions (excluding the two
French divisions in Germany not under NATO military command). There are other disadvantages. One of these is the rela-
tive positioning of the forward units on each side. Soviet armored and mechanized divisions are positioned in austere,
mobile, tank and truck parks within sight of many of the main
autobahns leading through East Germany. The distance from a
soldier's tent or hut to his tank, truck, or armored carrier is a
matter of minutes. This is in sharp contrast to the positioning of
forward United States units. These troops live in barracks com-
pounds which are often a half mile or more from their tanks,
trucks, and armored carriers. The vehicle parks are not always
accessible to major road nets. Much longer than minutes is
needed to get U.S. Army troops on the road to their defensive
battle positions.

As an infantry captain commanding a rifle company stationed in Nürnberg, Germany, I was expected to clear my company from the barracks compound within ninety minutes of the
time that I received notification of a battle alert. The mess and
supply trucks were frequently unable to load and move in sufficient time to meet this deadline. Our enemy mission was to

move with the rest of our battalion to positions astride the road that came south from the town of Hof on the East German border. There we were to hastily dig in and prepare to hold for at least a half hour against the columns of Russian tanks and mechanized infantry it was believed could come rolling down through the "Hof Gap." It was a stand and die mission, though theoretically we were to fall back after the initial delaying period. Why was a half hour specified? Because this was the minimum time that U.S. military dependents in Nürnberg needed to load their cars and begin fleeing west over the same roads on which NATO troops would be moving east to reinforce us. We had no illusions about being able to fall back or being reinforced in time if the Soviets were to make a major attack through the Hof Gap. But would they? On the contrary, strategic considerations would probably motivate the Soviet armored forces instead to strike boldly across the flat North German plains along the historic invasion route to the Ruhr and the English Channel ports. The U.S. Army's insistence on defending the Hof and Fulda Gaps is due in part to the fact that this concept lends legitimacy to the continued positioning of Army forces near the Bavarian recreation areas.

A more profitable mission would be to help the scattered West German divisions and under-strength British Army of the Rhine defend the industrial heart of Europe—the Ruhr—and the Army's own supply lifelines from Belgium.

If the Soviets were to attack across North Germany, U.S. divisions would have to move considerable distances to the north to reach viable battle positions. If an attack came suddenly, as it did in Hungary and Czechoslovakia, the divisions would have to make this northward movement over roads jammed with other NATO troops, overrun with millions of refugees including many of their own families, and constantly attacked by low-flying aircraft.[4] Time would be critical in such a maneuver. Because of the more favorable positioning of the Soviet and East German forward divisions only hours would be

---

[4] When I served in a liaison capacity with the French Army in 1962, their General Staff estimated that as many as three to five million Eastern European and German refugees would come westward in the event of war.

available in which to intercept and stem the Soviet advance across North Germany.

Yet in the early stages of the Berlin Crisis of 1961, when serious consideration was given to sending United States divisions northward, *days* not hours were estimated as being required for the move. And those estimates were based on movement during *peacetime*. I clearly recall the hurried conferences that were held in U.S. Army Europe headquarters in the days before the Berlin Wall was built and in the weeks that followed. I had been working on Berlin contingency plans for several months when the first intelligence reports indicated the East Germans were planning to build the wall. We hurriedly flew fifteen bulldozer blades to our Berlin garrison. These were to be mounted on the M-48 tanks and used to push down the wall if Washington decided to adopt such a drastic course. Some East Berlin intelligence sources had reported that East German soldiers had been given orders to withdraw if there was any overt American resistance to construction of the wall. No decision was ever made regarding the wall, but U.S. Army Europe was queried as to whether it would be possible to use an American armored division to open the autobahn without becoming involved in combat with the Russians: a series of high-level conferences were held in response to this request. It was decided that such an undertaking would require repositioning the entire Seventh Army in order to place the divisions in more desirable battle positions. This raised a question of whether there was sufficient gasoline for such a large-scale movement.

An interesting culmination to that series of conferences was the coded message that was sent back to Washington. It informed the new President that U.S. Army Europe could give no "high assurance" that the Seventh Army could hold its own against the ten East German divisions it would probably have to fight if it tried to force its way up the Berlin Autobahn. It recommended that two of the regular Army backup divisions from the United States be moved to West Germany. President Kennedy then called two National Guard divisions to active duty to replace these two regular divisions. These regular units

were never sent to Europe. This was partly because it was discovered that the National Guard divisions could not be made
ready for combat in less than six months. Faced with uncer-
tainty of success against the East Germans and the strong likelihood that the Soviets would intervene with their twenty-plus
divisions and require United States forces to resort to tactical
nuclear weapons, Washington abandoned any thought of opening the autobahn with a U.S. armored division. Instead, one infantry battle group was sent up the autobahn as a trial force to
see if the Russians would permit its passage to Berlin. These
troops were ignominiously forced to dismount from their vehicles inside East Germany and be counted by Soviet officers before being permitted to pass to Berlin. This was the strongest
conventional response the United States dared risk at a time
when we had five divisions in Europe and a preponderant nuclear advantage.

Even assuming that U.S. Army combat elements have improved their flexibility and mobility since 1961, exhibiting these
qualities requires tactical air superiority. Assistant Secretary of
Defense Roger Kelley cited the importance of air superiority in
his April 15, 1971, testimony before the Senate Armed Services
Committee: "The most demanding situation for tactical air
forces is of course in NATO. . . . For attack capabilities to be
effective, tactical air forces must be able to gain the air superiority needed to permit air support of our forces. . . . The criti-
cality of this air superiority/defense mission is dependent on
the situation. . . . It could be crucial in a NATO war."

I know of no military planner who assumes that the U.S. Air
Force could attain absolute air superiority of the kind it enjoyed over Europe in 1945 in less than ninety days after the
start of any war in Europe. Many experts doubt our ability to
attain such superiority in any time period. One Air Force general has rated NATO's chances of gaining control of the air
over Central Europe as "somewhere between stalemate and
defeat." Air Force planning officers at conferences I attended
in Europe always reiterated that they could not guarantee anything more than local air superiority over a particular battle

area for a limited time. They always stressed that achieving even this local superiority meant stripping tactical air support from other sectors of the Central European battlefront.

Furthermore, Air Force planes, ammunition, and fuel supplies in Europe are nearly all in unprotected base complexes that are highly vulnerable to Soviet preemptive air strikes or capture by fast-moving Russian tank columns. It would be foolish to believe that the Soviet Air Force did not note the success of the 1967 Israeli preemptive air strike against Egypt's unprotected planes and bases. The Soviets could make a similar surprise sortie against the closely grouped cluster of United States fighter bases in West Germany, before launching a sudden ground attack. Early warning radar could give a few minutes of warning, but not enough to enable the United States to get all its planes airborne. Nor could our limited antiaircraft capability survive and defend against incoming waves of Soviet conventional-armed missiles and fighter aircraft.

But even if one accepts the optimistic planning estimates that are made to justify a continued U.S. Army force in Europe, and assumes that the U.S. Air Force could gain air superiority, could Army forces conventionally stop a sudden attack by Warsaw Pact Troops? Most military professionals will answer no. They would base their answer on several factors. One of these is the need for the Army to have a period of time in which to mobilize before it can begin to fight effectively. In the best traditions of World Wars I and II the Army in Europe assumes that war will come after a gradual increase of tensions between NATO and the Warsaw Pact. Such a gradual warning period would permit evacuation of most dependents, a repositioning of the Seventh Army, arrival of airlifted reinforcements from the United States, and a thickening of what is actually a thin forward defense in a very shallow NATO theater of operations in Central Europe. In any statement about United States conventional capability, Defense Department spokesmen are careful to include a long-standing but seldom-noticed caveat that: "After a period of warning and mobilization" and "NATO has a major conventional capability after a period of mobilization," or "Assuming a period of warning and military preparation by both sides NATO has a major conventional capability and under many circumstances should be able to stop a Pact attack."

These caveats are intended to protect the Department of Defense from full accountability for what the combat response would be to a sudden Soviet attack such as the one carried out in Czechoslovakia. The rapidity and coordination of that invasion astonished United States intelligence specialists and European field commanders, who had not believed the Soviets possessed the capability to mass and move so secretly or so swiftly. This demonstrated Soviet ability means that there is little likelihood that Army forces would have the comfortable mobilization period their contingency planning envisions. But if Army planners were to base their contingency strategy on the assumption of a sudden all-out Soviet attack rather than on localized probes, or an attack coming after a month of increasing international tension, they would seriously undermine much of the twenty-year rationale for keeping United States forces in Europe.

A sudden Soviet attack would make it impossible for the Army to fly in troop reinforcements from the United States. The Soviets would not only be able to preemptively knock out most of the tactical fighter aircraft that would be needed to defend the airspace over the fields where the airborne troop carriers would land, they could also make the fields unusable. They could do this by air, rocket, or ground attack. For example, it would be impossible to land C-5A transports at Frankfurt's Rhein/Main Airport (where Reforger trooplift exercises normally land) if Soviet tanks had covered the 178 miles from the East German border and were firing on the field. Before transports could land at any European airfield, the Air Force would have first to attain local air superiority over the field and the surrounding air corridors. Without such local United States superiority the big lumbering C-141 or C-5A transports would be sitting ducks for fast Mig fighters. Our heavy losses in men and transports over Sicily and France during World War II are grim reminders of what happens to airborne troops when friendly air and ground control is not firmly established. In order to attain superiority over the landing fields, the Air Force would have to divert tactical fighters from support of frontline Seventh Army troops battling to hold back Soviet tanks from breaking through and capturing the airfields. There is also the problem of weather over Central Europe. There are considerable periods during the year when high-performance fighter aircraft simply cannot operate over Central Europe—nor can troop transports land or take off. Mr. John H. Morse, Deputy Assistant Secretary of Defense for European and NATO Affairs, stated on July 21, 1971, "The best weather of any base in Germany is worse than the worst weather experienced at any air base in the continental United States." Since the Soviets have a decided edge in conventional ground power it would seem reasonable to assume that any sudden attack would be launched when weather conditions over Central Europe would be unfavorable for flying.

Even if Army reinforcements could land they would arrive without their heavy equipment. This equipment—tanks, trucks, and armored personnel carriers—is stored in prepositioned sites along various unused autobahn spurs in West Germany. Before moving to fight, these reinforcing units would have to remove the equipment from storage and put it in serviceable condition. This process usually takes about a week. Since it would take a week or more for the divisions to be airlifted to Germany, it would be at least three weeks before the reinforcements could be of any help to the Seventh Army. In a purely conventional war it is doubtful if the Seventh Army could hold three weeks on the east side of the Rhine. It would run the risk of being pocketed in the South German salient and eventually backed up against the Alps and destroyed.

Another problem for the Army is the lack of an effective wartime supply line (LOC) to American soldiers stationed in West Germany. Since France withdrew from NATO the Army has had to rely on a line running down from the port of Bremerhaven. This supply line is unusable in time of war. The United States European Command is still trying to secure approval from our NATO allies for twelve technical support agreements required to establish the infrastructure for a wartime supply line across the Benelux countries. If agreements can be reached the LOC will cost around $11,500,000. This will duplicate the costly LOC that was built and abandoned in France. During his 1971 appearance before the House Appropriations Committee, General David Burchinal, Deputy Commander in Chief of the United States European Command, stated, "Well, we either build that line of communications or we settle for a position that says we are going to commit American troops in combat and not provide for their support in wartime. It seems to me 'either—or.' Now, presently, for economic reasons, we are using the Bremerhaven port for most of our throughput [supplies] and that certainly is a lot more exposed than the Benelux LOC. It is about eighty-five miles from the Iron Curtain. I consider the Benelux LOC has its vulnerabilities, but I do not concede it would not be usable. It certainly is not as good as the old LOC through France, there is no question about that." [5]

A Little Bit Nuclear

So why has the Army insisted on continuing the Seventh Army in Central Europe if it is faced with such dire prospects in battle? The answer has two parts: first, Army planning is not predicated on a sudden full-scale Soviet attack and, second, several years ago the Army devised a formula for fighting a conventional-plus war in Europe. They allocated a large portion of the seven thousand tactical nuclear weapons stockpiled in Europe to the Seventh Army. Simple! This could enable U.S. Army

---

[5] In 1961 I worked on contingency planning for the Benelux LOC while assigned to the Office of the Assistant Chief of Staff G-3 of the U.S. Army Communications Zone Europe in Orléans, France. This planning was in preparation for the time we might be forced from France. General Staff planners estimated the Bremerhaven LOC would be cut by the Soviets on the first day of battle and we feared that even if we obtained a Benelux LOC it too would be cut by Soviet tanks within two to three days after the beginning of combat. This is a serious tactical risk, because it means that American troops in Germany would be cut off from any source of re-supply through the channel ports.

conventional forces to offset Soviet advantages in positioning and combat manpower by exploding large numbers of nuclear devices against them from the earliest moments of their attack.

The Army has been training for years on the basis of such planning. Simulated use of tactical nuclear weapons is written into the scenario of most major Army unit-training exercises in Europe. In one NATO exercise in which I participated over a hundred simulated nuclear devices, from Atomic Demolition Munitions to nuclear shells, rockets, and bombs, were used. The exercise began with aggressor forces making a localized military probe into Bavaria from East Germany. This happened after thirty days of increasing international tensions between NATO and the aggressors. During the period of increasing tensions the scenario indicated that Seventh Army troops had taken up battle positions to defend against an aggressor attack through the Hof and Fulda Gaps. In the initial three-day phase of the exercise NATO troops were forced back in a wide arc toward the Rhine. However, once Seventh Army troops were behind the Danube River a hail of nuclear weapons ranging up to twenty kilotons was unleashed on the invaders. Much of this nuclear fire would have fallen on heavily populated areas of southern Germany. These nuclear fires stopped the aggressor probe at the Danube. Then nuclear-tipped rockets were used to "blow a hole" in the outer crust of the aggressor forces. Seventh Army tanks began racing through this nuclear-blown hole. The exercise called for them to be preceded by additional tactical nuclear rockets and bombs on aggressor units located in rear areas in East Germany. The scenario closed with Seventh Army units advancing behind these blazing nuclear fires and driving the aggressors back into East Germany, thus ending the probe. After this exercise our units mounted their vehicles and returned to barracks to clean equipment and await the flood of high-ranking visitors that would descend upon us from various United States headquarters.

This exercise, as well as others I participated in, was defined as a conventional flexible response to a localized probe on the part of a Warsaw Pact force. How valid is this definition? "Tactical" nuclear weapons include weapons of up to twenty kilotons, the same destructive power as the Hiroshima atomic bomb that burned seven square miles, killed 78,150, injured 37,425, and left 176,987 people homeless and sick. In terms of physical damage and indiscriminate loss of civilian and military lives, the one-sided use of such tactical weapons can scarcely be called conventional.

Britain's top military scientist, Sir Solly Zuckerman, made an analysis a few years ago of NATO war games in North Germany in which simulated tactical nuclear weapons were used. He discovered that military unit commanders tended to over-employ nuclear weapons to ensure victory. For example he found that the lowest-yield tactical nuclear weapons like the Davy Crockett are quickly put aside in favor of higher-yield weapons. In one of the smaller war games he analyzed, the simulated battle area was open ground with no large cities. Weapons of from fifteen to twenty kilotons were used. Both sides were calculated to have made five hundred to one thousand nuclear strikes during the first three days. Fighting could not continue after that time because of the extent of nuclear destruction.

Zuckerman estimated the human casualties would have exceeded more than half a million killed or fatally injured. Five million more persons would have been seriously harmed by radiation. The entire area of North Germany would have been so soaked with radiation that no human could have moved over it. There would have been only burned and ruined towns, radioactive land, food, and water. John Strachey, a former British Secretary of State for War, has written: "It is leading to a kind of situation in which the NATO forces in Europe, partly because of the nature of their equipment and even more because of the nature of their training, will feel themselves unable to undertake more than a border skirmish without the use of tactical nuclear weapons."

His concern is borne out by the statements of some U.S. Army generals. For example, General Goodpaster, the senior United States officer in Europe and current Supreme Commander of Allied Powers Europe (SHAPE), stated in response to a question during an appearance before a Senate Committee in 1970, "If an enemy were to come at us with all the forces that the Warsaw Pact could generate and were to sustain and press his attack regardless of the losses that he took, after a short period of time it would be probable that at least in some areas we would have to resort to nuclear weapons in order to hold." At another point in the same testimony, when asked what the NATO situation would be forty-five days after the outbreak of hostilities in Europe with both sides using only conventional forces, General Goodpaster replied, "I believe there is a probability that it would be necessary to resort to the support of tactical nuclear weapons." General Lyman Lemnitzer, SHAPE Commander from 1962 until 1969, stated it even more bluntly in 1970 in an appearance before the House Foreign Affairs Committee. He said, "One of the greatest problems that would confront NATO today would be a large conventional attack. Then we would be faced with a decision to use nuclear weapons or be defeated."

The U.S. European Commander already has authority to emplace Atomic Demolition Mines near the West German borders if he feels the threat to the Seventh Army justifies such action. If the Soviets attacked he would undoubtedly call on the Pentagon to secure Presidential approval for early detonation of those mines. That is what he is trained to do—and what he expects to do. General Burchinal, the Deputy U.S. European Commander, has stated his concept of using nuclear weapons as, "You try to have an increased range of conventional response before you resort to nuclear weapons. . . . But at no time do you disregard the nuclear response."

The President would be faced with a grave dilemma. He would have the difficult choice of authorizing the use of nuclear weapons—and thereby opening a nuclear war—or denying their use and writing off over half a million United States servicemen and their wives and children. Such a choice would not be an attractive prospect for any American President. Yet every President is faced with this grave decision as the result of efforts to maintain the fiction of an effective United States conventional-war capability in Central Europe.

The President would have very little time to make his decision. For example, the Atomic Demolition Mines would have to be detonated during the first hours to stop advancing Soviet forces. There would be no time for American constitutional processes to function effectively and military pressure on the President would be intense. He would have little other practical choice than granting permission for the use of tactical nuclear weapons. Such first use would cause the United States to be labeled as a nuclear aggressor and would give the initiative to the Soviets. They could respond on a slightly higher tactical nuclear level, or they could launch a massive nuclear attack on our cities. Could our defense planners afford to wait calmly to find out what their level of response would be? Unless United States officers assumed there would be no Soviet nuclear reply —a most unlikely event—there would be strong pressure for a massive United States preemptive nuclear strike to prevent a nuclear response from the USSR. By continuing the fiction of conventional-tactical nuclear "flexible" response in Europe we may be locking ourselves into a position where we could be forced to begin nuclear warfare as a result of any United States or Soviet misstep in Europe.

The Problem of Dependents

Another can of worms is the problem of evacuating the 225,000 military dependents from Europe if there is no period of mobilization. Each United States embassy has a "Country Plan" which is supposedly coordinated through various State-Defense liaison groups, but the Army gives priority to evacuating military dependents. Assistance to embassies and other Americans traveling or working in Europe will be provided only if the Army has any time or resources left over. Of the 225,000 military-sponsored dependents living in Europe, approximately 50,000 live in close proximity to the Iron Curtain.[6] These are to be evacuated first. Present contingency planning assumes a

---

[6] Twenty-five percent of the 225,000 dependents are children under three years of age.

grace period during which these dependents can either be sent home on the returning planes that ferry reinforcements into Western Europe or driven to certain designated "Safehavens" to await later evacuation to the United States.

If the Soviets attack suddenly, neither of these methods of evacuation is practical. The Deputy European Commander, General Burchinal, indicated this when he said, "There may not be time to pull the dependents out." This fact has long been recognized by Army planners. When I served as a General Staff plans officer on dependent evacuation, it was agreed that in the event of a sudden attack dependents would "stand fast." In other words they would be left behind when United States troops fell back to better defensive positions. To many of us it seems absurd to expect United States troops to fall back and leave their families to the Russians or the local German populace. The fact that a standfast plan exists is indicative of the irrationality of the situation. By standing fast dependents would not only be at the mercy of their attackers, but their own husbands and fathers might be required to direct nuclear-weapons fire on them in an attempt to halt the advance of the Soviet units. This is not a pleasant picture to contemplate, yet Army managers have been doing so for at least ten years and disregarding most of the risks.

In spite of the scope of this potential disaster, the armed forces opposed President Eisenhower's decision in late 1960 to stop further travel of dependents to Europe. In response to this opposition, President Kennedy rescinded the Eisenhower order in 1961, even though no effective dependent-evacuation plan had been devised by the Army. Nor is there an effective plan today.

What Is the Soviet Threat?

Having analyzed the U.S. Army ability to withstand a Soviet attack on Western Europe, we should examine the question of whether the Soviets intend to attack. According to Assistant Secretary of Defense Roger Kelley, "While we do not consider

an unprovoked aggression by the USSR likely, the fact remains
that the Soviets have a vital interest in preserving the status
quo in Central Europe. A crisis that could lead to a conflict
could arise if the political situation substantially changes in a
way which threatened the USSR. Such a crisis could escalate to
hostilities. Whatever the immediate cause the crisis could
trigger localized hostilities or mobilization by the Pact and
NATO." Mr. Kelley also said, "We assume that the Soviets are
deterred from attacking NATO by the high risk that a conventional conflict between NATO and Warsaw Pact forces would
escalate to the level of general nuclear war and pose grave risks
to the Soviet State itself."

If the United States does not consider an unprovoked aggression likely, then how can we envision "localized hostilities"
(that would remain local) being any more likely? Why would
the Red Army be inclined to conduct only a localized probe
against NATO when they are already quite aware that they
could rather handily win a purely conventional war? But if a
conventional war would admittedly escalate to a general nuclear war then what is the real purpose of the four and one-
third Army divisions stationed permanently in Central Europe?
These are questions that should be asked when the validity of
the mission of our European-based Army forces is discussed.

The Soviet reluctance to initiate either a probe or an all-out
attack is probably predicated on two factors. First, the Soviet
people would not be likely to support an aggressive war against
Western Europe unless it could be presented as a defense of
Mother Russia. They suffered far too much in World War II to
be receptive to an expansionistic grab of Western Europe with
the countless Soviet dead that such aggression would bring.
And second, Soviet leaders are aware that an attack on Western Europe would quickly escalate to general nuclear war.
They do not want such a mutually destructive war any more
than the United States does. The Soviets know they could win a
conventional war and give as good as they receive in a tactical
nuclear exchange. What they dare not risk is a massive nuclear
war. But massive nuclear deterrence does not require large

United States ground forces in Europe. It is already being accomplished through Poseidon submarines and United States based missiles.

Defeat of Senator Mansfield's amendment to withdraw two Army divisions from Europe and subsequent Presidential announcements that there will be no reduction of United States forces in Europe seem to indicate that we are going to continue to implement, at vast expense, the current irrational Army policy. This means that nearly 50 percent of our regular Army—always vital to our mobilization in times of emergency—will continue to be stationed out of the country. American armored-cavalry regiments will go on patrolling the West German border. And eight thousand American soldiers (plus their dependents) will continue to help man obsolete missiles in Northern Italy as part of the Southern European Task Force (SETAF). When will Congress and the American people come to grips with this situation?

Other Stations

In Korea, one infantry division has finally been withdrawn, eighteen years after the Korean War ended. But the Army's 7th Division (now renumbered the 2nd Division) still remains where it landed at the close of World War II (except for one year in Japan in 1949). To command and support this one division, the United States continues to station in Korea the Eighth Army, I Corps headquarters, and the 1st Logistical Command. And to improve the "experience" of the GI's remaining in Korea, a battalion of the 2nd Division will continue to be assigned guard duty on the South Korean border. This will help maintain an aggressive image for the Eighth Army. It will also give North Korean snipers and infiltrators a continued chance to gun down American soldiers from ambush as they have been doing for twenty years. "The best kept secret in the Army," as duty in South Korea is called, will go on, with senior officers still able to spend a year's "hardship" tour in Seoul with their young Korean mistresses. There is no valid military reason to continue to station even one Army division in South Korea, but there are many parochial Army reasons for retaining a presence there.[7] These include continuing emotional attachment to the scene of past combat as well as the desire to maintain as many divisions overseas as possible.

Much the same game has been played in South Vietnam. At the time of this writing there were 244,900 military personnel in South Vietnam according to Department of Defense sources. At about the same time the Secretary of the Army indicated that only thirty-four combat battalions remained in South Vietnam. Translated to force levels this meant that in June 1971 there were, approximately, 28,866 soldiers in combat units, 118,074 providing combat support, and 97,960 involved in combat-service duties. This is nearly the same Army infrastructure that was required in 1969 to command and support ten United States divisions in South Vietnam. The combat troops have been removed but the Army headquarters and support troops remain. Apparently the Army intends to retain between 40,000 and 50,000 of these troops in South Vietnam indefinitely as a "residual base force" to assure a Korean-style solution. This residual force, in the words of a Defense Department spokesman, will "remain until the time at which the Republic of Vietnam grows to sufficient strength and self-reliance to determine their own future." The supposition that this may take some years seems to be borne out by Army plans to assign advisers to eighteen-month tours of duty in Vietnam—accompanied by their families. And, as Secretary Laird has said, "We will have combat forces stationed [in South Vietnam] in a security role. These particular forces will carry on security missions and will be involved in combat." This not only sounds like a replay of the Army's experience in 1964–65, but it implies a semipermanent low-intensity war rather than disengagement of Army troops.

Officers and enlisted men also serve with the worldwide net

---

[7] The South Korean Army numbers well over 600,000 soldiers, while the North Korean Army has less than 500,000 men. Only in tactical aircraft are the North Koreans stronger than South Korea.

of military-assistance advisory groups (MAAGS). These MAAGS are frequently of questionable value to the national defense effort. Many have outlived their original purpose of helping American allies master United States equipment since most host countries received the last large shipment of United States military supplies some years ago. For example, in 1964 when I was stationed with the Army Element of the MAAG in Spain, my assigned duty was to advise the Spanish infantry. Yet nearly all of the United States supplied equipment in the Spanish infantry units was World War II vintage and has been in Spain since 1959. The Spaniards did not need either advice or assistance on how to use it. My principal job was planning the yearly trips made by senior U.S. Army officers throughout Spain. I made their hotel reservations, arranged for a military sedan and driver to transport them, and made sure their claim voucher for the government per diem payment of $13 a day was quickly paid. These "visits" were supposed to have been required by the surveillance provisions of the Foreign Assistance Act. However, the visits continued after these provisions were waived for MAAG Spain. I accompanied senior officers on several of these expense-paid trips. A visit consisted of a formal call on the local Spanish military commander, then a morning trip to a Spanish Army unit to look at United States World War II or Korean War equipment, followed by a *copita* (small cocktail party) or luncheon. The afternoons were usually free for sightseeing and shopping.

I vividly recall one shopping trip to Gibraltar. I had accompanied an Army colonel on a morning visit to a Spanish Army tank battalion near La Linea on the border between Spain and British Gibraltar. The tanks were all Korean War United States M-47 models, but their presence there constituted a considerable threat to the British forces in Gibraltar. After a perfunctory walk-through of the battalion, we crossed through the Spanish customs and entered the British colony. This had not been a simple matter to arrange, because Spanish customs officials were stopping all traffic in and out of Gibraltar. As our green Army sedan sped by the long line of cars waiting to pass customs, it was accompanied by some deprecating remarks from

American tourists waiting in the hot noonday sun. But we were on an official mission! Beefeater Gin was selling for 95¢ a fifth at Saccone and Speed in Gibraltar and we had a large number of orders from our fellow advisers back in Madrid.

After making our purchases we were browsing in front of a shop window when a woman asked the colonel, "Are you Yanks?" We replied that we were and she said, "Saw a lot of you Yanks, I did, during the war, but I never remember seeing that uniform before." I explained that the Army green uniform had been adopted after the war. "And what does the little blue patch with MAAG-Spain mean?" she asked. The colonel told her it meant that we were assigned to the United States military-assistance advisory group in Spain. "Do you mean to tell me you Yanks are advising them Spaniards how to run us off the Rock?" she asked belligerently. We hastened to assure her that was not our purpose, but she remained unconvinced. "Fine friends you are," she said. "What do you think they are going to do with all those tanks—hold a bloody holiday parade?" With that she flounced off angrily, while the small crowd that had gathered laughed.

Nothing much changes in any of the MAAG's. Visiting in Spain in 1970 I ran across an Army acquaintance with whom I had served during his first four-year tour. He had just returned for a second tour of three years. He was busy preparing the yearly schedule of visits to the same units we had visited in 1965, but the per diem had changed. It was now $21 per day!

The chief purpose of all too many MAAG's is to justify their continued existence and take advantage of as many local good deals as possible. In Spain as in South America the best deal was buying and selling cars. We all tried to use our diplomatic privileges to sell at least one car on the local Spanish market. A Mercedes-Benz costing us $2,800 would bring as high as $10,000. It was no problem arranging for delivery of a replacement car in the United States—an enterprising United States major in the Air Force section of the MAAG ran a new-car business from his official office in Madrid.

Another Army overseas deployment which contributes little to the combat defense of the United States is the U.S. Army

South (USARSO). This small force (less than ten thousand soldiers) located in the Panama Canal Zone is commanded by an Army major general. Its principal mission is defense of the Panama Canal. It has a brigade which commands two understrength infantry battalions, an air-defense battalion, and an assortment of support units. This command lavishes as much attention on its secondary missions as it does on defending the canal. These secondary missions include the Green Beret Special Forces Group that works with Latin American armies, the School of the Americas which trains soldier-specialists for Latin American forces, and the supervision of the Army Elements of the MAAG's and military groups scattered among the Central and South American countries. It is through some of these secondary activities that Army South Command involves the United States in the internal affairs of various Latin American armies.

When Che Guevara opened his insurgency in Bolivia, the United States offered to send Green Berets from Panama to train and equip a special ranger battalion in the Bolivian Army. An agreement was made with the Bolivian Army Chief of Staff that once the troops were trained and equipped they would be used in a counterinsurgency role and would be kept on active duty at least eighteen months. Green Beret "A" Teams from Panama were airlifted to Bolivia, along with quantities of light machine guns, M-2 carbines, and ammunition. They worked feverishly to train the Bolivian conscript soldiers in counter-guerrilla warfare. Units from the battalion had a hand in the final capture of a wounded Che, although the Bolivian sergeant who later executed him with a carbine was not from the battalion. Shortly afterward the battalion became a reserve bodyguard for the Bolivian president and was disbanded within a year.

Many other activities of Army South are simply ineffectual. The School of the Americas is one example. This U.S. Army School is financed by military-assistance funds. It is commanded by a colonel and staffed with Spanish-speaking United States officers and enlisted men. It has trained hundreds of Latin American soldiers in a variety of military skills. These soldiers have often been unable to utilize this training in their own armies because the skills were not applicable or they were reassigned to unrelated duties. Despite this the United States military group in each Latin American country goes on filling its quota of local army students to attend the school. This steady flow of students justifies the continued existence of the MAAG's and the school. Some Latin American soldiers have even become "professional students" and have helped United States military groups fill their quota by attending two or more courses at the school. Not much thought is given by USARSO to the number of Latin American soldiers that have been trained at United States taxpayer expense and are not being utilized in their newly learned skills.

Featherbedding at Home

All of the Army's paunch is not bulging out overseas. There is a considerable amount of fat in its stateside organization. There is not enough space in this book to describe all of the Army's complicated tangle of fragmented administrative and logistic commands. A representative example of the proliferated organizational structure is the system of Army geographic Area Commands. The fifty states are divided into four area commands and the Military District of Washington. Each area is commanded by a three-star general with a large headquarters and staff. He is responsible for all Army units and installations located within his area but these are largely support organizations. He supervises few active Army combat units. For example the First Army has no active combat divisions, but it has two or more corps headquarters (which should be capable of commanding two or more divisions apiece).

The Third Army has at least two corps headquarters to supervise one combat division. The Fifth Army has two corps headquarters to help supervise three and two-thirds combat divisions. The Sixth Army supervises only one combat division.

None of these headquarters has direct control over training the five divisions they supervise. This is the job of the U.S. Continental Army Command (USCONARC) at Fort Monroe, Virginia, which is headed by a four-star general. Subordinate commands are required to submit an unbelievable number of reports to all of these headquarters. There are status-of-training reports, maintenance reports, housing reports, disciplinary reports, personnel-status reports, manpower utilization reports, safety reports, storage reports, and so on. There are so many reports that military managers and civilian clerks have little time to read them as they file them away. Annual reports breed quarterly progress reports, and they in turn breed interim or "one-time" reports.

To keep up with this flow of paper large general staffs have been created at every command level from division up to the office of the Secretary of the Army. Each staff level is organized along similar lines. There is a commanding general, a deputy commanding general, a chief of staff, and a G-1 chief of personnel, G-2 chief of intelligence, G-3 chief of plans and operations, G-4 chief of logistics. The sections headed by each of these chiefs are quite large. For example, in the Pentagon Army General Staff, the G-4 section has over two hundred officers, civilian managers, and project officers. These are just the supervisors. The total work force includes many more lower-ranking officers, enlisted men, and civilians.

The Fitzhugh Commission Report on Pentagon management and organization probably best summed up what these numerous staffs actually do: "Functional analysis of these staffs reveals an astonishing lack of organizational focus and a highly excessive degree of 'coordination,' a substantial portion of which entails the writing of memoranda back and forth between lower echelons of parallel organizational elements which serves no apparent useful or productive purpose."

One of the duplicative staff levels that could be eliminated is the G-2 Intelligence sections in each division, corps, and army headquarters in the United States. The mission of these G-2 sections is to collect tactical intelligence data. Since only internal domestic intelligence can be collected within the United States boundaries these sections do not have valid missions. Many, like the G-2 at Fourth Army, have been used to handle matters of protocol and look after VIP guests. At other headquarters, such as Fort Carson, Colorado, the G-2 has been put to work collecting intelligence on local individuals and agencies which in its estimation could be "dangerous" to Army security. This loosely defined mission has allowed local G-2's far too wide a latitude in gathering and filing information on many Americans both in and out of the military. After I had published an article critical of the Army in the May 30, 1970, issue of the *New Republic*, a friend in Army Intelligence Command headquarters called to tell me that a confidential dossier had been opened on me, as a "danger to the Army."

In all too many instances these layers of headquarters and staff sections are maintained to provide jobs for Army field-grade and general officers. And by their excessive number and size they create the bureaucratic inertia and red tape that cause much of the Army's inefficiency. Posts like Fort Sam Houston and the Presidio of San Francisco are retained chiefly as preretirement stations. Older generals, senior colonels, and noncommissioned officers are sent to pasture at posts like these to while away their final years before retirement—by playing golf and looking for a civilian job.

Still other areas of duplication of effort can be found in the activities of Army Recruiting and Army Reserve and National Guard advisers. Active Army recruiters are stationed at various towns and cities throughout the country. In many of these towns and cities National Guard recruiters and Army Reserve recruiters are trying to recruit the same young men. One recruiter in each area could solicit for all the Army components, yet each year the Army budget requests separate funding for three categories of recruiters.

Being an Army adviser to the National Guard or Reserve is like being an adviser to a foreign army, except the language is the same. An Army adviser is expected to keep reservists and guardsmen abreast of current Army training and doctrines, maintain surveillance over government equipment, and certify the payrolls of Army Reserve units. This can be a most difficult task. As adviser to a reserve infantry regiment I once refused to certify government pay for reserve officers who had not performed the part-time active duty for which they were claiming pay. My Army superior urged me to certify the payments to

"avoid any trouble." When I refused I was transferred to another job. Other active Army advisers, who came to work at 9
A.M. and left at noon, counseled me, "Take it easy, Ed, you're
not supposed to do anything on this job but show up in the evening and stand around while the unit has a meeting. Do that
and don't ask any questions about the payroll and you'll get the
Army Commendation Medal when you leave. You start rocking
the boat and these bastards will fix your career for good
through their political friends." [8]

On my new job I was responsible for inspecting 188 Army
Reserve units. I reported that obligated white reservists were
not being assigned to illegally segregated all-black units in east
Texas. And I gave previously rated "combat-ready" units with
rusty weapons and vehicles that wouldn't run ratings of unsatisfactory. An active Army adviser once asked me to give a rating of excellent to a reserve unit that was in terrible shape. He
was retiring in a few months and had a job lined up with the reserve unit commander. He was fearful that an unsatisfactory
unit rating would cause him to lose the job. He said, "They
have always gotten superior ratings and if they get below excellent they will blame me and I won't get the job that I've been
working for three years to set up." I rated them unsatisfactory;
I never learned whether he lost the job because I was sent
overseas shortly thereafter. It should not be forgotten that the
nation's ultimate defense depends on these National Guard and
Reserve units. It seems unrealistic to equip them with military
hand-me-downs—while giving our newer weapons to the Army
of South Vietnam.[9]

---

[8] One of the reserve officers who saw to it that uncooperative active Army
advisers were removed was Brigadier General William J. Sutton—who was
later called to active duty, promoted to major general, and until recently
served as Chief of the Army Reserve!

[9] It is unrealistic to spend $1,261 million in FY 1971 to maintain an Army
National Guard and Reserve force of 660,000 men of whom 568,700 were non-
prior-service personnel serving in paid drill status. An additional 39,537 active
military and civilian personnel were required to support these inexperienced
forces. Yet during the Vietnam War only 17,415 Army Reserve or National
Guardsmen were involuntarily ordered to active duty to build up the active
forces.

Chapter 7

Favoritism and Neglect

☆ ☆ ☆ ☆ ☆ ☆ ☆ ☆ ☆

Manpower is the Army's most important asset and the one it most misuses. Frequent changes of station are necessary, according to the Army, to expose the soldier to a wide variety of jack-of-all-trades career-rounding experiences and to promote a seldom-achieved bureaucratic ease of operation. Yet the Fitzhugh Commission Report submitted to the President on July 15, 1970, stated, "Officers and enlisted men are rotated among assignments at much too frequent intervals. It is clear from the evidence that the rotation practices which have been followed result in (a) excessive and wasteful cost, (b) inefficiencies in management and (c) difficulty in fixing responsibility."

Misusing People

Vietnam is a prime example of manpower mismanagement. Manpower demands could have been reduced if the number

and size of headquarter and support commands had been restricted to an austere minimum. Fewer rotations would have
been needed if career officers and noncommissioned officers
had been required to serve a single term of eighteen months instead of two separate one-year tours. Tours of soldiers serving
in noncombatant assignments should also have been extended
beyond one year. Only combat soldiers should have been rotated after one year. A shorter tour for combat service would
have provided an incentive for combat duty and a fair reward
for those who risked their lives.

Officers and NCO's should not have been permitted to volunteer for Vietnam while serving in another overseas area. For
career reasons certain officers serving in Europe have asked to
be assigned to similar command or support jobs in Vietnam and
have been moved before their tours were ended. The government and the American taxpayer have had to move the officer,
his family, car, and household goods back to the United States
and then send another officer and family to Europe to replace
the first officer. The taxpayer also pays for relocating the first
officer's family in the United States. Storage and/or shipment
of the household goods of military personnel being rotated between assignments cost the taxpayer $350 million in 1970.

This constant moving about is even more costly in human
terms. It has contributed to the disruption of the morale and
family life of many members of the Army. Insecurity and lack
of roots have manifested themselves in an increasing number of
divorces and broken homes. The soldier can never stay in one
place long enough to build up any form of estate or future for
his family beyond life insurance and a hoped-for retirement.
Too frequently, lack of stability in job, environment, and home
and family living combine to produce frustrated, disgruntled
soldiers, dissatisfied wives, and rootless children who hope that
the next move will enable them to escape from a situation that
is oftentimes sure to be repeated. Dissatisfaction with constant
money worries and the frequent separations required by Army
policies are prime reasons many skilled soldiers leave the Army.
Yet these separations are often unnecessary—the soldier is

being sent to fill a busywork job which does not contribute to national defense.

The unending debt in which many military men are constantly embroiled is due in large part to this frequent moving. For the poorly paid lower-ranking soldiers, each move can be a traumatic experience. Although the move is supposedly made in the best interests of the Army it is the soldier who bears a large share of the cost and the inconvenience. The small amount he receives for travel and dislocation allowance (less than fifteen cents per mile for travel expenses of family members over twelve years of age and an additional $105 total for dislocation costs) hardly covers the travel costs. He has the added expense of maintaining his family in a motel or rooming house until he can find some type of low-cost rental housing.[1] This can be very difficult in the United States. Overseas it is not only costly but quite uncomfortable. The soldier can draw up to six months' interest-free advance on his base pay when he receives permanent change-of-station orders, but he must pay this advance back within six months. This means he must manage his finances very carefully during the repayment period. If he is imprudent with his finances this can mean trouble with his commander over unpaid debts. Many young enlisted men have become entrapped in a vicious debt-repayment-debt cycle.

In settling into a new assignment the lower-ranking soldier is frequently forced to accept living conditions which are far below the acknowledged United States poverty level. He is gouged by profit-seeking landlords who rent substandard housing near military bases at far more than its value. I once looked at a concrete-floored garage in Junction City, Kansas, that had been converted into a one-bedroom apartment with the shower

---

[1] The armed services have recently inaugurated a program of building on-post motels to provide low-cost temporary housing. The Army plans to build thirteen motels at a cost of $9.3 million in nonappropriated funds. Unless some action is taken these facilities will be used chiefly by higher-ranking officers and NCO's. These are exactly the Army members that can best afford temporary civilian accommodations. It is the lieutenants and sergeants (E-5) and lower ranks who most need this type of accommodation. In these low-cost motels the old Army motto of RHIP (Rank Has Its Privileges) should not apply.

next to the kitchen stove. The monthly rent was $105 per month excluding utilities. (My quarters allowance was $102.60.) When I remarked that the rent seemed high for a partially converted garage, the landlord replied, "Well, if you don't take it, someone else will 'cause there's a new batch of you soldiers coming in next week and there just ain't that many places around here to live." Overseas, the low-ranking married soldier, who does not qualify for government-furnished quarters, fares even worse. A young Puerto Rican corporal whom I once visited in a small village near Nancy, France, was living with his wife and two children in one room. A cheap pink curtain had been strung up to divide the sleeping and living area. One bare light bulb provided light for the entire room. In one corner was a small kerosene stove, which provided the heat and cooking facilities for the family. The bath was in another corner and consisted of a washbasin with a cold-water tap. A pipe protruding from the wall and dripping into a metal floor stand was the shower. The toilet was an outhouse located about twenty yards from the back door. The few odds and ends of furniture had been purchased from the local Army salvage depot. The rent was the equivalent of $90 per month. Yet the soldier considered himself lucky. Finding this place allowed him to have his wife and children with him while he served for three years as a warehouseman. Four months after he finished living in these slum conditions he was killed in Vietnam. Near Orléans, France, I saw black soldiers and their families living in barns around the tiny village of St. Jean de Braye, while the soldiers served as laborers at the U.S. Army logistical headquarters.

Dr. Fletcher Hamilton of the 130th Army General Hospital in Nürnberg, Germany, is quoted in a Reuter News dispatch of January 21, 1971, as saying that thousands of Army enlisted men stationed in Europe are living in poverty. He stated that low pay and lack of resources have led to a significant number of nervous breakdowns among GI's. Fletcher said the low-ranking enlisted men could not afford to bring their wives to Europe. He added, "A lot of the breakdowns are directly attributable to the fact that the G.I. is here without his family, or if here, the marriage is in serious trouble because the soldier has to live in a constant state of poverty and indebtedness."

Both overseas and in the United States the Army tells the soldier where he can't live. It does little to help him manage to live decently unless he happens to hold sufficient rank to qualify for on-base government quarters. The bulk of the pay raises have been in base pay, which has gone to those who have sufficient rank to warrant government quarters. Quarters allowances were raised in November 1971 for the first time in over ten years. The lower-ranking soldier has continued to go into debt to be with his family.

As far as officers are concerned, a Fitzhugh Commission staff study of Army, Navy, and Air Force promotions to general and flag-officer rank in 1969 showed the following situation: there were 174 officers in the group and their average service was twenty-four years. These officers had been given 3,695 assignments, or an average of twenty-one per man. Average duration per assignment was fourteen months. Looked at another way, the average officer had spent eight years in operational assignments, five years in service schools and other educational assignments, and eleven years in staff assignments. This is a small sampling of service assignments and rotation policies, but it seems fairly typical of the prevailing career pattern for most officers. For example, I was assigned to a mortar company in Germany for five months, then transferred to the division noncommissioned-officer academy as an instructor for twelve months. Next I was moved to an infantry battalion as an assistant operations officer for five months, before being given command of a rifle company for thirteen months. When that company was ordered home in a rotation plan called "Gyroscope" I was returned with it to maintain "continuity of command." [2]

---

[2] Gyroscope was a 1956 Army experiment under which divisions were to be rotated regularly between Europe and fixed United States posts. In theory it was expected to provide a degree of stability for career soldiers. In practice it resulted in the unnecessary movement of thousands of soldiers. This movement created countless hardships for many soldiers and their families, and cost the taxpayer thousands of dollars. It also reduced combat-readiness. The rifle company I brought home from Europe was part of a division that had been rated

Within four months I was on orders to infantry school. After nine months of schooling I was sent to Dallas, Texas, as an Army Reserve adviser. Twenty months later I left that assignment to attend a six-month Spanish-language course before being returned to Europe to serve on a general staff in France (where I had to learn French).

This system of rotation leads inevitably to deficiencies in management. An officer or NCO simply does not remain assigned long enough to learn his job thoroughly, become familiar with the people working for him, set attainable goals, and make plans for carrying the work through to a successful conclusion. In combat situations it means that the officer or NCO frequently does not have time to know his own troops well, is inexperienced in local combat techniques, the past characteristics and tactics of enemy troops, and the climate and terrain over which his troops are fighting. Another consequence, as the Fitzhugh Report points out, is that officers and NCO's are often automatically moved out of assignments at a critical point in the job. Frequently this move is dictated by the career needs of the incumbent officer and is accomplished before a replacement arrives to assume the job.

Present rotation policy not only fails to provide skilled experienced management and leadership, but, as the Fitzhugh Commission has found, "has deficiencies in accomplishing its stated purpose—the development of the officer himself. Men are not developed by being observers, they must have responsibility to assure growth." Through a process of constant change of job and environment a soldier is encouraged to do no more than learn the rudiments of his job. He then coasts until he is moved to another job where he repeats the process.

"Opportunity for promotion provides the motivating force and greatest incentive for the military officer," according to the

---

the most combat-ready in the Seventh Army, but before returning home it was reorganized and filled with soldiers ready for discharge. When we finally arrived at our stateside post the division had less than 50 percent of its authorized manpower, weapons, vehicles, and communication equipment. Despite the fact that this made it ineffective for combat, it was listed by the Pentagon as one of the Army emergency back-up divisions for general war.

Fitzhugh Report. In today's Army, this is unfortunately quite true. It was not the motivation for the Marshalls, Eisenhowers, and Bradleys of the pre-World War II Army. Those soldiers wanted to render service to their fellow citizens and their country. Yet today nearly all Army personnel programs and policies are geared to the concept of rapid promotion as an incentive for service in the Army. Such slogans as "Up or Out" for officers and "Promotions Come As Fast As You Handle Them" for enlisted men emphasize promotion as the motivation for service. This is admittedly a more realistic sales pitch for wartime than for peace. According to Pentagon figures published by the United Press International, in 1960 it took an Army officer thirty-three years and two months to move from second lieutenant to full colonel. But at the 1970 promotion rates, an officer might be able to move from second lieutenant to full colonel in thirteen years and four months.

Almost from the time he is commissioned, an officer begins to worry about the "image" he is presenting on his efficiency reports. These reports are a vital part of the promotion process. They are drawn up annually, or whenever an officer or his rater is transferred. Up until the early 1960s each career branch kept what was known as an OEI (officer efficiency index) on each officer. This OEI was a numerical rating which reflected the accumulated score the officer had achieved on his efficiency reports. Officers holding OEI's above 130 were considered superior officers and given the choicest assignments and advanced schooling. Those with ratings between 115 and 130 were considered as "quality" officers. The below average group had OEI's under 115. If an officer received a low numerical rating on *one* report there was a good chance that his OEI would drop to a point that he could not qualify for good assignments or further schooling, both of which are vital for promotion. To be passed over twice for promotion is to be caught in the "Up or Out" criteria. This has forced some officers out of service after fifteen years even though they had been consistently rated as average.

Unfortunately, an officer has little opportunity to rebut unfa-

vorable allegations on his efficiency report. Indeed, under
Army regulations, he has no automatic right to see his report
unless it contains an unsatisfactory rating. If he wishes to examine his ratings he must visit his career branch in Washington,
D.C., or authorize someone to visit for him. This means that an
officer is at the mercy of a rater who does not even have to face
him and tell him what he has done wrong. In fact and practice,
all a rater has to do to blackball an officer for promotion is to
describe him as excellent in the word picture but give him middle scores on the numerical ratings.[3] To recount a personal experience of how the system works—I had been serving in a
noncommissioned-officer academy in Germany for over a year
when I asked the commandant if he objected to my requesting
return to regimental duty. He told me he had no objection and

---

[3] Letters to the Editor, *Army Times* newspaper, January 19, 1970, Fort Bliss,
Texas: "Over one-third of the captains I have known in the past two years are
seriously considering resignation. It is the consensus of opinion among them
that career mismanagement by DA [Department of the Army] and the present
OER [Officer Efficiency Report] systems are the culprits. While some officers
seem to enjoy long tours to choice areas, one right after another, others have
had to endure frequent short tours.

"Due to its inherent inflationary structure, the present OER system allows
any rater or indorser, who so desires, to effectively 'kill' a subordinate's career
by simply rating him what would seem to be average. The rated officer cannot
rebut this rating unless he receives a 5 rating on the report somewhere or a
definite bad comment in the comments section. It is widely known that a long
series of 2's and 3's will do the job and no special justification is required on the
part of the rater to assess these ratings.

"The rated officer has not even got the right to be shown his report before it
is submitted. The rationale behind this ruling is that some raters would be
afraid to show a low report to a subordinate, especially a friend. Are not the
men who lack this intestinal fortitude the type the Army could do well without?

"Has not the time come for the Army to require periodic formal counseling
of junior officers? Should not each rater be made to show the report to the
rated officer? Should not the rated officer be allowed to comment upon and
sign each report? Should not all reports which are above or below standard be
accompanied with documentation, CMMI results, Article 15's, counseling records, etc., instead of a page of vague platitudes?

"DA seems to ask everyone but those involved what changes are needed.
The time has come for DA to survey its junior officers and learn how they feel
on the subject. DA speaks frequently of justice, but my contemporaries and I

signed the request. But when I submitted the request to the division headquarters for final approval, a friend serving in the adjutant general's office told me the commandant had asked them not to approve my transfer because he could not afford to lose my services. I insisted that his signature constituted approval and my transfer was ordered. Before I left, the commandant called me into his office and showed me an efficiency report which rated me as an outstanding officer. A few days later, my friend in the adjutant general's office told me he had received my efficiency report for forwarding to Washington and it was a "kindness"-type report which would lower my OER. I went to his office and looked at the report; it was a completely different report from the one I had been shown. And there was nothing I could do except write a letter alleging the change. The rating remains in my permanent efficiency report file.

If an officer receives an *unsatisfactory* rating, he is given an opportunity to reply in writing to the ratings on the report. But this does him little good since the report still goes into his permanent rating file. The rating and endorsing officers can deliberately "take care" of an officer who is not conforming to the demands of the Army system by writing a so-called kindness report. Most senior officers are well versed in the use of innocent-sounding phrases that give no hint of downgrading to the uninitiated but are instantly recognizable to the personnel report graders as derogatory statements.

Another tactic frequently employed on the OER is to state that the quality in question was merely not observed.[4] This

---

would like to have DA explain where the justice is in an officer finding out, after five or ten years' labors, that he has been retained in grade or passed over due to an efficiency report he never saw or knew about.

"This disaster has not happened to me, yet, but I have seen it ruin the lives of many good men.

"Capt. David G. Skehan

"S-4"

[4] Army raters and endorsers are asked to grade officers, on a scale of 1 to 5, on such diverse qualities as: "AMBITION (*seeks and welcomes, within the bounds of military propriety, additional and more important responsibilities*)," "APPEARANCE," "LOYALTY (*faithful and willing support to superiors and subordinates*)," "MORAL COURAGE (*intellectual honesty, willingness to*

technique, while seemingly harmless, is in fact designed to lower an officer's overall rating because anything "not observed" in army parlance is assumed to be negative. And there are the raters and endorsers who just decide between themselves that an officer under their command needs to be straightened out and set out about doing so by writing comments so derogatory that they ruin his career.

Such a rating system encourages the Army officer to please the man who writes the word picture and fills in the blocks that determine his numerical standing. It enforces conformity by frightening officers at all levels into supporting the views of their immediate superior. Any real or imagined mistake can result in a derogatory rating in the efficiency record and become a bar to future promotion. This means that officers tend to cover up natural errors. As a consequence, a young Army adviser in Vietnam may not feel free to report to his superior rating officer that the situation in his district is steadily deteriorating. To do so would be to admit failure and that failure would be duly noted in his efficiency report. The cover-up at MyLai came as no surprise to anyone familiar with the Army efficiency report system.

The purpose of the rating system should be to factually evaluate demonstrated ability and merit. It should not continue to be based on a secretive process which intimidates more than evaluates. The efficiency report title should be changed to "Duty Evaluation." This evaluation should be rendered in letter form and should be used only to help promotion and assignment boards better understand a soldier's strengths and weaknesses. It should not be used as a final determinant in any personnel action because, as one human's assessment of another, it is susceptible to human error and prejudice.

Another important component in the promotion process is the selection boards. Each officer serves varying periods of "time in grade" before he comes into the "zone of eligibility"

stand up and be counted)," "NON-DUTY CONDUCT (*keeps his personal affairs in order*)," "SELFLESSNESS (*subordinates his personal welfare to that of the organization*)," "SOCIABILITY," "STAMINA," and "TACT."

for selection for promotion. The announcement that a selection board will meet to consider eligible officers for promotion is a time of nervous apprehension for officers who do not have a West Point background, or have not been able to get the right assignments or "ticket punches" to assure selection. Only one who has lived it can understand and appreciate the inward feelings of a man when he learns that a board will meet shortly in Washington to consider whether he will be promoted to a rank he has been dreaming of attaining for years while he has been waiting in grade. Those feelings can be close to panic if he risks being passed over because he has obeyed orders and served in duties that did not count much for promotion. For example, combat-arms officers need a record of at least one successful company- or battery-command tour for promotion from captain to major. But there are more officers than there are company units. Extensive maneuvering through friends or classmates is often necessary if officers are to obtain one of these commands before coming up for promotion.

One of the surest ways to obtain promotion is to be well known to a member of the selection board. Such acquaintance-ship tends to be particularly advantageous if one has an "old Army family name." [5] Selecting officer-promotion boards is by

---

[5] Letter written *Army Times* in February 1971 in response to an article that I had published in that paper:

"Dear Sir:

"If my letter is published I will be amazed. . . .

"First off I am an Army wife—my husband is a Colonel in the U.S. Army and a West Point man. One might have the Academy behind him—but the right people and the right places are more significant. I am inclined to think that the right people on the promotion board help myself. We found this out already. If the name is well known from World War II—you have it made—no questions asked—we all realize this. Check your list for certain names—who cares what he has done, the name is familiar and this is what counts.

"Sincerely,

"An Army Wife."

There are no secrets in the Army about promotions. The promotion boards meet and a list of selected officers is published in official Army circulars and the *Army Times* newspaper. Within hours of their publication everyone on a post knows who made it and who didn't. After a few days the hurt passes for those who didn't make it, but they are marked by their unchanged rank as inferior to

law the prerogative of the Secretary of the Army. But in practice the Army Chief of Staff determines which officers sit on the board and he controls the names of the officers submitted to the board for consideration. This fact of military life has not encouraged criticism or questioning attitudes among Army officers. No member of the officer corps is going to deviate from the views of the Chief of Staff as long as the Chief determines who is to get promoted. The current selection process also weakened civilian control over the Army, as has Congress and the President's perfunctory approval of Army promotion lists. A career officer knows the real power lies with his military Chief of Staff and he usually has been careful to cooperate with the desires and parochial objectives of his service regardless of his personal views.

The ratio of officers to enlisted men is much higher in the United States armed forces today than it was in World War II. In 1969 with a total armed force of 3.5 million men there were 1,338 generals and admirals on active duty, or one general or admiral for every 2,900 servicemen. (The ratio in the U.S. European Command was even higher—one to 2,343 enlisted men.) In World War II with a total armed force of 12 million men there were fewer generals and admirals on active duty. This was also true of colonels and Navy captains. In June 1969 there were 18,277 colonels or captains on duty in the armed forces. On June 30, 1945, there were only 14,898 colonels or captains on duty. In 1969 there were 407,951 officers of all ranks in the armed forces—a ratio of an officer for every eight servicemen. There were at least twice as many noncommissioned officers as officers on duty which means there was one officer or one NCO to supervise every two enlisted men. It is no wonder that NCO's are frustrated at being unable to exercise command. With so many officers as managers, supervisors, and commanders, there is little supervising left for the thousands of NCO's to do.

Many of these officers and enlisted men are assigned to jobs

their contemporaries. As a lieutenant colonel friend said after being twice passed over for colonel, "All my friends are colonels now but me."

as aides, butlers, cooks, chauffeurs, or houseboys for general officers. Others perform administrative or housekeeping duties at bases in Europe and Asia. They are community-relations officials (maintaining relations with a people who speak a language they don't understand) and golf pros, athletic-field supervisors, hobby- and craft-shop supervisors, officer and NCO club managers, post engineers, household-goods clerks, private-automobile registration clerks, dependent-furniture supervisors, post firemen, veterinarians, filing clerks, office-briefing chart makers and artists, messenger boys, mail clerks, photographers and movie cameramen, and maintenance personnel. Over one third of all Department of Defense personnel are involved in maintenance—yet in 1969 the Fitzhugh Commission found the maintenance system "needlessly inefficient and wasteful, and far short of the potential for effectiveness of support of combatant commanders."

A first-class sergeant I knew in the Security Division of the Joint Chiefs of Staff was assigned to Germany as a household goods and furniture supervisor. He was responsible for storage and movement of incoming and outgoing household goods of other soldiers being rotated to and from Germany. To enable the sergeant to perform this noncombatant duty the government transported his wife and six children to Germany by air. It shipped their car and a part of their household goods there and provided a special school, post exchange, and commissary system for his family and the thousands of other dependents. One officer friend was shipped with his wife and four children to Frankfurt, Germany, to serve as a textbook officer in the military-dependent school system. Another went to Munich to become a post billeting officer. He supervised hotel lodging for soldiers visiting the Garmisch recreation area.

Such noncombatant assignments are increasing, partly because each senior Army command is a different general's separate fiefdom. Each command determines and justifies most of its own manpower requirements through manning tables based on job descriptions prepared by each supervisory echelon. These separate job descriptions are consolidated by the com-

mand personnel office and used by the commanding general as
the basis for manpower requests. These manpower requests
must be approved by a general at a higher level of command
but such approval is usually automatic. The higher-ranking
commander is a friend, classmate, or fellow graduate from
West Point. Few staff officers want to risk their careers by encouraging their commander to turn down another general's request—they are too likely to be caught in the middle between
two old classmates.

Each command is subjected to periodic "manpower utilization surveys" by teams from higher headquarters. But these
teams work under two limitations: (1) if they report too many
unsatisfactory manpower practices in a subordinate command
they will cause their own command level to look bad because it
has failed to prevent the unsatisfactory conditions; and (2) if
they report too many discrepancies they risk antagonizing the
local commanding general by making him appear negligent in
his command supervision—this may result in his calling the
higher commander and complaining about their performance.

The pressure for additional jobs often begins at the supervisor level. For example, suppose an aggressive, ambitious colonel takes charge of a staff section or a support command. He is
aware that the way to higher rank is to be known as one who
gets things done while supervising a large number of workers.
He sets out to expand his mission. Broadening the scope of his
mission gives him justification for additional manpower. He has
his subordinates make up job descriptions to justify a larger
staff. These he has approved by personnel specialists and
passed up the chain of command for approval by higher-ranking officers who also are interested in expanding the mission of
their command. If the expanded mission proves insufficient to
keep the new workers busy, they will generate reports from
subordinate commands to occupy their time. Busywork will be
created to justify the continued existence of their jobs and possibly a further expansion of the work force. Converting to an
all-volunteer army or civilianizing more military jobs will do little to reduce manpower requirements or improve efficiency if
the Army continues to waste personnel in superfluous jobs.

One reason why no Army member seriously questions the need for additional manpower in headquarter and support commands is because it fits with the oft-stated Army mission of providing the "best" for its soldiers. If some outside agency like the General Accounting Office inspects a command and attempts to find out its true manpower needs, it will be vigorously resisted. I remember a mission and manpower survey conducted by the GAO on the Joint U.S. Military Group/Military Assistance Group in Spain. Members of the advisory group were told before the survey to appear to be cooperative with the inspectors, but not to reveal anything regarding the scope of the visits made to Spanish Army units. Only favorable reports were left in the files and records of man hours devoted to military advisory duties were falsified to reflect more hours than were actually being spent with the Spanish units. After the GAO report was filed the entire advisory group spent many hours attempting to discredit the unfavorable portions which recommended reducing the size of the advisory group. No consideration was given to the possibility of accepting the report and no evaluation was made of the unfavorable findings.

Sterile Education

One reason the Army has had problems with its privates is that they don't trust the noncommissioned and commissioned officers. If the Army is going to improve its leadership, it must first improve professional education. The Army career-school system should start trying to stimulate imaginative, creative thinking rather than enforcing World War II dogma. Student individuality should be recognized and encouraged. Faculty members should be more carefully chosen for teaching ability. Officer education should be made more relevant to existing and probable future roles of the Army. Instruction in long-range planning techniques should begin to take more cognizance of the intangible limitations that are imposed on an Army planner by such domestic civilian problems as inflation, urban decay, deficit spending, poverty, and so on. The officer student should learn early in his career that he cannot ignore such considerations. He can no longer assume that America can and will make available whatever he decides is necessary to accomplish an Army mission. The career-education process should stress austere organization and operation of the Army.

The place to start educational improvement is at the pre-commissioning level. For example, West Point has become an educational anachronism—a second-rate engineering school. It is too costly a way to produce a second lieutenant. For example, West Point's operating costs in FY 1972 have been estimated by the Department of Defense at $57,551,000. According to the Department of the Army each FY 1972 West Point graduate will cost the taxpayer $53,200—as compared to $12,800 for an ROTC scholarship officer (computed at the approximate national average college cost of $2,000 per year for four years plus $1,200 per year ROTC student scholarship allowance).

West Point perpetuates the old-boy syndrome of favored, clique leadership which has insulated the Army from reform. Most of the instructors hold only master's degrees (while civilian Ph.D.'s are unemployed) and teach only a few years before being rotated to other Army duties. Qualifying these officer instructors in the disciplines they teach is also costly to the citizen. For example, two or three West Point graduate captains or majors are assigned to the universities of Madrid, Heidelberg, and Paris each year. These officers are shipped to the school at taxpayer expense with their families, private car, and household goods so they can learn a language which they will teach at West Point for two or three years and then in all probability never use again. At the same time the Army trains other officers to speak the same languages in the Defense Language Institutes on the east and west coasts of the United States. Why couldn't West Point language instructors also be trained at the Defense Language Institute? Or why couldn't qualified civilian language teachers have been hired to teach permanently at West Point?

The inbred characteristic of the West Point graduate is produced by the narrow viewpoint of the military faculty. Allegiance to the Army is stressed above all else, whereas a broad liberal-arts education could produce the creative thinkers so desperately needed by that Army. Such thinkers could be obtained through civilian college and university scholarship programs that would require a smaller overall investment in tax dollars. For years the Marine Corps has successfully used a civilian scholarship program to obtain most of its career officers. The Army could do the same and save the costs that accrue to the taxpayer in keeping West Point open. Students selected for four-year government-paid military scholarships at civilian institutions could be given as much military training as is presently received by West Point cadets. For example, the scholarship students could attend ROTC classes during the school year, receive intensive military training at Army summer camps, and attend the basic officer-training course. An officer commissioned under the scholarship program might be required to serve five years of active duty after graduation. If he showed outstanding academic aptitude he could be granted an additional one-year scholarship to complete a master's degree. Under such a program the Army would gain the benefit of the officer's advanced studies as soon as he entered active duty and the taxpayer would be spared the extra cost of returning an officer to college in mid-career when his salary is higher and he has a family to move.

The Army officer career-school system also needs to be reorganized. Career schooling is predicated on a long-standing assumption that all officers must be trained to assume higher command responsibilities in time of emergency and full mobilization. Such an educational system has ensured that an officer has either forgotten the training he received by the time he achieves the rank he has been trained for, or that the training and doctrines he has learned have become obsolete by the time he has an opportunity to apply them. For example, young, newly commissioned second lieutenants are given eighteen weeks of training in how to serve as a company-grade officer. In the infantry this means learning how to be a platoon leader and the rudimentary duties of a company commander. First lieutenants and captains are eligible for a nine-month advanced course on how to be battalion and brigade commanders. Majors or lieutenant colonels may be sent to the Command and General Staff College at Fort Leavenworth, Kansas, to be trained as division general-staff officers and as two-star division commanders, three-star corps, or four-star Army commanders. Only a small fraction of these officers will years later attain such commands. Such an educational system is not only unrealistic, it ignores the growing reservoir of relatively young retired generals and colonels available for recall in the event of full mobilization. These men already have the knowledge that the Army is so feverishly trying to instill each year in lower echelons of officers.

The current training system encourages conformity. The student slogan at the Command and General Staff College is "Cooperate and graduate." Course work is centered on faculty-prepared "school solutions" to tactical problems. The student quickly learns that if he wants to receive a top grade and rank high in his class standings (and this influences his chances of attending the War College) he must feed back the recommended solution taught by the school. In the final division offensive-tactics map exam that I took at the Command and General Staff College there was a situation that the school solution had said called for the use of nerve gas. Not to have applied this instruction would have resulted in a grade-cut on the exam. So despite the fact that I disliked the idea of using gas in an offensive role, I, along with the rest of the class, got out my gas kit and made the necessary calculations to wipe out an enemy division in Europe with nerve gas.

This fetish with standardized responses means that an enemy commander can quickly learn what nearly any U.S. Army division, corps, or Army commander will do under a given set of circumstances. It also discourages innovative thinking which does not conform to stereotyped military faculty war-gaming and lesson planning. This method of career schooling has been a major cause of the Army's inability to recognize the problems and come up with creative solutions to its dilemma in Indochina.

Another problem is the quality of the instructors and the content of the courses at all levels of the career-school system.

Instructors are not selected on the basis of educational background or teaching ability. They receive their assignments because they have a high efficiency report record and are rated as "comers." Civilian educators hired on long-term contracts could do a much better job than most of the Army officers who are rotated in and out of their teaching positions. Also, civilian instructors could expose the student officer to the thinking and priorities of the civilian society he is sworn to defend. The career officer has too frequently been forced to spend most of his adult life in military ghettos in civilian communities near Army posts, or on bases in the United States and overseas. He is often out of touch with the problems of the civilian community or feels unable to voice his concerns because of his status as an officer. Yet the bulk of the training courses deal with nuts-and-bolts tactical problems. Only slight attention is given to broad reading and mind-developing study. Little emphasis is given to foreign policy, socioeconomics, international political-military affairs, or domestic priorities or problems. These subjects are reserved for surface coverage by the Army War College, despite the fact that many graduates of the Command and General Staff College go directly to assignments in which they need a broad knowledge of these and other nontactical fields. Even the tactical courses are frequently patterned on World War II concepts of battle in Europe.

Many school solutions to tactical problems are of questionable practicality. The Leavenworth solution to an offensive mechanized-division map problem in Central Europe was to send a mechanized brigade over the summit and along the length of a hill heavily forested with pine trees. When the class protested that such an attack would be inordinately slow because the armored personnel carriers would have to knock down the trees to advance, the instructor answered that this was true but faculty war-gaming has shown it to be the best route. He laughingly admitted that as an armored officer he personally would look for a less difficult route. He cautioned us that "we would see this one again" (a CGSC instructor's way of telling a class that a certain point would appear on a later exam).

The noncommissioned officer, like the commissioned officer, needs a career-school system which educates him for his military duties, while developing his potential as a leader in daily contact with the soldiers of today's Army. Education of the Army noncom is presently a haphazard, hit-or-miss affair. Some of the young NCO's are given six to eight weeks of instruction at NCO academies or leadership schools set up by division or Army area commands. The curricula at these schools will vary, depending on the idiosyncrasy of the particular commander, but for the most part are predominantly troop-leading procedures, weapons employment, and small-unit tactics. Not all NCO's receive this very basic leadership training. Those above the rank of platoon sergeant receive no formal education or professional training. They are expected to have learned their trade on the job. This sounds more realistic than it actually is. Since most senior NCO's change assignments every two or three years, they do not have an opportunity to gain in-depth training through on-the-job experience. They must educate themselves through years of trial and error. As a consequence, the NCO is often looked on by the soldiers he must lead as a reactionary "lifer" who can do nothing more productive because of his limited education. Yet lack of skill in a particular job is often partly due to frequent reassignments, which cause an NCO to appear less competent than he actually is.

What is needed is a career-education program which would train corporals through platoon sergeants as troop leaders and enable sergeants first class and above to gain an education in higher-level management and administrative skills. This would allow the NCO to assume broader responsibility and release more costly commissioned personnel from many of their present administrative duties. One of the goals of such a program should be to broaden the perspectives of the NCO as to the mission of the Army and its role in American society. As much time should be devoted to the development of the man and his intellectual grasp as to sharpening his professional skills. His increased educational development will be of more overall benefit to the Army over the years than the possession of one or two narrow skills.

Lock Step Training

The Army is still using the World War II training-center format as the basis for training its soldiers. It is not the best or most economical way to train. Under this system, the Continental Army Command (CONARC) and four Army area-command headquarters supervise the operation of five reception-training centers located throughout the country.[6] Young men entering the Army take the symbolic step forward in dingy recruiting offices or armed forces induction stations. Then they board planes or buses for the trip to one of the five training centers. There they are issued new Army green uniforms and fatigues and taken to hear martial music and a "welcoming speech" by a field-grade or general officer. Later they will receive another welcome by the commander of the training battalion and finally a speech by the captain or lieutenant commanding the training company to which they are assigned. The new soldiers then settle down to eight weeks as a faceless number in an assembly-line process that pushes them relentlessly through repetitive, fear-motivated training classes. The new soldier is passed from the training control of one committee after another and with each one he is subjected to a monotonous yet confusing and exhausting schedule which stresses that he must remember all that he is being taught or he will fall victim to an enemy bullet in combat.

His instructors are frequently young sergeants or lieutenants who are still learning troop-leading procedures and have little practical Army experience. Few experienced officers or non-commissioned officers willingly serve in training centers, where the hours are long, the work boring, and the career rewards meager. For that reason the Army has to assign sergeants involuntarily to "volunteer" jobs as drill sergeants. Some instructors teach about weapons they have fired only once or not at all and lecture on tactics that they frequently learned about from

---

[6] Forts Dix (New Jersey), Jackson (South Carolina), Leonard Wood (Missouri), Ord (California), Polk (Louisiana).

reading a "canned" lesson plan in the BOQ the night before the class. Most of the officers and NCO's, from the commanding general to the three-stripe buck sergeant committeemen, are living for the day they get their orders to leave the training center. (The young soldiers undergoing the training are living for the same thing.) Such a training cadre is unable to indoctrinate homesick young men with much belief in either the Army's concern for their welfare or the value of their services.

The recruit is marched to closely adjacent classes and motored to those that are far enough from the barracks to tire him if he had to march (centralized CONARC training schedules don't allocate training time to marching, this is supposed to be accomplished on "company commander time"—since few company commanders relish five-mile road marches, little marching gets done). At each class a sergeant or lieutenant tells a dirty joke (to "loosen up the students"), or "motivates" them by telling a war story about what dire consequences will result if they don't pay attention. Occasionally a firecracker is thrown among them to gain attention.

After seven weeks of studying charts, watching training films, firing at pop-up targets on the rifle range, fearfully throwing live hand grenades, negotiating muddy or brick-hard infiltration courses shouting his lungs out that the bayonet is to "Kill! Kill! Kill!" and experiencing nighttime harassment by cadremen, the recruit goes to "bivouac in the field." [7] For a week he sleeps on the ground and learns a few of the rudiments of squad tactics. Then he returns to camp to take a proficiency test. If he passes this test (and few fail because the company commander and committee chiefs who have conducted the training will all be held responsible by senior commanders if over 10 percent fail), he will have successfully completed basic training and will be permitted to go home for leave before beginning advanced individual training. He has received practically no effective training in how to operate in the dark, which

<hr>

[7] Nearly every training-center company commander has had recruits "freeze" on the grenade range because they were too frightened to throw a live grenade. Much of this fear comes from scare-type instruction.

is one of the reasons the American soldier has often been unduly fearful of night operations.

During the eight weeks of basic training the recruit has been more confused than trained. He has learned to overly fear combat (particularly mines and booby traps) and most of the weapons he must fire. His excessive fear arises in part because of the inexperience and exaggeration of his instructors. He has learned to obey almost any order for fear of punishment if he does not. Too many soldiers look back on their training as a period of harassment during which they were depreciated as soldiers and degraded as human beings. The buck private often feels he is a helpless number on the mindless conveyor belt of a huge monolithic "Green Machine" that moves him relentlessly toward danger, seemingly without any logical purpose. He may begin to doubt the Army's sincerity, or become convinced that it is hopelessly inefficient. In any event his initial impressions of the Army have been formed. In too many instances those impressions disgust and disillusion him to the point where he decides either to tolerate his service skeptically, doing only what he must, or actively to resist further service. Too often the new soldier leaves basic training hating the Army he initially desired to serve. I do not believe this is the fault of the soldier, but rather a failure of training methods.

In advanced infantry training the soldier is forced to fire a bewildering variety of weapons. He will not be given time to master any of them. Many soldiers leave the sixteen weeks of basic and advanced individual training as ill-trained jack-of-all-trades who have to be largely retrained in the first regular unit to which they are assigned. Some have not even been adequately trained in basic soldiering as evidenced by the number who were killed in World War II, Korea, and Vietnam, shortly after being assigned to combat.

One of the reasons the training system is so ineffectual is because it is geared toward mass production of a certain number of soldiers in accordance with the requirements of the centralized CONARC training schedules. Quality is secondary. During the training period, command emphasis is placed on com-

piling impressive statistical records instead of on effectively
training the soldier. Even the final proficiency test is manipulated to make the training appear more effective than it actually is. No real attempt is made to probe the degree of learning
achieved, partly because of the pressure to certify at least 90
percent of the trainees for overseas duty.

This is not only harmful to the trainee but undermines the
integrity of the training cadre. As a training-center company
commander I suspected that my noncommissioned officers
were using "M-1 pencils" to falsify scores made by recruits on
the rifle range and on the proficiency test. The NCO's did this
so our company averages on the training status report to headquarters would compare favorably with that of other companies who were doing the same thing. This widespread cover-up
and cheating was considered essential if one were to survive a
command tour and receive sufficiently high efficiency reports
to stay in the race for promotion. If my NCO's had reported
the actual percentage of recruits who failed to qualify on the
rifle range, both my battalion commander and myself would
probably have been immediately relieved from command. All
company commanders knew this. We all submitted padded
scores and did not question the figures our training NCO's
(usually a college-graduate enlisted man was assigned to this
statistical duty) maintained on the graph-data "training progress chart." This chart was supposed to reflect the amount of
training each soldier had received and whether or not he had
successfully completed it. If one wanted to remain a company
or battalion commander, one's unit training charts had better
show that over 90 percent of the personnel in the unit had satisfactorily completed all scheduled training. If a soldier missed
training because he was on a work detail like kitchen police,
cutting grass, picking up papers and cigarette butts, or "beauti-
fying the area" (digging flower beds, lining up whitewashed
rock sidewalk borders, or other such eyewash), the chart had to
show that he had "made up" the training. His make-up normally consisted of the training NCO marking an X in the
"training completed" box on the graph. If the recruit missed

the class on how to use a rifle grenade for example, it didn't matter—until he was shipped overseas!

Except in periods of full-scale mobilization, it would be less costly and more efficient for the Army to train its recruits, or volunteers, in the regular tactical units where they would spend their first period of service. At present most regular Army units in the United States are maintained at somewhere between 70 to 90 percent of authorized strength. Vacancies in these units are filled by soldiers who have finished advanced individual training. These newly trained replacements must be assimilated and retrained when they join the regular units. Also, they must be moved at government expense from the place where they enter the Army to the basic-training center, from there to the advanced training center, and from there to the regular unit.

If recruits were assigned directly to the regular unit for training this would reduce the cost and disadvantages of moving men about like unappreciated numbers. It would eliminate the need for continuing Army training centers and allow for the reincorporation into combat units of the thousands of regular army personnel now assigned to those centers as cadre. This would eliminate much duplication of effort and allow the regular units to be maintained at full strength. More importantly it would give the new soldier a feeling of belonging and of being part of the defense effort from his first days in the Army. It would also remove him from the automated, dehumanizing assembly-line feeling that permeates the average training center.

A new soldier should enter the Army at an area reception station, where he could be administratively processed into the Army. During his brief one- or two-day stay in this station, he should begin to be indoctrinated on why he serves and how that service relates to the hopes and aspirations of his fellow citizens and the priorities of the country. He should begin to receive fundamental training in the history, customs, and traditions of the U.S. Army. He should not be required to perform work details during the time he is in this station, nor should he be formally and completely sworn into the Army. Entry into the U.S. Army should not be relegated to a perfunctory group oath routinely administered by some unconcerned field-grade officer. A soldier should be sworn into the Army after he has completed a period of rigorous training that qualifies him for entry. The ceremony, like those of baptism and marriage, should be sufficiently memorable to impress the new soldier with the importance of his service and the value his fellow citizens and the Army attach to it. Such a ceremony should be conducted in the presence of his fellow soldiers, his friends, and his family. Its central theme should be that entry into the Army is an earned responsibility of citizenship and an accomplishment the soldier can be proud of.

PART III

Chapter 8

Some Outgrowths
of the Problems

☆ ☆ ☆ ☆ ☆ ☆ ☆ ☆ ☆

Under technocratically oriented leadership the Army's emphasis has shifted from individualism to the team player and centralized control from Washington. The subsequent downgrading of individual dignity, and the dehumanizing effect this has
had on all soldiers, has played a large part in converting the
Army from a close-knit society into a depersonalized big business. All levels in the Army have felt helpless to do anything to
stop the growing centralization of power and relegation of field
commanders and middle managers to the roles of buckpassers.
The foot soldier who does most of the doing and dying has been
increasingly ignored by the management. Soldiers have come to
distrust the established channels of complaint against grievances because these channels have become the tools of management. The Army Inspector General is charged first with

protecting the reputation of the Army and second with reporting and correcting discrepancies and grievances. The chaplains' corps is called the "Establishment's Pillow" by young GI's because all too often the chaplain is more an agent of the commander than the comforter of the soldier. Like other officers, he too wants a high efficiency rating. The chaplain of the 11th Armored Regiment, under the command of Colonel George S. Patton III, prayed "for wisdom to find the bastards and strength to pile on," to back up his commander's motto of "Find the bastards and pile on." Chaplain-soldier relations would be improved if chaplains did not hold any military rank. An officer's rank separates him from the soldiers he is supposed to serve. Neither should there be permanent chaplains. More of these men should enter the service at varying stages in their civilian careers and serve a few years before returning to civilian life. This form of service could eliminate any tendency for ministers to develop a vested career interest in the military establishment.

The enthusiasm for corporate growth has led the Army away from any serious attempt at austerity into nearly two decades of expanding experimentation carried on in close harmony with the defense industry. This has resulted in an unending race to obtain more and more sophisticated weapons. Part of the motivation has been the soldiers' natural desire for newer and supposedly better weapons with which to fight. Another has been the Army's urge to keep up with the Air Force and the Navy in the battle for defense funds. Still another factor has been the built-in bureaucratic need for self-perpetuation and aggrandizement of mission. And it is for the latter reason that Research and Development (R&D) has become an ever more important part of the Army management structure. Army planning for future operations is heavily influenced by the exotic weapons on the drawing boards of the R&D people.

Tactical organization and doctrines are often written to support the use of certain sophisticated weapons being conceived by Army General Staff planners and the Army Combat Development Command. For example, Army planners working with R&D researchers foresee a need for a tactical vehicle that can meet a certain number of specified "requirements." R&D is then supposed to come up with a creative solution to the requirements they helped create. At this point R&D scientists begin to sketch out the specific capabilities which the new weapon must have. Then these specifications are furnished to defense industries which might be interested in producing such a weapon.

This procedure has gotten the Army involved in such unsuccessful or overly sophisticated ventures as the Nike-Zeus (which was started as the trouble-plagued Nike project in 1944, subsequently became the highly inaccurate Nike-Hercules, and continues today as the erratic Sprint missile in the ABM system), Lacrosse missile, Crawler and Mule land transport vehicles, VTOL (vertical takeoff and landing) aircraft, M-14 rifle (which was quickly replaced by the M-16 that is far more difficult to maintain than the Soviet-made AK-47 but no more lethal), the Cheyenne helicopter, the Sheridan recon vehicle, and the Main Battle Tank. The Sheridan reconnaissance assault vehicle has cost the taxpayer over $1 billion because its four basic "requirements" were predicated more on what armored and airborne officers thought would be nice to have for operations in Europe than on what was actually needed for national defense.[1] This vehicle hasn't functioned at all well in the jungles of Vietnam (the first official report listed 345 deficiencies), performs poorly in desert tests, and is unsuitable for places like Alaska, yet the Sheridan continues to cost the taxpayer roughly $100 million a year to develop.

The Main Battle Tank is another example of an oversophisticated gold-plated weapons system. Development of this sixty-ton monster was first shared with the West German Army. When agreement could not be reached on the validity of the "requirements" (the U.S. Army considered certain specifications essential which the Germans with their panzer experience

---

[1] Sheridan has to be able to ford small rivers and streams, be air droppable for airborne operations, have a missile-firing capability, and be able to fire a combustible cartridge. Some officers called it the "hide-a-bed" because it was neither a decent tank nor a decent missile launcher.

of World War II thought superfluous), the Germans withdrew. The Army has continued to work on this "dream tank" of the 1970s, although there are serious problems with its gun turret and fuel consumption. The high silhouette is undesirable because it makes a better target for enemy gunners and there have been widespread differences of opinion as to what is the most suitable type of main armament for the tank. Some have wanted to install the Shillelagh missile system, others (including the Germans) have favored a conventional tank cannon. Despite these problems development goes on toward an unknown production cost now estimated by the Army at over $700,000 per tank (some critics estimate the final cost at nearer to $1 million a tank)—with 324 tanks planned for each of the four active armored divisions. This development is occurring at the same time that serious questions are being raised within some Army circles as to the feasibility of using tanks in future warfare. The possible end of the draft and the accompanying reduction in the proportion of highly educated troops also have important ramifications for a piece of equipment that requires a large number of skilled personnel for its maintenance, without which it will be next to impossible to keep the Main Battle Tank in operation.

The military project manager for the Main Battle Tank probably is aware of all of these problems, but he, like the project manager of the ill-fated Cheyenne helicopter (which is still in the R&D stage despite repeated foul-ups and failures that caused the original production contract to be canceled), will undoubtedly continue to make optimistic predictions regarding eventual production.[2] If he were to state the negative aspects of producing such a costly—and at this point questionable—tank, he would be considered disloyal to the Army and would

---

[2] Since 1964 the Cheyenne helicopter has cost the taxpayer $265,200,000. The Army estimates it will cost an additional $103 million to complete development of the helicopter. Procurement costs for each helicopter are estimated at another $3,900,000. Original plans called for buying 375 models. Yet a recent Seventh Army report indicated that it is very doubtful if the Cheyenne would be effective in accomplishing its primary mission of providing anti-tank protection and gunship fire support for our forces in Europe.

be removed as project manager. The project manager's responsibilities do not include questioning the validity of an Army weapons system. He is charged with managing the weapon through to full production, just as the R&D scientist is charged with developing a weapons system that provides "solutions" to "requirements" generated by different groups of officers pushing varying degrees of vested branch interest. Evaluation of need is secondary to achievement of a new weapon—and career rewards are predicated upon that achievement. There is no incentive to save tax dollars by eliminating either technological gold plating or an entirely unrequired weapons system.

Although the Army has been channeling billions into development of oversophisticated weapons systems, it has spent little on equipment to save the lives of soldiers. It has failed to develop a new helmet that would reduce GI combat deaths resulting from the present World War II helmet. Dr. James Hopkins, a combat surgeon in World War II, has done extensive research on helmet and armored-vest protection. He claims 15,000 soldiers' lives could have been saved in Vietnam by better head and body protection. Colonel Charles J. Horn, an Army researcher, has been quoted as saying, "We're searching for the 'optimum helmet,' we want a helmet that has everything—light weight, good fit, and best protection possible." Dr. Hopkins says, "The Army really doesn't care. They have so many men available for replacements, it's just a numbers game with them." The American soldier still goes into battle carrying a 1914-style metal canteen and canteen cup that rattle enough to give his movement away while on patrol and make seating in vehicles difficult. The canteen catches on the turret hatch of tanks and armored vehicles, making his entry and exit dangerous. While money and research personnel are being squandered on developing heavily armored tanks, there has not been enough interest to develop an effective lightweight suit of body armor for the combat GI who still fights with only the protection of a fatigue jacket or wears a heavy, hot, ineffective armored vest designed during the Korean War. The GI is given no special way to carry his hand grenades, so he carries them into battle in a sack or his pocket where the safety pins either get bent and are difficult to pull before arming or work loose and explode, killing or maiming him. Frequently he attaches grenades to his belt or shirt pocket flaps where they, along with his cumbersome steel helmet, bounce off as soon as he begins to run and maneuver under enemy fire.

The soldier eats his meals in the field out of a World War II-styled metal "mess kit" or "meat can" that ensures that the food is mixed together like slop and will be cold when eaten no matter how hot it was when served. And this happens in a decade when prepackaged, self-contained food service has become a byword. The heavy ammunition that the Army now fires in such abundance must be hand-moved by soldiers or locally hired stevedores from the ship to the gun that fires it—and this occurs in an age of containerized shipment of heavy materials. But there has not been sufficient R&D money or personnel to develop solutions to these mundane requirements of United States soldiers.

Yet the theory of "nothing is too good for our boys" has been the reasoning behind Congress' almost unlimited allocation of tax dollars to development and production of weapons. The Army has used this catch phrase to accumulate complex equipment and electronic gadgets that require more of "the boys" to maintain and repair. Such gadgetry includes a mind-numbing number of complex radio sets, electronic detection devices (that seldom work), and jeeps and trucks with automatic transmissions (which are less efficient under combat conditions than regular standard transmissions and require more maintenance). Procurement of complex equipment has been a major reason why the logistic-support tail of the Army has grown to the point where it now wags the whole Army by consuming over 60 percent of the total manpower. Instead of improving Army mobility as claimed, this overly sophisticated equipment has actually reduced overall mobility by creating a need for a large, vulnerable rear-area supply and maintenance-support structure. Under current Army doctrines and standards it is essential that this support infrastructure be in position before large-scale combat operations can be undertaken. The crash construction of the huge Cam Ranh Bay logistic-support base was essential before U.S. Army combat power could be used in Vietnam. This is not a favorable indication of the Army's ability to wage a mobile war in the absence of, or any distance from, large fixed logistic-support complexes.

Army officers have worked in close cooperation with representatives from defense industries in the development and production of new weapons. I have seen this system in operation for many years and on one occasion in Spain I participated in it. In our United States military advisory group contingency planning it was considered desirable that the Spanish Army have a mechanized capability. The Spanish were very much in favor of this idea, but the problem was how to find the money to buy the Armored Personnel Carriers (APC's) and get the trained personnel to operate and maintain them. Solving this problem became my responsibility. The manufacturer responded most cordially to inquiries regarding the possible sale of M-113 carriers to the Spanish. United States military assistance funds would pay the manufacturer's price for the APC's and as part of the sales package the manufacturer would send over a technical team to instruct the Spanish in maintenance techniques. Military-assistance funds would finance the training of additional Spanish technicians in the United States. Shortly before the Army Materiel Command negotiated the contract for the package, a sales representative of the company arrived in Madrid with charts, brochures, and a sales pitch (in English) extolling his product. I was assigned to translate the material into Spanish and present it to the Spanish Central General Staff.

Afterward I was invited to the company representative's plush suite at the Castellana Hilton Hotel for drinks, taken to dinner at one of Madrid's most exclusive restaurants (where the bill was more than I earned in a day as a major in the Army), and noncommittally asked what I planned on doing after I retired from the Army. The representative's affluence was most impressive—almost overwhelming—to a thirty-three-year-old major earning less than $800 a month. I was flattered to be part of such a seemingly important international effort in "defense" of my country. There was a feeling of power about the negotiations that obscured the fact that the armored personnel carriers would contribute little to the defense of the United States. My first suspicion that all of the seemingly important briefings, conferences, and contract meetings might not really be in the best interest of my fellow citizens arose when I had an opportunity to read the contract and discover that the defense company was collecting an extra $30,000 sales commission from the United States Government for the work I had done in "selling" the Spanish Army on buying the armored carriers. When I mentioned this to one of the GS-15 Department of the Army civilians whom Army Materiel Command had sent to Spain on temporary duty to assist in settling the contract, I was given a patronizing look and told that was the way "these things are always written."

A year later when I was assigned as a Spanish-language briefing officer at a display of the most modern United States manufactured weapons, radios, and electronic equipment, I was not so naïve about the purposes of military assistance to our allies. A C-130 transport plane flew in from Germany loaded with some of the latest models of U.S. Army weapons and equipment. About sixty Spanish-speaking United States soldiers accompanied the equipment as demonstrators. This large team stayed in Madrid for a week while another Spanish-speaking United States officer and myself briefed group after group of high-ranking Spanish Army officers on the advantages of American equipment. As one senior United States general put it, "This will sure as hell whet their appetites for some of this new equipment." It did. The problem was who would pay for it. To record the event for posterity, the U.S. Army Signal Corps flew a special movie team to Madrid to film the entire operation. This, of course, was also at the taxpayers' expense.

It became clear to me that an Army officer is not normally prepared by background or training to mix with defense contractors without being unduly overawed by their affluence and their pseudo-friendly attitude. The officer's primary motivation is career promotion. His orientation is toward accomplishing set objectives as a means of personal recognition. He is not oriented toward profit-making. In fact, he is accustomed to living on an income which does not permit him many luxuries. The seemingly incredible affluence of the defense contractor tends to impress him. The promise that he might be able to join this affluent way of life after he retires is often a powerful incentive to be cooperative and friendly in contract negotiations. And the contractor plays on the officer's tendency to be a "doer" who wants to "get things done," and see a project through to an early and successful conclusion, no matter what the cost. The military officer is inclined to be trusting of the motives of those with whom he works; he automatically assumes that the defense contractor is motivated primarily by a desire to defend America. Though this is undoubtedly true to some extent, the contractor has frequently been able to use the trusting naïveté of the military officer to serve the profit motives of the defense corporation.

The wide disparity between the motivation, working principles, and life-styles of the officer and the defense contractor has been a contributing factor to the imbalance in defense-procurement practices. The ultimate justification for all Army procurement practices is the extent of the so-called threats to United States security. Where do these threats come from? The obvious answer is that they are posed by Soviet or Chinese Communists. This is only partly true. The intelligence establishment receives information from a variety of sources such as earth-orbiting satellites, spy planes, paid informers, agents, military attachés, travelers, foreign diplomats, and others. These data are assimilated and then evaluated to determine their impact on national security. This evaluation is made by military officers or career civilian employees, who are influenced by their job situation. The military officer must respond to the desires of his service if he has any hope of advancing in his career. The civilian employee knows he will incur the displeasure of his superiors if he habitually downgrades the "threat" that the intelligence he evaluates is supposed to present. All of this is particularly true of the operation of the Defense Intelligence Agency and to some extent of the Central Intelligence Agency.

Consequently it is the custom of the intelligence and defense establishment to accept the worst possible case analysis as the parameters of the threat that the United States must normally defend against. They do this because it is often easier to evaluate intelligence in this way and it eliminates any possibility of underestimating the dangers. It is the intelligence officer's way of covering his ass. It also frequently suits the budget objectives of the Department of Defense to overestimate a potential threat to the national security.

When the Soviet-assisted construction of a fishing port at Cienfuegos, Cuba, took on the characteristics of a possible submarine base in 1967, this was not considered a particularly important threat. Yet in 1970–71, when the Navy was battling to maintain the size of its carrier force and trying to get more money to modernize the fleet, this same threat suddenly took on ominous proportions. By this time the Navy desk officer who had handled the "threat" in 1967 was close to promotion and he was not at all inclined to state that the threat from Cienfuegos was no worse in 1970 than it had been in 1967. In keeping with the worst possible case analysis, the threat of a Communist uprising in Peru in 1967 was the basis for the U.S. Army sending forty additional 105mm. howitzers to the Peruvian Army. The threatened insurgency proved to be mostly illusionary, but the U.S. Army advisers who had foretold the threat, and the Army officer in DIA who embellished on it, both achieved improved efficiency reports for their good work in curbing Communist expansion—while improving U.S. Army relations with the Peruvian Army.

Threats based on the worst case analysis have all too frequently been used to rationalize the procurement of oversophisticated weapons. The worst case analysis should be replaced by a more realistic assessment of the potential enemy's capabilities. This assessment should be used to determine the validity of strategic-force deployments as well as defensive-weapons requirements. To do otherwise is to deceive the American people.

Another matter which has traditionally been handled in a deceptive manner is the status of the Army Reserve and National Guard forces. On August 21, 1970, Secretary of Defense Melvin Laird declared, in a major shift of policy, that National Guard and Army Reserve units—instead of draftees—would be relied upon to back up the regular Army in future emergencies.

Similar statements were made after World War II and the Korean War. The results were disappointing largely because of the great disparity between the declared Army Reserve readiness and the actual state of training and equipment. Increased readiness of National Guard and Army Reserve forces supposedly made it possible for Secretary of Defense Louis Johnson to reduce active forces to skeleton status before the war in Korea. Yet in that war most of these ready-reserve units remained at home while individual reservists and draftees were rushed piecemeal into battle. Of the half dozen Army National Guard divisions called into federal service in 1950, two finally saw combat a year later, after considerable additional training and equipping.

This record did not inhibit another Secretary of Defense from announcing in 1955 that increased Army Reserve readiness would again permit large-scale reduction of active Army forces. The test of this combat readiness came during the Berlin Crisis of 1961. Two Army National Guard divisions were called for emergency duty. Neither was ready for combat despite the fact that they had been repeatedly rated combat ready by a series of regular Army advisers. The advisers had been more interested in keeping local National Guard commanders happy and making themselves look good to their regular Army superior than in reporting the true state of conditions in the National Guard divisions. The result of this cover-up was that a United States President was badly misinformed about the true ability of the Army to respond to crisis. If we are to believe Mr. Laird's statement, the next result of habitually covering up the low state of training and combat readiness of the National Guard and Army Reserve units could be the failure of the Army to fight effectively in defense of national security.

In any event, full reliance on the National Guard for backup of the Active Army in any future general war raises fundamental questions regarding the assigned role and missions of the National Guard. Since 1962 the Army National Guard has been used only for civil disturbances and riot-control purposes. It has not carried out this function very well. To combine the general war–riot-control functions and ignore their dichotomy of purpose could lead to more Kent States. Equipping young, green, marginally trained guardsmen with automatic rifles and then sending them out to control campus disorders shows a lack of reasoning. For one thing, the M-16 rifle is much too lethal for crowd control. The standard Army riot gun is a far more practical weapon for controlling civil disturbances, but despite the fact that the Army has had a large stock of these less lethal weapons in its inventory for years, few have been issued to the guardsmen performing riot-control duty. Like its search for the optimum combat helmet, the Army is continually researching for better riot-control agents, but few, if any, ever reach the hands òf the National Guard troops who need them. It is no answer for the Army to publish information on its research. What is needed is an intermediate response between throwing tear-gas canisters and mowing citizens down with automatic M-16 rifle fire. One possibility is the water cannon, which does not kill and which European security forces have successfully used for years in crowd control.

The Secretary of Defense and the Army should not continue to delude themselves and the American people with the belief that the Army National Guard is equipped or trained to perform a general war role or effectively accomplish the mission of riot control. The lack of substance in such DOD imagery regarding the Reserves is a serious matter. Sporadic training, hand-me-down weapons, and press agentry are not going to prepare the Army Reserve and National Guard to perform an effective role in national defense—and this is about all they have received from the active Army.

Chapter 9

Blueprint for Reform

☆ ☆ ☆ ☆ ☆ ☆ ☆ ☆ ☆

The Army needs reform.

But only public pressure can bring about substantive changes. The habit of protective rationalization and covering up is too strong to be broken by members of the officer corps. It is unrealistic to believe that the military and civilian members of the Army are willingly going to change a system which provides them a comfortable livelihood and a secure retirement. This is the rock upon which internal Army reform has always foundered. Only if it becomes apparent that reform is the way to make "stars" will Army leaders become interested. They have a tendency to get on bandwagons.

Recent attempts at reform have been mostly cosmetic. Top Army leaders still hope to ride out the current wave of discontent by petty bureaucratic vindictiveness and superficial changes. A lack of awareness of the problem was shown by General Westmoreland in his annual Army Posture Statement of March 1971, when he said, "I have made it a personal goal of mine to press home to every leader in the Army—from senior generals down to the newest corporal—the need for absolute honesty and morality in everything they do." He did not mention how he intends to reform the system which today makes it virtually impossible for any officer to practice official honesty and morality and at the same time succeed in the Army.

How can the Army be reformed? How can the nation overcome bureaucratic inertia, as well as the added problem that any criticism of the Army is characterized by some as patriotically suspect if not quasi-treasonable? Obviously there will be obstacles of intrenched service and congressional attitudes that must change before any effective reforms can be made. Here are some reforms that I believe to be essential:

1. A greater effort should be made to guarantee soldiers their First Amendment rights. A soldier should not become a second-class citizen by swearing an oath to defend his country. Perhaps he cannot be given the same broad latitude of expression he enjoyed as a civilian, but there is no justifiable reason to limit his freedom of expression without *substantive* evidence that it adversely affects the good order and discipline of the Army. Soldiers should not be restrained from commenting on matters of concern to ordinary citizens. The Chairman of the Joint Chiefs of Staff, Admiral Moorer, has stated that servicemen must give up some of their freedoms so that others may keep all of theirs. What is the meaning of that remark? If servicemen are to give up any First Amendment rights it should be after thorough review by competent civilian authority, including the courts. It should not be the prerogative of Admiral Moorer or any military officer to express judgments or to limit the exercise of constitutional rights.

The capricious restraint that has been imposed by various military commanders on freedom of expression of soldiers has frequently been unconstitutional. Some soldiers have been vindictively punished for making public comments on national issues. During an Army-sanctioned interview, a Tomb of the Unknown Soldier guard, Sergeant Michael Sanders, commented to a reporter from the *Louisville Courier-Journal,* "It's unfortunate that when people see me here on duty they will associate me with the Vietnam thing. I am very much opposed to our Vietnam involvement and I think so is practically everyone else on duty here." When a copy of the newspaper story was received by Army Chief of Staff General Westmoreland it was "routinely ·investigated" by the commanding general of the Military District of Washington. Sergeant Sanders (who had only eight months of service remaining) was then "routinely" reassigned to duty in Vietnam.

There was, in fact, nothing routine in the Army treatment of Sergeant Sanders. His public statement about the war displeased General Westmoreland and he was sent to Vietnam as punishment. This not only violated Sergeant Sanders' constitutional rights, it served notice to other members of the Army that public disagreement with the views of any senior officer was grounds for punishment.

Specialist Fourth Class James J. Stone expressed his feelings in a letter he wrote me from Vietnam: "Freedom of speech in the Army is a myth. You can say anything you want, but, to be sure, there will be a penalty, whether being sent to the field, doing details for the rest of your tour, or being denied normally-given privileges." Stone went on to tell about what happened to his platoon sergeant: "My platoon sergeant has been in the Army twenty-two years. He is one of the few career men I have served under in the Army who has the admiration and respect of all of his men. He is a man of deep understanding of the attitudes of lower ranking enlisted men. He works right alongside of his men and often works longer and harder than any of them. A while back he felt that there was something wrong in the way things were being done and he had enough moral integrity to try to remedy the situation. What he finally did was to use one of the few constitutional liberties that are open to servicemen, he wrote his congressman. Well, a copy of the letter got back to his commander and was put in his permanent record. My platoon sergeant, as good and as capable as he is, will never be promoted because of this."

Active and retired Army members should also be permitted to participate more fully in national political affairs. Paragraph 42 of Army Regulations 600–20 is an example of the restrictions imposed: "Members of the Army while on active duty may not participate in political management or be members of political committees, nor may they take an active part in other political activities, including but not limited to political conventions and campaigns, political speeches, the publication of articles, and any other activity designed to influence the outcome of an election or solicit votes for themselves or others. The foregoing statutes are applicable to retired Regular Army personnel also." Such restrictive regulations in effect bar Regular Army officers from practically ever participating in the political life of their country. If career soldiers are to be barred from exercising free speech and participating in normal political activity, they cannot be expected to have as much concern and understanding for the interests of the nation as for the parochial goals of their branch of the armed forces.

2. The Uniform Code of Military Justice should be revised to bring it into accord with the American legal code. The rights of the serviceman must be better protected. Army judicial and nonjudicial punishment should be made uniform and just. At present nonjudicial punishment is more often influenced by a commander's prejudices and desire to maintain a good statistical image for his unit rather than by a desire to dispense justice to the soldier.

Pretrial investigations and court-martial proceedings are also heavily influenced by the views of commanding officers. In order to eliminate such influence, it may be necessary to establish a separate Army judicial command staffed by civilian and military judges and lawyers. Such a command should be under the direct control of the Secretary of the Army.

Lower-rank enlisted men being tried by courts-martial should not be denied judgment by their peers. The current practice of assigning only officers and higher-ranking career noncommissioned officers as members of courts trying lower-ranking enlisted men is discriminatory and ensures harsh verdicts. Paragraph 4 of the Uniform Code of Military Justice clearly did not intend to establish such a practice. It states, "Any enlisted person on active duty shall be eligible to serve on general and special courts-martial for any enlisted accused who has requested that enlisted persons serve on it." Summary courts-martial which are conducted by one officer who acts as judge and jury should be abolished from the Uniform Code of Military Justice.

The Department of the Army has recently taken an important first step toward better protection of the rights of its soldiers by requiring that nonjudicial punishments be reviewed. This belated move should be followed by others such as stopping abuses in Army stockades and base correctional-custody facilities. Soldiers should not be confined for minor offenses. Those that are confined for other offenses should not be subjected to degrading conditions and sadistic jailers.

The Army must not be allowed to continue taking the easy path of eliminating soldiers from service rather than rehabilitating them through effective leadership. The burden belongs on the Army leader to gain willing compliance and obedience through quality leadership rather than force or fear. Habitual criminals and drug addicts should be eliminated. But too many young Americans have had their lives blighted by officers or noncommissioned officers who disliked them for one reason or another and harassed them into committing some act for which they could be punished. The Army disciplinary system should not condone stigmatizing soldiers as misfits by placing them in "eight-ball" units for committing minor offenses.

3. Discrimination and favoritism in the Army must be stopped. Soldiers experience discrimination for a variety of reasons: because of their ethnic heritage, their religion, family background, or color of skin. Subtle career favoritism is also practiced by the elitist leadership.

For the past five decades it has been almost axiomatic that Army general officers and senior NCO's were white Protestants from solid Anglo-Saxon middle-class backgrounds. Generals have frequently been the sons of generals and have come from one of thirty families that have sent succeeding generations to West Point. Having one of these family names has been as important for promotion to general as an outstanding record of service. An example is Brigadier General George S. Patton, III. He is a capable officer but not outstanding enough to have merited promotion from lieutenant colonel in 1968 to brigadier general in 1970. It has not been in the best interest of the Army or the country that an elitist West Point leadership has dominated the Army. Only tough civilian control can eliminate such favoritism. The civilian leaders of the Army should be men with sufficient military background to enable them to understand and control the Army General Staff. The civilian secretaries and the Congressional Armed Services Committees need to pay closer attention to the records and backgrounds of generals assigned to key Army command and staff positions. The Armed Services Committees should use more fully their right of approval of general officer promotions by requiring officers nominated to three- and four-star rank to appear before one of their subcommittees prior to confirmation. Periodically, random selections of officers nominated for promotion to colonel and brigadier general should also be summoned to appear. Such hearings would give members of Congress an opportunity to evaluate the judgment and foreign-policy orientation of officers up for promotion and learn something about attitudes and conditions within the officer corps.

The Army should stop assigning soldiers on the basis of personnel requests which state, "officer of Italian descent preferred," or "not suitable assignment for an officer of the Jewish religion." The covert policy of assigning only a restricted number of officers of Puerto Rican or Mexican-American heritage to duty in Spanish-speaking countries because they are not considered representative of the Army should also end. Officers and NCO's must be made to understand that "closed-shop" attitudes will not be tolerated against any member of the Army. Favoritism in assignments should cease. Major Peter Dawkins (West Point 1959 and All-American football player) has achieved his rank while spending seven of his twelve years of

Army service in schools, either collecting advanced degrees or instructing at West Point. None of his contemporaries has received equal treatment.

Inspector generals must cease to be the agents of the status quo. They should not only sincerely investigate complaints of discrimination and favoritism, but actively seek out such practices for correction. Distinctiòns between types of officers on active duty (reserve, regular) should be abolished. Equal opportunity must be given more than lip service. Each soldier should be encouraged to seek and to remain at the level to which his ability can carry him. Today's emphasis on constantly striving for higher rank as the way to remain on active duty overlooks the advantages to a unit of the experience and stability provided by the career buck sergeant or company commander. The British Army has had career squad and platoon sergeants for generations.

Soldiers are also the victims of discrimination by those they are sworn to defend. This ranges from the black soldier who is unable to rent a decent home near his duty station to the soldiers who are preyed upon by loan sharks and profiteering car and insurance salesmen. There is the more subtle discrimination that comes from feeling that one's fellow citizens consider a soldier a second-class citizen without much ambition because he chose an Army career. The Army should take a more positive approach toward helping dispel this discrimination. Present off-base housing rules to prevent racial restrictions are important. The Army should also develop policies which aid the soldier in obtaining a decent home. More liberalized Veterans' Administration mortgage loans for lower-ranking soldiers would be one way. Another would be leasing off-base housing and renting it to enlisted men at nominal rates.

The Army should protect its lower-ranking soldiers from the questionable businessmen that it permits to solicit on its posts. The Army should cease to act as a coercive collection agent in behalf of debts that are frequently the result of unfair business practices. The soldier should work out his own debt problems without paternalistic coercion and interference by an officer. The Army should change Paragraph 36 of Army Regulations

600–20 which states, "If a commanding officer believes that a member of his command has dishonorably failed to pay his just debts, disciplinary action may be initiated [articles 15, 133, and 134, UCMJ]." All too frequently commanding officers feel they *must* rather than *may* take disciplinary action against the soldier. Too often personal indebtedness is used by officers and NCO's as an excuse to punish a soldier they dislike.

4. The Army must make better use of its manpower. This misuse begins in the Tables of Organization and Equipment (TOE). All of these tables should be reviewed on a line-by-line basis by committees of broadly experienced combat officers and NCO's. This review should stress organizational austerity and simplicity as its goals. Accompanying the review should be a change of Army combat and support doctrines. The emphasis should be changed from creating layers of supporting headquarters to streamlining combat capability by using small austere support forces to back up an increased number of combat units. The present concept of two divisions being required to support one combat division (in which half the soldiers are also involved in support duties) should be eliminated. The initial support increment of an Army division should be structured so that it could provide the entire support required by the division. Such a support force should not exceed eight thousand soldiers. More soldiers within the combat division itself should place fire on the enemy. The Army's TOE's should deal solely with the formation of units designed for the defense of the United States. It should not provide for specially tailored units to fight "internal defense" or "low-intensity" wars in the underdeveloped world. If the Department of Defense follows the recommendations of the Fitzhugh Commission Report and reappraises the armed forces unified-command concept, the past military impulse to use special forces to intervene in the affairs of other nations will be checked.

After the TOE's have been changed to form more austere combat-oriented Army units, the Secretary of the Army should have a man-by-man study made of what all of the Army's soldiers are doing. This study should be upgraded annually. Its findings would most surely show that 60 percent or more of the

Army's manpower is assigned to other than combat duties. The Secretary should personally enforce redistribution of a majority of the Army's manpower into streamlined TOE combat units.

5. A reduction in the present number of nonessential jobs would mean fewer soldiers would be needed in the United States and overseas. Length of duty tours could be longer and assignment policies more flexible. For example, length of tours in Europe could be made optional. A soldier could volunteer to serve there for fifteen months without his family or forty-eight months with his family along. If he performed his duties in a satisfactory manner and desired to remain overseas, he should be allowed to extend his tour up to eight years. The needs of the Army should take precedence over the career desires of the soldier. But those needs should be valid and they should not involve constant movement of manpower.

A worldwide listing of available assignments should be published each year. Officers, noncommissioned officers, and enlisted men with over three years of service should be allowed to volunteer for the jobs they want. Assignment boards could then select the most qualified men to fill Army positions. Those that failed to qualify for their first choices could be assigned lower choices.

6. Promotion policies should be revised. Too much importance is attached to time in grade as a criterion for promotion. If time in grade is to continue to be used, it must be more consistently applied. It should not take some soldiers seven years to satisfy grade requirements that others satisfy in three years. The main criterion for promotion should be ability to accept higher levels of responsibility. This determination should be made on the basis of comprehensive examinations and demonstrated professional and cultural development. Outstanding soldiers should be advanced to levels where their ability can be best used. If promotion vacancies are not available these soldiers should be given brevet promotions which would entitle them to wear the rank appropriate to higher-level duties. Soldiers performing satisfactorily in brevet rank should after one year be considered for "below-the-zone" accelerated promotions.

Order of priority for attendance at service schools and advanced civilian education should be based on the same criteria as promotions. Competitive examinations must be controlled and not allowed to become of all-consuming importance. For example, officers who have demonstrated outstanding ability during their time-in-grade minimum, but score poorly on examination for promotion should be reexamined within three months. If the officer scores well on the second examination his name could be added to the end of the current promotion list. Officers who fail the examination should be allowed to retake it after one year. A second failure and a below-average performance of duty would necessitate the officer's appearing before a board of his peers that would decide whether he would be retained in grade or eliminated from commissioned status. Noncommissioned-officer promotions to grades sergeant (E-5) through sergeant major (E-9) should be based on the same criteria as officer promotions. Promotions to private first class (E-3) and corporal (E-4) should be based on demonstrated performance of duty.

Promotion selection boards should include at least one representative of a grade lower than that of the men being considered for promotion. The file of each nominee for promotion should be submitted to the board by number rather than name. Before the names of officers selected for promotion are made public, all those not selected should be notified by letter. Reasons for nonselection should be given in this letter and the officer should be counseled on whether or not to plan to continue his service.

7. The present rating system, which relies upon efficiency reports containing numbered blocks and fill-ins, should be abolished. It should be replaced by a word picture of the officer being rated. Such a word picture should not include an evaluation of the rated officer's potential for promotion, schooling, and type of future assignments. The rating officer is seldom qualified to make such important evaluations and doing so gives him excessive control over the lives and futures of officers under his command. Attached to the word picture should be specific examples of job performance which substantiate state-

ments made in the descriptive picture. An officer or noncommissioned officer should be rated once during each calendar year and should sign the word picture after reading it. Additional reports would be submitted only if a rater considered them necessary and he should be required to state his reason for the special submission. All reports submitted should be accompanied by summaries of the occasions when the rater counseled the rated officer or NCO on shortcomings or failures mentioned in the word picture. These records of counseling should be signed by both men. If the rated commissioned or noncommissioned officers disagree with the counseling report or the word picture, they should be allowed to submit an accompanying letter stating reasons for disagreement. Higher commanders who endorse officer or NCO word pictures should be required to comment on the statements of disagreement. Each commissioned officer should also be encouraged to submit an annual letter to his career branch stating how he views his professional development and his career objectives for the coming year.

Evaluation of noncommissioned officers should emphasize job performance and a brief word picture of the soldier. NCO's performing technical duties should be tested annually on job proficiency. The results of these tests should be included as part of the annual report. The senior NCO should also be encouraged to submit periodic letters to the noncommissioned branch stating his objectives of service and how he views his professional progress. Annual word pictures on enlisted men should include copies of any record of punishment and counseling related to this punishment.

8. Present salaries for senior officers and senior NCO's are more than adequate when compared to comparable civilian wage scales. They continue to be inadequate at lower officer and enlisted ranks. Recent congressional action to improve these conditions will be helpful. But further action will be needed to balance out the inequity between the salaries of senior officers and NCO's who usually qualify for immediate low-cost on-base government housing, and the salaries of lower-ranking personnel who seldom qualify for such housing.

Once the pay inequities have been balanced, future pay increases should raise the pay of lower-ranking soldiers proportionately to prevent the imbalance from occurring again. If defense-budget cuts should ever necessitate reduced pay raises, the top of the pay structure should receive the smaller increases. A general can manage on $2,998 a month, but a corporal is hard-pressed today to feed and shelter his family on $390 a month.

Further attention should be given to recommendations that the total value of the soldier's pay should be made more visible to him. For example, in addition to showing him the monthly amount he is paid for quarters and rations, he should also be shown the amount of his medical and retirement benefits. Soldiers could be given an option of receiving a fixed monthly amount for medical care of their dependents or utilizing government medical facilities.

9. The value of Army awards has been cheapened by a too liberal policy of conferring them on senior officers. Decorations should no longer be routinely awarded to senior officers as farewell tokens when they leave a job. Combat medals should not be routinely awarded to battalion, brigade, or division commanders for doing what they are paid to do—lead their troops. According to a news story in the *Washington Post*, a public-information officer was awarded a Bronze Star medal for his year in the fleshpots of Saigon.

Only personnel assigned to combat brigades or separate fire-support battalions should be eligible for combat decorations. The Army award and decoration system should be revised to include a combat-support medal, which could be given for an outstanding job in noncombatant-support assignments. Noncombat-support personnel should not be awarded a campaign service medal with the same battle stars as the soldier who actually does the fighting. There should be a distinct logistics campaign ribbon (without battle stars) awarded to soldiers who serve in a war zone in administrative, support, and logistics assignments. The fighting soldiers should receive a different campaign ribbon and be entitled to wear the battle stars they earn in combat.

The combat infantry badge should be awarded only to soldiers who serve under enemy fire in infantry companies and battalions. Medical, armor, and artillery personnel who serve with these infantry units should also be eligible for this award. Soldiers of the Army should not be allowed to continue to wear foreign decorations on their uniforms. They should be permitted to accept such medals but they should not use them to adorn their uniforms.

10. One of the strongest motivations to Army service is the military retirement plan. Yet today this plan encourages soldiers to leave the Army at twenty years. It also is the reason that many soldiers hang on in the Army serving time until they qualify to retire. Under present law there is no way that a soldier can leave active service short of twenty years and recoup any part of his invested retirement benefits. After a soldier has ten years of service he is firmly "hooked," and no matter how much he may dislike his service he will remain until he completes twenty years for retirement. It would be more economical, and better for the Army, to allow a soldier the option of leaving after ten years' service and collecting a lump-sum payment for accrued retirement benefits.

The soldier should be allowed to retire at twenty years but it should be made less attractive to do so. Under the twenty-year retirement plan too many good soldiers are encouraged to leave at the peak of their productive years. Retirement at twenty years should bring less than half of base pay. Thirty-year retirement should entitle the soldier to half of his base pay. A prorated scale should be established to increase the percentage of base-pay entitlement each year after thirty years of service. For example forty years of service could bring payment of 90 percent of base pay.

A retirement system oriented toward providing incentives for longer active service need not cause stagnation in the Army. Stricter control over the number and quality of persons allowed to enter career status and a selective program for those retained beyond thirty years could prevent such an occurrence. The Army should recognize that it cannot realistically expect the taxpayers to continue to support twenty-year retirement.

Retirement must be retained as an incentive for long service rather than as a means of encouraging career soldiers to leave to provide slots for the promotion of others.

11. The officer-enlisted relationship should be modified. There has not been a serious review of these relationships since the Doolittle Board of 1946. The President should appoint a commission of civilian and military leaders (including a young junior officer and enlisted man) to study this matter throughout the armed forces.

Attitudes of caste superiority that have caused many commissioned and noncommissioned officers to look on lower-ranking soldiers with disdain, and even contempt, must be changed. The individual dignity and value of the lives of ordinary soldiers should be reemphasized. The use of terms like "grunt" and "animal" to describe lower-ranking soldiers should be forbidden. Use by an officer or an NCO of personally derogatory profanity toward a soldier should be stopped. Officers and NCO's should cease to use their authority to berate verbally and belittle enlisted men through so-called ass chewings.

Army customs and rules should be reviewed to see if they are still pertinent for today's generation. For example, what is the need for the excessive and subservient use of "yes, sir," or "sir" uttered in almost every breath when an enlisted man addresses an officer or a junior officer addresses a senior? And does it *really* promote better discipline to constantly be saluting out of formations? Neither of these customs is much observed in combat where the daily threat of death removes much of the false role-playing of rank and caste superiority. I question their real value in daily Army life. Rather than promoting discipline they promote a false sense of superiority among officers and create unnecessary resentment among enlisted soldiers. Members of the Army should address each other by rank and/or name. Wes Storrs, the young man who traded places with a soldier brother in Vietnam, has pointed out how ridiculous this custom has become. When asked how he managed for several weeks in the Army without any training he said, "I just saluted when everyone else did, ended every sentence with 'sir,' and acted stupid the rest of the time. I didn't have any trouble."

12. The professional education of career commissioned and noncommissioned officers should be of better quality, more relevant and comprehensive. Present officer schooling trains him for future duties rather than the ones he is likely to perform. Today at the Command and General Staff College majors with eight years of service are taught how to perform as lieutenant generals. This is both unrealistic and inefficient. At each level of Army education the officer should be trained for the duties he is likely to perform between graduation and the next educational level.

Course content in schools like the War College and Command and General Staff College should be of sufficient length and academic quality to qualify a graduate for an accredited advanced degree. One way to improve the academic quality of Army professional education would be to hire larger numbers of civilian educators. Civilian instructors could be used to teach needed courses in international economics, political theory, diplomacy, international law, public administration, history, and so forth that are not included in the curriculum of today's Army school system. The presence of civilian educators would not only provide better-qualified instructors but would add a leavening of civilian attitudes and experience to the presently sterile military teaching environment.

Some courses should be lengthened and others curtailed or eliminated. The length of the officer basic course, for example, should be curtailed. After four years of officer training in college, it should not be necessary for an officer to attend an eighteen-week familiarization course before serving.

The Army maintains twenty-two military installations as school posts. Sixteen of these posts house the staff, faculty, students, and support troops of branch-of-service schools (Fort Benning, Georgia—infantry school; Fort Monmouth, New Jersey—signal corps school; Fort Sill, Oklahoma—artillery school, and so on). Significant savings could be made by consolidating these scattered branch-training facilities. For example, the average annual expense of operating Fort Benning, Georgia, is $36.2 million.

Fragmentation of Army schooling should be eliminated. All

combat-arms schooling (infantry, artillery, armor) should be taught at a Combined Combat Arms School under the direction of a combined-arms staff and faculty. Technical service corps subjects (quartermaster, ordinance, engineers, and so on) should be taught at a Combined Technical Service/Logistics Support School. Higher-level career schooling now being conducted at the Command and General Staff College, Fort Leavenworth, Kansas, and the Army War College, Carlisle Barracks, Pennsylvania, should also be consolidated at one post. This could be done at West Point.

The United States Military Academy (like the Naval and Air Force Academies) is too expensive on a cost-per-student basis for the quantity and quality of its product. The undergraduate military academy should be closed and Army officers obtained through less costly civilian college-scholarship programs and direct entry from ROTC. The facilities of West Point should be converted into the senior-school center of the Army. The Army War College, Command and General Staff College, Senior Noncommissioned Officer School, and Army Museum and Library should be located there.

A streamlined Army school system would consist of only the three school centers. At both the Combined Combat Arms School and the Technical Service/Logistics Support School noncommissioned officer courses for grades E-4 through E-7 should be taught in residence and by extension. Each of these two combined schools should also teach basic NCO courses. Attendance at these courses should not be only on a quota basis, but based on competitive applications.

13. In fiscal year 1972 the Army will operate five military installations as training centers. The average annual operating cost for each one of these centers is $22 million. At the Fort Dix, New Jersey, training center 14,240 persons are required to command and support the training of 16,140 soldiers. This ratio of cadre personnel to trainees is similar at other Army training centers. Each center wastes both money and manpower.

All Army basic and advanced individual training should be carried out within the regular division structure. The training functions of the Continental Army Command should be assimilated by the Department of the Army and the Army Area Commands. The Continental Army Command should be closed.

Soldiers assigned as training-center cadre should be transferred to divisions based in the United States where their training skills could continue to be used. Overseas replacements could be drawn from stateside divisions and they in turn could train additional soldiers while carrying on combat-readiness training. Training and duty in regular divisions would add the now missing ingredient of a new soldier's service—a sense of purpose. Only in time of national mobilization should the Army return to the present mass-production training-center system.

Closing the training centers and beginning training in regular units will not be enough. The fear-motivated, lock-step training methods must also be changed. The large amount of time currently devoted to repetitive step-by-step-type training should be reduced. This World War II concept of training was predicated on a much slower learning ability than today's soldiers possess. Childlike repetition turns off a member of the television generation and Army training should become aware of this fact. The principal objective of the basic phase of a soldier's training should be to teach him to handle his rifle and live under field conditions. More time should be devoted to realistic combat training in rifle marksmanship, technique of fire, field living and sanitation, road marching, and physical training.

The manner of the instruction should be serious and forthright—which it is not today. The soldier is aware that his life may rest on the quality of the instruction. He is disillusioned by poor instruction and "Mickey Mouse," just as he is repelled by constant use of fear of death as motivation to learn. Motivation through fear of death in combat was a learning device developed during World War II. It does more to breed unreasoned fear and apprehension about combat than it does to instill a desire to learn in a homesick young man. More positive motivation to learn must be used in future Army training. If the quality of the training and the instructors were improved it would be possible, for example, to stress proficiency as a motivating

factor. To promote quality the Army should relax the standardized centralization that has removed most of the innovative incentives from training commanders.

14. Army research and development has become too large
and has lost sight of its intended purpose. Rather than providing for the needs of the Army's combat soldiers, it has become
an agency for justifying sophisticated weapons systems to enhance Army interservice prestige. It is inexcusable that the
Army's soldiers entered the Vietnam War wearing a World
War II helmet and without effective lightweight body armor.

The number of Army R&D commands and the personnel assigned to them should be reduced. All Army R&D activities
should be consolidated at one military installation. The mission
of the Combat Developments Command should be restated to
encompass only scientific development and testing of weapons
and equipment necessary for austere combat operations. The
guiding objective should be to develop less complicated items
at the lowest possible cost. The emphasis should be changed
from developing weapons systems to developing items to improve the combat capability and protect the life of the individual soldier.

15. The Army must be more forthright about the value of its
overseas deployments. Divisions should no longer be kept overseas because their presence justifies a proliferation of headquarter and support commands. Korea is an excellent example.
There is no valid military reason to continue to station nearly
thirty thousand soldiers there, nor is Eighth Army Headquarters (with a four-star commander and three-star deputy), I
Corps (with a three-star commander), and a large logistical
command necessary to supervise and support one U.S. infantry
division containing fewer than ten thousand American soldiers.
These headquarter and support personnel should be reduced.

Europe is another example. As we have already seen it takes
111,000 American soldiers to command and support the 59,000
who serve in combat divisions there. This is due to faulty Tables of Organization for combat and overstaffed headquarter
and support units. These units should be reduced. An Army
corps consisting of one armored and one mechanized division

reinforced by an armored cavalry regiment and an antiaircraft brigade would be a realistic United States contribution to NATO defense. Such a force positioned along a line in Germany running north-south from Bremen-Hanóver-Kassel, with supply lines back to Rotterdam or Antwerp, could offer a stout contribution to NATO defense against any Soviet inclination to make an armored sweep across the North German plains. This is something U.S. Army Europe can't accomplish from their present positions in Bavaria using an exposed supply line running south from Bremerhaven close to the East German border.

Headquarters U.S. Army Europe/Seventh Army, one corps headquarters, and two and one-third Army divisions should be brought home from Germany. The Theater Army Support Command should be reduced to a logistical command and its excess personnel returned to the States. Prepositioned heavy equipment for one armored and one mechanized division should be moved to covered storage sites in Holland and Belgium. Supplies and equipment stored in West Germany should be reduced to thirty- or forty-five-day levels. Only one Army infantry battalion should be stationed in Berlin. The eight-thousand-man U.S. Southern European Task Force (SETAF) stationed in northern Italy should be withdrawn. The limited-range obsolete missile fire support it provides the Italian Army is of negligible value and could be accomplished in other ways.

With regard to Japan, the nearly ten thousand Army support troops stationed there should be withdrawn. Their mission should be assumed by the Japanese Self-Defense Forces. All troops should be withdrawn at once from Vietnam. The U.S. Army has been advising and supporting the South Vietnamese Army for sixteen years—that is long enough. Its continued presence there will only lead to the U.S. Army's complete disintegration.

An Army organized along austere lines could plan on a FY 1975 year-end strength of 500,000 soldiers manning as many as nineteen divisions. Two of these divisions could be in Europe, one in Hawaii, another in Alaska, and the remainder in the continental United States. All of them should be manned and equipped at least 90 percent of authorized strength. Six divisions could be under command of a corps in the Fifth Army area. Five others could be assigned to a corps in the Third Army area (including Fort Knox, Kentucky). The divisions in Alaska, Hawaii, Fort Lewis, Washington, and Fort Ord, California, could be under a corps in the Sixth Army area. When reorganizations and school consolidations are finished, Forts Belvoir, Devens, Dix, Leavenworth, Monmouth, Monroe, Gordon, Hamilton, Stewart, McClellan, and Carlisle Barracks should be closed.

16. Miscellaneous points. (a.) The Chaplain and Army Medical Corps should be changed to permit lateral entry and exit at varying times. Qualified, experienced civilian doctors of divinity and medicine should be allowed to enter these corps at different age levels, serve for a few years, and then return to civilian life. They should serve in a contract status and should not hold officer ranks or be made part of the Officer Corps promotion system. Their purpose is to serve the soldier but officer rank hinders instead of facilitates this function. The permanent corps of officers serving as chaplains and doctors should be replaced by a small nucleus of career directors supervising the work of professional contract civilians. The battle-zone status of such contract specialists could be the same as war correspondents currently enjoy under the Rules of Land Warfare.

(b.) The Chemical Corps should be abolished. Personnel assigned to this small corps should be transferred to the Ordnance Corps. Its functions should be restricted to planning duties and a small amount of laboratory experimentation. One of the reasons for the rapid acceptance of CBW warfare in Army doctrines has been the existence of the Chemical Corps. Chemical officers have been as anxious as other technical-service corps to advance the prestige of their corps. They have worked diligently to have chemical and biological warfare included in Army tactical doctrine. Today CBW is taught as standard tactical doctrine at all Army schools. This should be changed, because in war soldiers do what they are trained to do. It is through such mistaken training that use of these terrifying agents may some day become a reality.

(c.) The Infantry, Artillery, and Armor Branches should be grouped under a Combined Combat Arms Branch with officers assigned to duties on an interchangeable cross-branch basis whenever possible. The technical service corps of Quartermaster, Ordnance, Signal, and Transportation should be grouped under a Logistics Support Branch with the officers of these corps also assigned to duties on a cross-corps basis when possible. Lateral entry from civilian life or reserve status should be open to specialists who have needed logistic skills. This concept of lateral entry could also be used in the Judge Advocate General and Women's Army Corps. Civilian lawyers should be allowed to enter military service for specified periods. Such entry should be based on the need for the lawyer's experience rather than determined by his age. Experienced women technicians and secretaries should be given entry into the Women's Army Corps at whichever levels their skill and experience qualify them.

(d.) The Inspector General should report directly to the Secretary of the Army, rather than through the Chief of Staff. Officers assigned to the office of Inspector General should serve for five years and should be responsible only to the chief of the IG Department. Reports of inspections or investigations should be sent directly to the Chief Inspector General and not be subject to review by local commanders. The Secretary of the Army should decide the action to be taken on all Inspector General reports of unsatisfactory conditions.

(e.) The numerous staff agencies of the Department of the Army should be streamlined and consolidated. The department's staff should be limited to a ceiling of three thousand officers and enlisted personnel. The Army General Staff should be restricted to the office of the Chief of Staff, and the deputy chiefs of staff for logistics, operations, personnel, and intelligence. The size and number of Special Staff agencies should be drastically cut back. The following is only a partial listing of the offices and commands that could be reduced: Advanced Aerial Fire Support System Office, Army Exhibit Unit, Army Materiel Command, Research and Development Office, Directorate for Civil Disturbance Planning and Operation, Combat Developments Command, Foreign Science and Technology Center, Military Traffic Management and Terminal Service, Personnel Operations Office, Support Services, Aeronautical Services Office, Army Audit Agency, Army Command Information Unit, Computer Systems Support and Evaluation Command, Army Field Operating Cost Agency, Army Information and Data Systems Command, Army Management Systems Support Command, Army Strategy and Tactics Group.

(f.) Army officers and Department of the Army civilian employees assigned to civilian procurement or project-manager duties should be more carefully screened and more adequately trained in the responsibility of their jobs. They should be better indoctrinated with their obligation to conserve the needless expenditure of tax dollars. More comprehensive controls of procurement and project-management practices should be initiated.

(g.) There must be more integration of the activities of the Army Reserve and National Guard with the Active Army. One way to bring this about would be dual-basing of active and reserve divisions. By pairing divisions, the Army could make better and more economical use of its equipment, as well as improve coordination and teamwork. This also would help destroy the prejudice that many Active Army personnel feel toward the Army National Guard and Reserve. Retired regular and reserve commissioned and noncommissioned officers under age fifty-five should be allowed to serve voluntarily in Army Reserve units. Under present regulations retired personnel are prohibited from serving in reserve units and maintaining their military skills.

Chapter 10

A Look to
the Future

☆ ☆ ☆ ☆ ☆ ☆ ☆ ☆ ☆

There are several things that the U.S. Army can do after it is
withdrawn from Vietnam. One is to try to recoup its fortunes
and reputation in another counterinsurgency effort or internal
defense, as it is now called, in some other corner of the world.
Planning for this contingency has already begun. The Military
Assistance Officers Program (MAOP) is underway at Fort
Bragg, and young General Staff majors and lieutenant colonels
are busily at work in the Pentagon updating Army contingency
plans for South America to meet what General Bruce Palmer,
Army Vice Chief of Staff, envisions as a "real and apparent"
threat.[1] For the ambitious officer, and the ones who just like to

---

[1] General Palmer gained fame during the United States intervention in the
Dominican Republic, where he was the chief advocate of an unnecessarily
large build-up of Army forces. As in Lebanon, the Army wanted to prove it

fight and kill, the place where the action will be in the future is in military-assistance efforts which can be built into little "internal defense" wars. As "the Colonel" (David H. Hackworth, who has served five volunteer tours in Vietnam and collected two promotions and a sackful of medals in the process) was quoted as saying in Ward Just's book *Military Men,* "Well, now I'm going to study Latin American affairs. That's where it's going next, because the bastards think they can win it all now. Yessir, Latin America COMUSMACL. I guess I just like war." And for the young West Point ticket punchers who don't like war very much, but like to pin on general's stars and read about each other's promotions and decorations in the West Point alumni magazine, it is the only way to get there.

More Counterinsurgency and More Foreign Wars

So if the U.S. Army is not reformed and civilian leadership is not restored, the fathers and mothers of America can look forward in another five to ten years to seeing their sons go off again to defend the United States from "Communism." The next place that young draftees can die so officers like Colonel Hackworth can "take that battalion and mold it just like I would a piece of clay, take those kids and make them into the best fighting force that I could. The best in the country. And by God, I made it go," would be Chile and Bolivia. Again, the professional killers and organization men can line up for six-month combat tours and finish out the year by serving in the headquarters of the Combined United States Military Advisory Command Latin America (COMUSMACL).

The contingency planning now going forward in the Department of the Army, and the Military Assistance Institute (formerly the John F. Kennedy Special Warfare School) at Fort Bragg, starts with certain basic assumptions. The scenario for the contingency planning will probably read something like the following:

---

could move its forces more rapidly than the Marines. This excessive build-up of Army combat power was costly to the American taxpayer and provoked the Dominican people.

1. Assumed: that a completely Communist government has ousted the Socialist-Communist government of President Allende and has refused to hold national elections in Chile. A Communist-appointed Chilean Minister of Defense has invited an Eastern European military mission to Santiago and has concluded an agreement for early shipment of sophisticated Soviet military equipment to Chile. Previously dissatisfied junior officers and colonels of the Chilean armed forces have replaced all older senior officers who held steadfast loyalty to the democratic institutions of the country. Labor unionists have been armed to form a paramilitary force capable of containing any elements of the army inclined to support the previous elected government. The situation in Chile is chaotic and the American ambassador has indicated his concern over the safety of United States citizens living and working in Chile. He has also expressed his concern over the increasingly close contacts that have been opened between the Communist government of Chile and the leftist government of Bolivia. The American ambassador in Bolivia has reported that there are rumors that an East European military mission is expected momentarily in La Paz.

2. Scenario: the situation in both Chile and Bolivia has steadily worsened. All American business interests have been expropriated by the Bolivian government. The American ambassador in La Paz has ordered all American citizens to leave the country as their safety cannot be guaranteed. Mobs have attempted to set fire to the Embassy in La Paz and the country is under martial law. Major elements of the Bolivian Army are supporting the leftist military regime. But certain Army units in the Cochabamba and Santa Cruz areas have declared their opposition to the regime. Fighting has broken out and threatens to increase in intensity. United States military-assistance officers in Bolivia are recommending that "democratic" units be assisted and a reinforced U.S. airborne infantry battalion be immediately deployed to La Paz to protect American citizens and families of embassy and military advisory-group personnel who have assembled there for safety.

In Santiago, Chile, citizens have begun arriving at the United States Embassy for evacuation from Chile. An East

German freighter has docked at Valparaiso and unloaded a second shipment of Soviet tanks and armored personnel carriers for units of the Chilean Army loyal to the Communist regime. However, battalion-sized elements of the Chilean Army and Carabineros in the south of the country have declared that they will not support the newly installed Communist government and have demanded immediate national elections. Fighting has broken out between these units and armed labor unionists supported by elements of the Chilean Army loyal to the Communist government.

United States military-assistance officers with the dissident Chilean forces have recommended immediate aid in the form of weapons and Green Beret "A" teams to assist in training. This recommendation has become more urgent as a result of the lack of supplies and losses sustained by the democratic elements fighting to reverse the Communist takeover. As a result of a series of incidents between United States citizens in Santiago and local nationals, the ambassador has requested that a U.S. military force be dispatched to safeguard the lives and property of citizens. In response to this request the President has directed that one U.S. airborne infantry battalion be flown at once to Santiago. In addition he has directed the Joint Chiefs of Staff to prepare to furnish military equipment to the democratic forces fighting in Chile. This equipment would be accompanied by sufficient United States military-assistance personnel to train and assist the democratic Chilean forces in its use. End of scenario.

In this way, COMUSMACL would be established. From a few advisers and Green Berets, the force could quickly grow, particularly if the U.S. infantry battalion protecting American lives had a case of nerves and mistakenly fired on Chilean troops (as in the Dominican Republic), or Washington called for an increased U.S. military presence in Chile to stop "Communism short of the Texas border." The trained MAOP officers would be in on the ground floor of their own war. Soon U.S. battalions in Chile would be replaced by brigades and with any luck at all by a division or two and that would justify field army and corps headquarters and a huge supply base at Valparaiso.

And of course the Marines would be allowed to land a battalion or so somewhere on the south coast of Chile to establish a base to move inland and assist the beleaguered democratic forces. The airborne battalion protecting American lives and property in La Paz would have grown to the entire 82nd Division. And there would be excitement and adventure for the Green Beret teams that would be high up in the Andean wilderness leading Bolivian and Chilean insurgents who would be fighting to restore the democratic status quo.

Such a scenario could be duplicated in Africa. There are absolutely no limits to the possibilities for further war that this low-intensity or internal-defense concept provides for the Army. It will become the "wave of the future" unless the American people stop such nonsense now before contingency planning and MAOP training go forward to a point where we find ourselves in another foreign civil war that is none of our business.

Despite the bitter experience of Vietnam, Army managers have not yet learned that the U.S. Army cannot involve itself and the nation in the internal problems of underdeveloped countries without becoming engaged in a massive protracted military adventure. The Army system must be changed to provide a role for the Army which does not demand war as the principal way to achieve career success.

The civilian leadership must begin to provide the political guidance and restraint that was so notably lacking in the early days in Vietnam. Another such misguided, ill-conceived adventure would surely result in far more deaths and damage to our national fabric. In Latin America the people would unite to fight against any military intervention from the hated "Yankees." It is absolutely impractical even to consider ideas like those held by Colonel Harry Jackson regarding insurgency in the *altiplano* of Peru and Bolivia. Colonel Jackson, head of the MAOP academic board, is quoted by Ward Just in *Military Men* as saying that an insurgency operation in Peru wouldn't have been nearly as tough as Vietnam. "Oh look," he said, "get in there early, get in there very early and really analyze the situation. Analyze the revolution. Find out all about it, the people, the methods, the particulars. Get in there early and form it, shape it." It is exactly such naïve, uninformed thinking as Colonel Jackson's that got us involved in Vietnam.

Not only is this not the way to counter a civil war in the *altiplano*, it is not even an accurate assessment of the dangers and difficulties involved in fighting there against local soldiers. This is the type of monomaniacal self-delusion and Madison Avenue catchphrasing that has overwhelmed the U.S. Army. Such shallow thinking is the wellspring of poorly thought-out doctrines.

The U.S. Army Military Assistance Institute should be closed. If not closed it should be closely scrutinized and placed under control of the Department of State. The Army (nor any of the other armed forces) should no longer be permitted to operate schools which go far beyond the sphere of military tactics and strategy. If the public does not want continuing wars for the next two decades then they should demand that these questionable activities cease. The road to peace is not paved by war. And the Nixon doctrine of nonintervention in the internal affairs of our neighbors is not going to be assured by training our Army to seek ways of placing itself in the middle of civil wars. Counterinsurgency is a bankrupt concept; it should be discarded.[2]

Volunteer Army and Repression

As a result of parochialism, poor leadership, faulty organization, and plain stubborn selfishness, the Army now finds itself beset on all sides. Its reaction has been predictable. The majority of career and noncommissioned officers have tended to blame the "outside" with paranoid ferocity. The increasingly

---

[2] An example of the continuing Army desire to get involved overseas is contained in an Associated Press dispatch written by Fred S. Hoffman, appearing in the September 11, 1971, edition of the *Washington Post*: "Looking beyond Vietnam, Army planners hope to form a two-division mobile force ready to move swiftly from the United States to an overseas emergency. . . . Military officials say, the 82nd airborne at Fort Bragg, North Carolina, is now the only full Army division in the United States in shape for quick-reaction deployment to the Middle East, Latin America, or elsewhere."

obvious failure of Army tactics and policies in Vietnam, Europe, and elsewhere have as usual been ignored. Apologists like General Westmoreland have blamed political restraints for lack of total victory. They have tried to delude the men of the Army and the country into believing that the Army has been successful in Vietnam and that the unenlightened will eventually realize this. General Westmoreland and his adherents delude no one but themselves. But in the inexplicable way of bureaucracy these are the men who continue to manage the Army.

They are managing it into further disaster. Their approach is typical—allow longer hair and beer in the mess halls to heal a gravely wounded Army self-confidence. These managers will surely botch the volunteer army concept even if it does come to fruition. They secretly oppose such a concept because they know that it is only truly feasible with an Army of about 500,000 men and then only after drastic internal reform. Besides, a smaller Army would reduce the chances for high rank and plush overseas living. The leadership is making the required noises in support of the volunteer concept, but this is superficial rhetoric that will be accompanied by as many roadblocks as possible. The hope is that after a year the idea will go away with the Presidential election and the "club" can go on as before.

This must not be allowed to happen. An end to the draft is necessary except during times when war is declared by Congress. But a volunteer army should not be recruited chiefly by money. Excessive pay scales will only encourage mercenary time servers to become volunteers. The Army must offer a legitimate means of providing service to the nation before a volunteer concept can be translated into reality. The Army could become increasingly involved in settling domestic disputes between poor, disenfranchised black and white Americans and the forces of government supported by some middle- and upper-class citizens.

Let's try to imagine a situation within the next eight to ten years whereby a well-paid volunteer army has become a reality under the command of the existing Army Officer Corps. Lack-

ing reform, the lower ranks of this volunteer army would consist of underprivileged Americans. To them the Army would
represent an opportunity for financial security unmatched elsewhere. These young Americans would come from groups that
have traditionally been excluded from most of the benefits of
society. To compensate, they have learned to look down on
those whom they can rationalize as being socially and cultur-
ally inferior. It is easy to instill the "gook" mentality in such
young soldiers. And a gook does not necessarily have to be Asiatic. Young, long-haired students, left-leaning academics, Jewish businessmen, peaceniks, and radical-liberals could all become gooks if they were in opposition to anything the Army
was ordered to protect or enforce.

Our recent past demonstrates this possibility: the confronta-
tions at Little Rock, Arkansas, at the University of Mississippi,
the riots at Watts, in Detroit where it took Regular Army
Major General John Hay two days to stop guardsmen's wanton
and indiscriminate shooting, the military reaction to the march
on the Pentagon, the Washington, D.C., riots, and the killings
at Jackson and Kent State. It could come to pass that an army
of economic volunteers led by an officer corps of careerists
might be called upon to go into the streets of some American
cities to settle the issue between unemployed blacks and whites
and an unresponsive government. Many members of the Army
would have difficulty in carrying out such duties. For others,
however, it would be no more problem to follow orders and
shoot American "gooks" than it has been to shoot Asiatic
"gooks" in Vietnam and Korea. As the young National Guards-
man said after obeying orders to fire into a crowd of students at
Kent State, "It was an order just like an order to clean a latrine." Many members of the officer corps would have little
hesitation over ordering volunteers to fire on Americans whom
they believe to be responsible for their defeat in Vietnam.

Once such an Army was committed as part of the law and
order forces to control the actions of Americans, a great deal of
pent-up hate and frustration would be vented on the first
groups confronted. If these equally frustrated and angry groups
use weapons to strike out at an elitist system that they feel

holds them in bondage, the Army might respond with excessive overkill. These initial encounters could set the tone for a later bitterness that might cause an irreconcilable split in our nation.

There would be little doubt as to the outcome of such a confrontation. The Army would "win" in the streets of America the victory that eluded it in Vietnam. The Republic would be saved from a takeover by "Communists." American political leaders would owe a large debt of gratitude to the Army for manning the secret $1 million Civil Disturbance Center in the basement of the Pentagon, and coordinating activities of the Army, National Guard, police, and intelligence operations in rounding up suspected Americans. This round-up could be facilitated by the use of those previously "destroyed" computer tapes that have been secretly stored at the Army Intelligence Center and the dossiers that Army intelligence units continue to maintain on Americans they believe pose a threat to the Army.

The Army manager/generals might not be satisfied with mere political gratitude. Most of these generals would be products of Vietnam. They would have served as battalion and brigade commanders there. They might want to be sure that the Army maintained its freshly restored image as the savior of the country. Also they might want to be able to exercise influence on the shaping of future domestic and international policies. So there could be a strong reluctance on the part of the top Army leadership to relinquish full control to a civilian political leadership which they are convinced has used them in the past as scapegoats for its own mistakes and failures.

There would be no coup mentality. There would be no conspiracy or intent to subvert the civilian government. None of the top-level Army managers would even seriously consider such a thought. And yet those same men could help in the evolution of the Army into the real power in America. How? By first assisting political leaders in restoring "order." Because of the force they would command, their power would be the actual power and it would be spread throughout the country. Where there was little or no fighting, that force would probably represent stability to the American people. The leaders of

that force would also represent a return to the virtues of law
and order and respect for established authority. Army leaders
would regain the confidence of a nation that might have lost respect for the government in Washington and the men who
serve it in a political capacity.

If the civilian government seemed to be drifting or moving in
a direction which the Army leaders felt was contrary to the
best interests of the Army, they might find it necessary to remove or undercut those politicians who opposed Army policies.

The Officer Corps wouldn't have to use much, if any, force
to do this. The Army has learned how to manipulate national
public opinion. Through its widespread units and public relations media, the Army would be able to influence much of the
thinking across the country.[3] The Army's objectives would initially be to continue the Army's restored prestige, return the
country to the status quo, and make sure that the United States
keeps ahead of the Russians in the nuclear-arms race. But as
the influence of the Army grew it could attempt to build a mili-
tary-hero state dedicated principally to a battle to the death
with "international Communism."

Elected and appointed officials who cooperated with the
Army would be left in their official positions and manipulated
to serve Army purposes. Those who had the temerity to oppose
Army policy could be overtly or covertly removed. At an early
point in this evolutionary seizure of power the Army would
have to come to terms with the Air Force and the Navy. This
would initially be done by some practiced log-rolling in the
Joint Chiefs of Staff. The armed forces would be frightened by
the first outbreaks of civil resistance and would unite quickly to
save the nation. As Army power grew, its bargaining lever with
the other services would be the lure of increased military prestige and power in the councils of the central government, plus

---

[3] As General Maxwell Taylor replied in answer to questions concerning *The
New York Times* publishing the "Pentagon Papers" on decision-making in Vietnam. Question: "Well, what do you make, General, of the principle of the people's right to know?" Answer: "I don't believe in it as a general principle, a citizen should know those things he needs to know to be a good citizen and
discharge his function."

the possibility of a stronger military posture at home and abroad. By the time that the other services became suspicious of the Army's motives it would be too late. All effective power would be in the hands of the Army. It would rest there with the willing support of the mass of the American people, who would have given up many of their freedoms and chosen military rule as an exemplification of law and order and return to stability.

Evolution of the Army Into a Force for Peaceful Change in America

What are the alternatives to involvement in continued counterinsurgency wars or a usurpation of national power by the Army? The answer is early thorough reform from top to bottom, of the type that I have tried to outline in Chapter 9. Concurrently with this reform, most of the Army should be withdrawn from overseas bases. Once the majority of the Army is at home it will be much easier to reorganize and rebuild its structure and morale.

But what should soldiers maintained to defend our borders do? There are enough large bases within the fifty states to accommodate seventeen active divisions and furnish sufficient terrain for annual maneuvers. All of these personnel would not be constantly involved with combat or support duties. Rather than continue to occupy their time with busywork, they should be returned to their early frontier role of helping fellow citizens build the country. The small limited program in nation building that General John Tolson began at Fort Bragg, North Carolina, in 1970 should be expanded to include all units of the active Army, the Army Reserve, and the National Guard. This would allow the physical assets of the military to be used in overcoming poverty in the rural and urban jungles of Appalachia, Mississippi, New York, and Detroit (instead of involving themselves in South Vietnam, South America, and Africa). Under such a program the money, equipment, and know-how of military personnel could be used to help solve urgent domestic problems. For the threats to national security are not only foreign threats. They are also the threats of internal poverty, sickness, slum ghettos, poor housing, antiquated public health and sanitation facilities, and so on.

Service in defense of America should no longer be defined in such restrictive terms as standing at the butt end of a flaming M-16 or an M-60 machine gun. The men trained to man those weapons can also defend America at the handle end of a shovel, or from the seat of a bulldozer, or from behind a stethoscope.[4] As Assistant Secretary of Defense Roger Kelley has said, "America in the seventies will demand a military organization whose capabilities extend beyond traditional military effectiveness." If such reformed military forces are available to offer a real challenge to young Americans to serve their country, there will be no difficulty in filling the number of a 500,000-man Army with volunteers. There will probably be a waiting list even without the astronomical pay scales that are being envisioned to entice young Americans to serve. The problem is not that present-day young Americans don't want to serve, but that they do not want to serve in causes they know are not in the best interests of their country.

It is toward the goal of regaining the hearts and minds of America's citizens and soldiers that the U.S. Army must now direct its efforts. It once was the greatest army the world has ever seen. It can be again. Nothing less than the future of the United States depends on what it does to regain its sincerity and honesty of purpose. This is the challenge that faces the soldiers of today. I pray they can meet this challenge and find the answers to the problems that are destroying the Army that I long served and still hold in such tremendous affection.

---

[4] Perhaps some thought should be given to creation of a national service corps which would provide all young Americans with the opportunity of serving the country in the way that they feel best suited. They should have alternative methods of national service open to them, including the Armed Services, VISTA programs in schools, hospitals, institutions, and environmental clean-up.

Appendix

Excerpts from Letters

☆ ☆ ☆ ☆ ☆ ☆ ☆ ☆ ☆

December 10, 1968

Mr. Richard Nixon
President-Elect
Hotel Pierre
New York, N.Y.

Dear Mr. Nixon:

   After sincere deliberation I am writing you in the hope that I may offer some observations that might be of value as you address some of the issues which are of importance to the long term security of the United States. . . . These thoughts have occurred to me many times over the past ten years. . . . I can no longer contain them as I see what is happening to our country. . . .

If we learn nothing else from Vietnam, let it be the truth that our national armed forces entrusted as they are with the defense of the liberty of the nation cannot and must not be used as "management troubleshooters" in mercenary wars which are the end result of an out-dated, bankrupt foreign policy. . . .

To continue, or again repeat, such an unreasoned course as we have followed in Vietnam will not only lead to the destruction of the soul of the national armed forces, but will contribute to the growth of an officer corps which under the guise of obedience to civilian authority will become more concerned with personal promotion and decoration than with the well-being and liberty of the nation. Today military officers talk in terms of the need of securing command of battalions, brigades, or divisions in Vietnam rapidly before this war ends. There is little, if any, thought given to the sons of the American middle class and poor who make up these units and who must be maimed or killed in order that these combat commands may be achieved by men who will then within a few years formulate policy and decide whether or not we should get involved in another of these "dandy little wars." . . .

To realize that the deaths in 1952–53 were useless, just as the death and agony in Vietnam today is useless, is to ask more of American youth than we have a right to ask. They will die willingly for the . . . freedom of this nation. They hope they are doing so today in Vietnam, they thought they did so in Korea, they were sure they did so in World War II. But we owe it to them to be sure it *is* for the freedom of the United States . . . they are dying and not to cover political blunders. . . .

Were our efforts in Korea and are our efforts today in Vietnam truly directly related to the defense of the . . . liberty and security of the United States? Do we need a presence on the Asiatic mainland to truly defend the liberty of the people of the United States? I for one do not believe that Chinese can walk on water and since there would appear to be no other way they can decisively attack the United States, I am not convinced that if we don't contain them in Southeast Asia, the United

States is faced by any threat serious enough to justify American boys dying in Asia. Mahan clearly outlined our course of defense in regard to Asia a century ago. . . . What occurs in Southeast Asia . . . is unpleasant to our pride perhaps, but certainly not a grave enough threat to risk destroying the soul of our nation and our armed forces. Let us at least put our priorities in perspective and in doing so clearly establish what issue justifies American boys dying—the defense of the liberty of the U.S.—and what issues do not justify such a cost. . . .

In critically analyzing the military I would hope you would analyze areas which would:

Remove all the national armed forces from Vietnam at the earliest time, leaving absolutely no vestige of U.S. military presence in Southeast Asia; . . .

Revert the Department of Defense to its role of preparing for the defense of the nation and remove it from the foreign-policy-making role it has usurped since World War II;

Examine ways to provide more return on the tax dollar spent on defense by eliminating the present degree of luxury enjoyed by the armed forces and reducing the unnecessary and costly personnel turbulence which they continue to maintain. I refer specifically to the improper luxury of manpower epitomized by the incredible spectacle in Vietnam, where though over 525,000 American troops are committed to the area, at no time can over 100,000 be actually used to fight. Such waste is indicative of improper organization and will spell national disaster if we ever have to attempt to fight a major war with such a misuse of our manpower resources, particularly if we face the USSR. . . .

Direct the Department of Defense to carefully evaluate the actual danger inherent in maintaining four U.S. divisions in Europe in view of the USSR initial strike capability. . . . Assess what the loss of these divisions in battle would mean to your office and U.S. public opinion, and the feasibility of your authorizing the immediate use of nuclear weapons in their defense. . . .

Assess the value of continuing to maintain two U.S. infantry divisions in South Korea and the true military necessity that

one of these divisions be permanently positioned on the demilitarized zone where it is subject to continued casualties and possible war-provoking incidents at the whim of North
Korea. . . .

I have decided that rather than continue to be a contributor
to the tragic and useless waste of the lives of our servicemen in
Vietnam, I will terminate my 23 years of service in the armed
forces not long after you assume direction of the government. . . .

Sincerely
Edward L. King

✿   ✿   ✿

Office of The Assistant Secretary of Defense
Manpower and Reserve Affairs
Washington, D.C. 20301

2 April, 1969

Dear Mr. King:

President Nixon has asked that I reply to your recent letter
regarding an all-volunteer armed force and other matters. . . .

As you may know, the President has just appointed a special
Commission to develop a comprehensive plan for achieving an
all-volunteer force.

I believe it is reasonable to assume that the Commission will
carefully examine all aspects of an all-volunteer armed force,
including considerations such as you noted.

. . . It is regrettable that you intend to terminate your
lengthy service in the armed forces. We wish you success in
your future endeavors. . . .

Sincerely,
Albert Kay
Associate Director for Procurement
Policy and General Research.

✿   ✿   ✿

May 14, 1969[1]

Honorable John G. Tower
United States Senate
Committee on Armed Services
Washington, D.C. 20510

Dear Senator Tower:

I have this date received your letter in which you were kind enough to furnish me a copy of the Department of the Army reply to your inquiry concerning my retirement. . . . I hope the Army will soon stop deliberately delaying a decision on my request (March 28, 1969) which they have not had the courtesy to acknowledge. . . .

I believe retirement from service in an Army that provides . . . a depressive sense of hopelessness, frustration, and disillusionment at the futility of one's service . . . and the inability to contribute in any meaningful way to the sweeping reforms so urgently needed will resolve much of my malaise of spirit and body. . . .

After summarily removing me from the Joint Chiefs of Staff . . . I am doing nothing, because some organization-man in the Army leadership must attempt to disgrace and punish me for honestly stating my convictions. . . . This is the most vivid commentary I know of the type of command mentality that pervades our Army. Never evaluate fundamental issues, never look for the truth, never listen to any dissenting thought or ideas. . . . The answer is always subterfuge, evasion, even lies on occasion, protecting careers, seeking high efficiency ratings and promotion. . . . Then ruthless Mafia-like suppression and discrediting of any whisper of dissent or desire to reform a structure that is organizationally archaic and a leadership that is clique-ridden, and unconcerned and out-of-touch with the realities of actual conditions within an as yet only vaguely restless and dissatisfied Army. . . .

---

[1] The following letter was written while I was on convalescent leave after undergoing exploratory surgery at Walter Reed Army Hospital and shortly before I returned to my isolation at Fort McNair.

Nor will anything be done to face the issues . . . and this convinces me of the futility of any more service in an Army which because of this stubborn, blind refusal to face problems has now failed the nation in Vietnam. . . . It is foredoomed to fail again in another hour of national peril if some positive steps are not soon taken to correct some of the basic problems that exist within the leadership and organizational structure. . . .

The U.S. Army is going to, at some point, have to pick up a number of the chips for failing to properly use the vast manpower resources that the nation has so painfully provided and in failing to properly organize tactically to permit it a chance of winning. There has been a notable lack of demonstrated high-level skill, will, and ability. . . . An Army in failure has no excuse. This is, I predict, going to be a most difficult thing to explain to the thousands of young officers and men who have so bravely fought this war. The voices of recrimination are going to be loud and demanding and the long fingers of guilt are going to be pointed . . . toward an Army leadership which has failed and deluded them and itself. This is not imaginary Senator, it is going to come to pass because this Army is not prepared to accept any blame for the failure of Vietnam after having given its heart, soul, and blood in a no-win cause that is coming home to roost. I predict that if we ever want to see the U.S. Army take the field to win again we had better start now to repair the damage of Korea and Vietnam. . . . We better start now seeking the answers and beginning the reforms that Vietnam should tell us are so urgently needed. . . .

I pray that I am wrong Senator, but I don't think we can wait around and continue business as usual in the Army and risk finding out I'm not. For that reason I know I must leave active service and remove myself to private life where I may do whatever God gives me the power and strength to do to alert my fellow citizens to these weaknesses before it becomes too late for Army and the nation. . . .

> Most sincerely,
> Edward L. King
> Lt. Colonel USA

Department of the Army
Office of the Adjutant General
Washington, D.C. 20315

20 June, 1969

Subject: Reconsideration of Request for Voluntary Retirement

Thru: Commanding General, Military District of Washington, US Army, Washington, D.C. 20315

To: Lieutenant Colonel Edward L. King 069711, Infantry

1. This is in reply to your letter addressed to the Secretary of the Army regarding reconsideration of your request for retirement on 1 August, 1969.

2. Your request for retirement has been carefully reviewed . . . and approved for 1 August 1969. . . . The decision to approve your retirement was based on a thorough review of the additional information you provided for reconsideration. In evaluation of this information, the conclusion could only be drawn that you suffered a complete reversal of the previously highly rated attitude and motivation reflected during your career. . . . Accordingly, the board decided that your release from active duty would be in the best interest of the Army.

3. In the near future, orders will be issued directing your retirement on 1 August 1969 (with relief from active duty on 31 July 1969).

BY ORDER OF THE SECRETARY OF THE ARMY:

C. A. STANFIEL
Colonel AGC
Acting The Adjutant General

°   °   °

August 2, 1969

Honorable Stanley R. Resor
Secretary of the Army
Room 3E 718, Pentagon
Washington, D.C. 20310

Dear Mr. Secretary:

As I voluntarily retire from over 20 years active duty . . . I want to express some of my thoughts and convictions concerning the present day Army you are appointed to lead. . . .

The attached letter I have received from the Adjutant General of the Army is incredible. The only conclusion that can be drawn as to the reason why an officer with my 20-year record of devoted service would fight, at any cost, to get out of the present day Army is found to be because of suffering an unfathomable "reversal" of attitude and motivation! Such obtuse reasoning is typical of the mentality of the present day Army organization yes-men, but it is a very long way from the truth.

My attitude toward the Army remains as loyal and devoted today as it has always been. My motivation to honestly and effectively serve the Army and the Nation remains the principal desire in my life. It is precisely because of these attitudes . . . that I have decided to leave active service in the Army. It is impossible to render honest, beneficial service to the nation or the Army in the atmosphere of fear, repression, injustice, and selfish personal career promotion and advancement-seeking that flourishes within the command levels of the present day U.S. Army. Existing conditions within that Army are a disgrace. . . . I could no longer serve as a part of the hypocrisy, fraud, deception and self-seeking yesmanship that characterize and dominate Army service today. The conclusion that correctly should have been drawn . . . was not that my insistence on retiring was because of an unexplainable "reversal" of attitude, but rather a quite explainable "suffering" of ten years disgust, revulsion, and disillusionment at the hypocrisy, injustice, waste, inefficiency, incompetency, unconcern and deception that exists in the so-called "Modern Army" of today. . . .

It should tell you something Mr. Secretary . . . when loyal servants are willing to fight to lay aside their lifetime career and attempt the difficult task of beginning anew in middle-age, so as not to remain in the frustration and futility of present day Army service. . . . How could veteran, productive soldiers become so disillusioned? It is not from suffering "complete reversals" and it cannot be blamed on Vietnam. The answer lies far deeper, it lies very near an almost total failure of leadership in support of honesty and justice by the high level leadership of the Army. . . .

My 28 March 1961 letter and the similar ones you have received from other equally loyal, dedicated, career officers should be an indication to you that something is seriously wrong in the Army. . . . You should not brush aside attempts to honestly inform you of conditions within the Army. . . . You had better start taking some action to make some long overdue changes and reforms and I say this in all loyalty and sincerity. . . .

The Army leadership must stop making excuses and attempting to shift the blame for its own repeated failure to provide credible, impartial leadership. . . . It must stop trying to evade its internal problems and stop making professional humiliation and court martial the persistent response to any dissent created by these problems and its own lack of leadership. . . .

The Army you are responsible for has serious internal morale and organizational problems Mr. Secretary. It is an Army on the wrong road and in trouble. It has failed the mission in Vietnam and has thereby failed the trust of the nation. Its leadership has given little but frequent excuses for their failures and waste of lives and money. Too often the concept of expediency and the end-justifying-the-means has been the basis for command action and decision. An Army in combat has no excuse for failure. We have strayed from our time-tested principles and precepts in Vietnam and we have failed the nation. In my estimation you have failed because you have been apparently unconcerned and weak and have too readily supported and accepted the distortions, platitudes and excuses that have been offered by the yes-men around you. . . . The present Chief of Staff in my estimation, failed first as the tactical field commander in Vietnam by his tactical deployments and battle strategy. He continues to horribly fail to provide credible, informed, concerned leadership as the appointed military leader of the Army. . . .

There is a crisis of confidence throughout the Army brought about by this leadership-by-image and the what's-in-it-for-me thinking of the organization yes-men that you listen to and permit to run the affairs of the Army as they see fit. You cannot fool either the young or old soldiers by empty words. . . . The real problem in the U.S. Army now and for many years has been the unconcern of the out of contact, high level leadership for the dignity and welfare of the men who serve. . . . With present day Army leadership it is do what I say, never mind what I do. . . . The Army . . . desperately needs a leader who will . . . sincerely understand and care about the welfare of the men in it. . . . Things are not wonderful, the image is anything but that of a "winner" . . . this letter, others like it and the ever-rising desertion and AWOL rates should among other things, give you some indication of how bad things really are. . . .

Unless the drastic, sweeping reforms that are so desperately needed are soon made, I am apprehensive about the future ability of this Army to ever again take the field to win. . . .

I would have liked to have continued to try, as I have in the past, to help implement the changes and reforms that are needed. . . . such a course is not possible in the present Army. There is nothing one can do except leave active service, or be cowed into the morally unacceptable position of serving as a fraud in Vietnam, responsible for death and agony of fellow citizens while attaining personal promotion and recognition. . . .

I hope that God may help you in the future to better understand and more effectively serve in your vital duties as Secretary of the United States Army. An Army which until recently has been considered as the greatest and most victorious the world has known. For my part I will forever remember my service to it and the majority of fine dedicated men who serve in it, with the deepest sense of humble pride, respect and affection.

Sincerely,
Edward L. King
Lt. Colonel USA (Ret.)

Enclosures:
1 Letter from Adjutant General
2 Thoughts and Ideas on Ways to Improve the U.S. Army (22 pages)

Index